T0208972

Joy IN THE MOURNING

Overcoming Bipolar Disorder

CLAIRE LIEBER

WESTBOW
PRESS®
A DIVISION OF THOMAS NELSON
& ZONDERVAN

WestBow Press books may be ordered through booksellers or by contacting:

WestBow Press
A Division of Thomas Nelson & Zondervan
1663 Liberty Drive
Bloomington, IN 47403
www.westbowpress.com
844-714-3454

ISBN: 978-1-6642-3517-5 (sc)
ISBN: 978-1-6642-3518-2 (hc)
ISBN: 978-1-6642-3516-8 (e)

Library of Congress Control Number: 2021910297

Print information available on the last page.

WestBow Press rev. date: 03/24/2022

To:
The Brave
Persevering
Overcomers
Whistle Blowers
Scapegoats
Forgiven and Forgiving
Includers
Lovers of Truth
And Lovers of God

Acknowledgements

The editorial team at Westbow Press for making what seemed to be impossible happen.

To Bill for telling my mother we could make it and for forgiving me for all the trouble bipolar disorder brought into our lives. I'm grateful and aware of your many kindnesses to me through the years.

My sisters for sharing my heartaches and hurts and trying to understand.

My three children and their spouses for taking time out of their busy lives to help their mom what I was overloaded by many dangers, toils and snares.

Aglow friends for your example of intercession for people around the world and prayers for even me. I love you Jane, Kay, Carol, Judy, Caryl, Barbara, Virginia and Judy.

Celebrate Recovery "sisters" who helped me so much by sharing your shameful and painful stories. My sponsor Vanessa—you are wise beyond your years. To Mary, Cimion, Liberty, Angie, Navi as well as my leaders Amanda, Danette and Christine. Special thanks to Cathy for ongoing encouragement and much gratitude to the people in my current Twelve Step group, Amanda, Danette and Angie.

Thanks to many friends who are part of this story. You know who you are! Special thanks to Cindy, Lisa and Ray, as well as those who read parts of the book and gave me invaluable feedback. Thanks to Jana, Jen, Sally, Polly, Lisa, John and Dave.

Thank you to my psychologists, counselors and many nurses on psych wards who listened and helped me.

Thanks to the alternative healers in my life—Dr. Albert Mensah, Dr. Judith Bowman and Heather Larsen.

Thanks to several pastors from the past and present:

Pastor Bill Hull for the many profound sermons that helped shape my faith as a young believer. Through you I learned that I don't lose my salvation every time I sin. I just need to confess my sins to God who is faithful and just to forgive me and cleanse me every time I ask. Thank you for also introducing growth groups to us.

Pastors Ken and Jana Shook. Thanks Ken, for instilling within us the importance of prayer through your teaching and by demonstrating prayer in your own life. I will always remember those all-night prayer meetings and prayer walks. Jana, for loving me and teaching me "how to chat" candidly and freely.

Pastor Dan and Beth Cullett of Celebrate Recovery. My husband says that you, Dan are the most approachable pastor he's ever known. I think that's the beauty of Celebrate Recovery. Leaders and participants are all in the same boat, forgiving those who have hurt us, confessing our sins against others and making amends as we are able. Thanks for not putting yourself on a pedestal where you are more likely to fall off.

Pastor Mark and Terri Canon for being there for us during those uncertain times in the last year of Bill's mom's life. And for being examples of God's sacrificial love in adopting your children and being a chaplain to the police.

Thank you to Pastor Scott and Michelle Reese for inspiration and releasing of the people of God to be the hands and feet of Jesus in the Quad Cities. Thank you for believing that Jesus still heals the sick and sets captives free.

Thanks to Tammy and Bill Shaver and your team for overseeing the physical and inner healing class at church. It is so wonderful to be able to receive hands-on-prayer from gentle, spiritually attuned people at church each week.

Thanks to Nancy for texting me and praying for me specifically whenever I ask and thanks to Ellen, my prayer partner. Thanks to Kenny for being there like a little brother when I was studying inner healing and learning to listen and pray for people like you who were willing to be a guinea pigs.

Preface

In 2011, I began writing a thesis called "Overcoming Bipolar Disorder." At the time, I was working on a master's degree in counseling through Christian Leadership University. CLU was established on the premise that Christians can and ought to "hear" God's voice on a regular basis. At the beginning, I took time to ask the Lord how to approach my writing. I sensed He was telling me to include "all the parts." In other words, He was telling me that there is no easy fix for something as complicated as bipolar disorder. So led by the Holy Spirit, with an advisor to guide me, I began a journey to get to the roots of an illness that baffles not only psychologists and psychiatrists but also clergy and prayer counselors.

When I mention to people that I struggle with bipolar disorder I rarely know what they think or if they really have an understanding. My mother-in-law thought I had Attention Deficit Disorder, just like her pastor. Some don't want to hear about it, others avoid me like the plague or think they know all about it. A psychologist told me that if he were to choose a psychiatric disorder to have, he would choose bipolar. "Yeah, if it weren't for the threat of suicide, bipolar would be great," I replied, as I made a note to myself to find a different counselor.

Another psychologist told me once that if I needed to know anything about bipolar disorder I should ask her. I was floored. I could hardly believe she said that to me. **I** was the one fighting against bipolar. Maybe *she* should ask me. The next time I saw her,

I asked if she had ever been in a psych ward. She replied that she had several times during her training. Then I asked, if she had ever spent the night in the psychiatric section of a hospital. She admitted she had not. I went on to suggest that being housed in a psych ward wasn't easy, after all there are *crazy* people in there! Such a place can be scary especially at night. Just try sleeping when you don't feel secure. Now, I might add that psych wards are often harboring humble, gifted, caring people. Some are nurses and aides; others are patients. Whenever I was pronounced well enough to go home, I always hated to leave my friends.

Other "helpers" have no idea what the medications actually do to a person's body and brain. My most recent psychiatrist, was all about the medication. During the time I was his patient, I too, was hoping for a magical, pill-for-every-ill kind of cure. But this particular psychiatrist didn't want to read the book I had given him about alternative/natural treatment, nor talk to a doctor I discovered who based her therapy on the works of Carl Pfeiffer and Abram Hoffer. He didn't have time. I have come to believe the hard way that psychiatric drugs are not the answer. I also believe that many psychiatrists have been brain washed by their profession.

Well-meaning friends have said, "You're not bipolar." I want to say, "What then, is this trouble that afflicts me?" It's like saying to someone with diabetes, "You're not diabetic." In part these friends are right. Bipolar is not my identity. I don't want to be labeled but at the same time I want those who love me, to know what I've suffered. It's not visible but the hurt and trauma associated with mental illness is real.

In this book, I tell of the lives and times of my parents, recognizing that my story is very much rooted and intertwined with theirs. My trouble with bipolar disorder did not begin with my first break down. Events from my young life and even the lives of my ancestors set the stage. I'm not trying to imply that my parents or relatives in past generations deliberately did anything to contribute to my problem. Bipolar Disorder is a complicated illness. My first encounter with psychosis began in 1971 when I was fifteen. The book concludes in 1977 when I was 22—unsettling years in the world of mental health. There have been significant advances in understanding and solutions in several areas since then, even recently.

My life journey and quest for answers has taken many twists and turns. My search was not confined to computer research or the memoirs of others who suffer with bipolar disorder. In the years of 2017 and 2019, I was hospitalized in local psychiatric wards five times. Those years were extremely confusing and difficult for me, my husband and our children. Yet, that was also an educational period. I am overcoming. Because the Holy Spirit dwells in me, all things are working together for my good (Romans 8:28). I know that God in His wisdom does not grant heavenly rewards to cowards, and I hope and pray to be courageous.

Anyone who has the misfortune of landing in a psychiatric ward usually comes to grudging acceptance of the need for medication that produces horrible side effects. Sadly, in our time, the main function of most psychiatrists has been to grant each patient a fifteen-minute check up to see how the meds are working. I found this approach to be entirely insufficient and even damaging. Yes, I am physical, but I am also a soul comprised of my mind, will and emotions as well as a spirit which gives me life. Today's typical psychiatrist neglects gifts and personalities as well as light filled human spirits which cannot be touched by pills.

Psychiatric medicines are not a cure. They have no nutritive value for our bodies or brains. They harm important organs. All complicated problems are comprised of multiple contributing factors. In the past few years, I have doubled down in my search for solutions. If I have a bone to pick, it is with the pharmaceutical companies that promote one-size-fits-all toxic solutions that seriously hurt people and shorten their lives. Our bodies are miraculously and wondrously made (Psalm 139:14). We are not mechanical, merely in need of gas, oil, or wiper fluid. It is past time for change! I hope for a major revolution not only in psychiatric medicine but also in the treatment of physical ailments such as high blood pressure and cancer.

Since the turn of the 20th century our entire nation has been under the dominating influence of pharmaceutical companies and medical schools originally financed by tycoon John D. Rockefeller who owned 90 percent of the oil refineries in the nation. As far as Rockefeller was concerned, the best thing about manufacturing medicines made with petrochemicals was that vitamins could be synthesized and medicinal drugs could be patented and sold for high profits. But there was one problem with Rockefeller's plan for the medical industry: natural/ herbal medicines were very popular in America at that time. Almost half the doctors and medical colleges in the U.S. were practicing holistic medicine. So Rockefeller sent a contractor named Abraham Flexner into the medical colleges to convince them to use and prescribe allopathic, petroleum-based medications.

Part of bringing a halt to the craziness in society is to return to our Creator and ask for His forgiveness for turning from His ways. As a people we need to feed our bodies and brains with substances that nourish, build up, sustain and heal. We need medicine that is derived from fresh, life-giving, unpolluted earthly substances. God help us all.

While writing this book, I read several memoirs concerning bipolar disorder and schizophrenia. I had read *The Bell Jar* by Sylvia Plath as a teenager, but several more authors particularly stood out to me: Carrie Fisher, Mark Vonnegut, Melody Moezzi, Jack Deere, Matt Samet, Elyn Saks, Kevin Hines and Mark Lukach.

I loved each and every story but I want to highlight two of them. Keven Hines' book *Cracked not Broken: Surviving and Thriving after a Suicide Attempt* highlights the danger of suicide for people suffering from bipolar disorder. I recently met Kevin at a local event meant to promote suicide awareness and prevention. After the session I stood in line, waiting to talk with him.

When my turn came, I briefly shared the suicide part of my story. With a knowing kindness in his eyes, he shook my hand and said, "That's two of us." Kevin and his wife Margaret travel telling their story as a warning to parents and people who work with and care about children. They also share a common bond and comfort with those who are grieving and traumatized by loved ones lost to suicide.

Mark Lukach's book *My Lovely Wife in the Psych Ward* touched me deeply. Mark's story of his wife's struggle with bipolar disorder depicts his steady concern and care for Guilia. He makes clear *how* mental illness causes tremendous stress for the entire family. I identified strongly with the tensions Mark describes. My husband Bill and I have experienced similar difficulties in our attempt to live a meaningful life while not only dealing with bipolar disorder but also seeking to prevent the dementia that plagued his dad and my mom.

Several doctors highlight research into the nutritional aspect of healing. Dr. Natasha Campbell-McBride has written a fascinating treatise on the difference diet can make in the treatment of mental illness. *Gut and Psychology Syndrome* goes into detail explaining the importance of having a healthy intestinal tract. Casein from milk and gluten from grains can turn into substances with chemical structures like those of opiates. The colon is sometimes referred to as a second brain because important neurotransmitters are manufactured there. Dr. Natasha explains the importance of a healthy colon in truly healing people with various mental issues. Her book includes a protocol, recipes, and lists of gut-friendly foods, as well as a list of foods to avoid. I like what Dr. Natasha suggests. I have tried many of her recipes. Even though I find her protocol difficult to follow, I have adapted most of her philosophy to my lifestyle.

Dr. William J. Walsh is another author who discusses the importance of proper nutrition for brain health. *Nutrient Power: Heal Your Biochemistry and Heal Your Brain* tells of his research into the world of psychiatric disorders. Covering topics ranging from the halls of an Illinois penitentiary to the microscope slides that delineate one brain cell from another, Dr. Walsh expertly explains the differences in the chemical makeup of various disorders. In this book he offers help for Schizophrenia, Depression, Autism, Behavioral Disorders, ADHD and Alzheimer's Disease. Dr. Walsh is currently working on finishing a book specifically about Bipolar Disorder. Stay tuned.

I regularly visit Dr. Judith Bowman who practices with Dr. Albert Mensah at Mensah Medical Clinic in a Chicago suburb. Mensah Clinic is associated with Dr. Walsh and the doctors use much of his research to inform and guide the treatment of their patients. When I first visited Mensah in 2011, blood and urine tests revealed that I was undermethylated with pyrrole disorder, which is fairly common. Pyrrole disorder causes a severe deficiency in both zinc and B6 (pyridoxine) which are swept from the body before having a chance to be absorbed. This is a critical defect because zinc and B6 are used by the body to create important neurotransmitters for the nervous system. Anyone, experiencing a lot of stress can suffer from pyrrole disorder. Krypto pyrroles are overproduced molecules and by products in the of the production of hemoglobin. The Kryptopyrroles attach to B6 and zinc which are excreted from the body. This is serious for people who have been diagnosed with a mental illness. Vitamin B6 is essential in the making of neurotransmitters and zinc is important because it balances copper. Elevated copper can lead to mania, violence and underachievement. When zinc disappears from the body, anxiety, dyslexia, nerve damage, depression and aggressiveness can result. Gracelyn Guyol in her excellent book *Who's Crazy Here?* poses the question-"Why don't pediatricians, internists, school boards and PTA's know about this?(p. 33)" Why don't law makers and parents everywhere know about this, I might add. Children are needlessly put on various expensive and harmful medications when adding inexpensive zinc and B6 could take care of so much.

Methyl groups act as transporters and keys to turn on neurotransmitters. In a recent zoom call conversation with Dr. Bowman, she explained to me that undermethylation is an inherited predisposition. People are born as either normally methylated, under methylated or over methylated. Undermethylation is the depletion of methyl atoms, which modify gene expression. I currently receive a mixture of nutrients from a compounding pharmacy that is uniquely formulated for someone like me who needs extra zinc and Vitamin B6 among other vital nutrients.

In the spirit of seeking, knocking, and asking, my husband and I also made several trips to a northern suburb of Chicago, to a clinic established by well-known psychiatrist Daniel Amen who often teaches on PBS. Our purpose was to obtain assessments of our brains and to undergo SPECT (single photon emission computed thermography) scans. This psychiatrist's research is similar to and dovetails with the works of Dr. Walsh and Dr. Campbell-McBride. In his latest book, *The End of Mental Illness*, he shares many helpful ideas, foods and supplements that can affect brain and whole body health. It was at Amen's clinic in Chicago that a psychiatrist recommended that I find a therapist I could meet with regularly. I followed her advice and began meeting with a local psychologist for a while.

Three years ago, while I was sequestered in the psychiatric ward of a local hospital, my husband got involved with a life-changing ministry known as Celebrate Recovery. Many years prior, Bill was arrested for drunk driving and jailed overnight. He had received the mandatory counseling but was afraid in August 2019 that the stress and anxiety from dealing with my mania and psychosis could cause him to revert to using alcohol. He found a counselor who recommended Alcoholics Anonymous as a support. Bill, however, found a group that not only dealt with addictions, but recognized Jesus as the higher power that people refer to in AA. While I was still in the hospital, Bill attended a couple of meetings and liked what he heard. A few days after I was released from the psych ward for the last time in 2019, I followed Bill to a large Baptist Church on a Friday night for worship, teaching and "open share" gatherings. We both decided to join twelve step groups in order to delve more deeply into recovery. Bill's men's group met each week on Sunday afternoons, and I joined a lady's group on Tuesday evenings as someone working on "life issues."

I am currently in my second twelve step group. I answer the probing questions and work to make amends to people the Holy Spirit brings to my mind. I've gotten to know several dear, humble women. These groups have been instrumental in helping me make true friends who sincerely want to be pleasing to God. My friends are helping me build trust in women. Through much of my life I had been so hurt by competitive, catty girls and women. The Celebrate Recovery ladies are real. They follow the admonition of James 5:16 to confess your sins to one another that you may be healed. They also seek to refrain from gossip. When I joined, I still felt shame and guilt about a number of things. As I confessed to my sponsor and other women in the group, I began to sense the comfort of God's forgiveness as the weight of troubling memories began to lift.

Though my mother warned us before Bill and I said "I do" back in 1977, we had no idea of the difficulties we would face in battling bipolar disorder. Some years were easier than others, and we were fortunate to have supportive parents to help us during the years our children were little. God has been faithful, and we have learned a lot. We have much to be thankful for. It certainly has not been easy, but we trust our Savior who never gives up on us.

I am experiencing and believing for a complete breakthrough in dealing successfully with bipolar disorder. I am taking classes at my Four-Square charismatic church to study the spiritual aspects of many maladies. We use books like one written by Randy Clark of Global Awakening. My church believes in healing. I regularly receive hands-on prayer and prophetic guidance on Sunday mornings. The pastors and staff are committed to maintaining the established church as a place of healing and training people to "do the stuff" that Jesus did.

I believe in healing by getting to the root of problems. The instructor of my church class advised staying on medication until given permission to stop by a doctor. If, at that time, I had been under the care of a holistic physician, I would have asked for permission. I did ask my psychiatrist if I could taper off Abilify but he said he wouldn't recommend it. So, I was on my own.

When I was younger, my parents were the ones who knew me well and loved me enough to oversee my withdrawal from both Trilafon and Elavil. My parents are gone now, so, in June of 2021, after research and careful deliberation with the agreement of my husband, I set aside my prescription for Abilify. Abilify supposedly regulates dopamine in the brain. However, I found that it did not bring me to a place of stability. Instead, it robbed me of my drive for living, causing me to want to escape from life and spend as much time as possible in a large recliner in our living room. I'd get up in the mornings, groggy, confused and unfocused. So, rather than following my psychiatrist's recommendation, I chose to get to the bottom of things. I knew I was taking a risk, but I could no longer endure the numerous side effects of Abilify or medications I have taken. Most notably I had taken Latuda in 2017. It seemed to work well for a while until my jaws became painfully locked. Currently I *am* experiencing nasty effects of withdrawal from Abilify. Yes, the symptoms of withdrawal are nasty, but on the plus side I'm getting my life, my energy and my hope back.

I also read everything I could find about the high blood pressure medication I was taking. I am painfully aware, that if I overcome bipolar disorder but neglect my blood pressure, the result could be a stroke which can lead to dementia- a fate just as debilitating as psychosis or depression. I began taking a supplements that are supposed to lower the stress hormone, cortisol. I exercise by taking walks and climbing hills. I've learned about detox pathways and the importance of assisting those pathways in their job of cleansing my body of debris. Hot Epsom salts baths and ionic foot baths have proven helpful.

In October of 2021 I discovered and began meeting with Heather Larsen, a holistic health practitioner in the Quad Cities.

My presenting problems were high blood pressure, kidney issues, insomnia and a desire to prevent colon cancer. On my first consultation with her, Heather made a list of my physical concerns and began teaching me her natural approach for treating a number of issues. She explained that our bodies and past trauma are very much connected with our emotional and spiritual health. She provides me with homeopathic tinctures, herbal remedies vitamins and minerals including iodine which can affect brain health.

On a psychological level I am asking the Lord to make me aware of destructive things I say and negative expectations that I harbor. Among other things, I came to understand that worry is a habit. Worry about my health and about my children kept me awake at night. Romans 8:13 Bible instructs us to "put to death" the deeds of the flesh. So, by faith, I renounced worry and asked God to bring worry as a habit to a halt on the cross. My husband Bill and I look for Bible verses to pray and declare over our children and issues that worry us.

I am heartened by a documentary video on Youtube called "Take These Broken Wings: Schizophrenia Recovery Without Medication." It tells the stories of two patients and two therapists who worked to overcome schizophrenia. In 1948 Joanne Greenberg, author of *I Never Promised You a Rose Garden*, began treatment with German psychiatrist, Frieda Fromm Reichman, a contemporary of Sigmund Freud. Through their work together, Joanne not only came to a place of healing, but she also wrote many books and served as a professor of anthropology at the Colorado School of Mines. Likewise, Catherine Penney began working with psychiatrist Daniel Dorman in 1967, who through patience, listening and teaching helped Catherine to a productive life. After watching the film, I had to deal with my own anger and grief that so much damage and misinformation has kept people in bondage to illness and dysfunction. Psychotropic medication creates a prison for those who have been caught in its sway.

Catherine Penney went on to become a psychiatric nurse. Hope rose in me after I watched the film. I then read Dorman's book called *Dante's Cure*. Dorman's method was good and I admire him for being so patient with Catherine even in the face or criticism from colleagues. Yet, it bothered me that he failed to warn her about having sex outside of marriage. I believe Catherine in her newfound freedom and attractiveness, experienced unnecessary stress because she got involved sexually with several men without the protection of marriage or a pastor.

Recently, I watched a documentary that exposed the dangerous connection of the FDA and pharmaceutical companies- *Generation Rx*. The greed and disregard for human life of the pharmaceutical companies must be held in check by an independent agency led by people of integrity. We need people in high positions who value truth above money and power. At tender ages, children are placed on Ritalin or other psychotropic medications. How many people have lost their lives to suicide because of trust in a pill?

Another important work for anyone seeking health and wholeness is *Medication Madness: A Psychiatrist Exposes the Dangers of Mood-Altering Medications* by Peter R. Breggin, M.D. His book tells story after story of tragic outcomes for people who have believed the doctors that they didn't need to talk, they just needed to take medication to alter their moods. The book you hold in your hand tells of my own nearly fatal experience with an anti-depressant as a young person.

Breggin is a psychiatrist who mostly uses talk therapy in ministering to his patients. I applaud and admire his pursuit of a better way that does not include drugging of people who need help. I hope for an increase in the number of psychiatrists who don't rely primarily on medication. I don't object to the temporary use of a drug to bring a person out of psychosis, but I do mind drugs being used ongoingly as substitutes for relationship, talk and understanding. His book *Reclaiming Our children: A Healing Plan for a Nation in Crisis* is a must read for anyone who cares about children and knows that the problems which afflict our children and our nation are complex requiring new and better solutions. Maybe one day soon, schools and hospitals will employ intercessors to pray for patients and children.

I am especially happy that my healing class at church addresses the issue of demons and deliverance ministry. Years ago, I had read M. Scott Peck's book *People of the Lie: The Hope for Healing Human Evil*. His book challenged me to think in a new way. Peck, as a nationally known psychiatrist did a study of evil and concluded that the devil does indeed exist and remains to torment human beings all over the earth. After I became involved in inner healing and prayer counseling, I decided I didn't care much for the deliverance aspect of the ministry. I decided I would leave that to other people. I have since changed my mind. The teacher of our class has told us stories of breakthrough in people's lives because of deliverance from a trained ministry team. I also learned that fear can be perpetuated by a demonic spirit—a spirit of fear! As with worry, I am considering fear to be gone from my life.

I remain vigilant concerning bipolar disorder. It is a complex illness with euphoric highs and depressive lows. By God's grace I am an overcomer. The Church, imperfect as it is, has proved to be the safest place for me to be. To use Brennan Manning's words, I know that the church Is a gathering of "Ragamuffins" just like me. Yes, I have experienced judgment, misunderstanding, and abuse from being used, but I have also gained friends who believe in truth, forgiveness of sins, freedom from guilt and shame, encouragement, prophetic words, access to the Holy Spirit, holy angels, worship, dancing, faith, hope and unconditional love that never fails.

I do plan to continue building my faith. Jesus is a healer, and the Church is meant to be a hospital, rehab center, a school, a place of worship and even a restaurant and grocery provider for people who battle poverty. The people of God are meant to walk in His example. We all need healing in our bodies, minds, wills, emotions and spirits. I would not be here today were it not for my Wonderful Counselor (Isaiah 9:6) who moves through His people to be His heart, hands, and feet upon this earth. May His will be done.

Introduction

In 1971, while on a trip to Texas with my high school orchestra, a boy showed interest in me. As we got to know each other, I fell in love, and within a few weeks of returning home, I was manic—high on the idea that a cool guy liked me and wanted to spend time with me. The mania turned to psychosis, and I was hospitalized until my high became low and the awful truth began to seep in around the edges. Contrary to what a doctor had suggested to my parents, I had not lost my mind because someone had slipped me LSD. Rather, I was battling a serious illness then known as manic depression.

This book details the therapies, medications, and nutrients that played a role in helping me move along a path to wholeness. Some therapies were practically worthless, but some gave life and hope. The medications were hard hitting, and one proved nearly lethal. I have come to distrust the use of psychiatric medication except in emergency situations—to be used temporarily.

Some of the people I met along the way were helpful. Encounters with others made me want to run and hide or give up altogether. Overall, I was met with misunderstanding of bipolar disorder and mental illness in general. Stigma still stains those who are afflicted.

In the first chapters, I share details from the lives of my parents and my early years before the breakdown. In our lives, there are numerous people and events that shape us. The blessings and sins of our parents are handed down to us. Mostly my memoir focuses on my high school and college years, from age fifteen to twenty-two.

In my first year away at college, I had another breakdown and later a serious bout of depression that landed me in the hospital again. I recovered enough to be able to hold down jobs and finish college in my hometown. During that time, I dated "normal" guys and eventually met and married my husband, Bill.

The first chapter was written when I was eighteen years old. Because I wrote that chapter so close to the actual events, it includes many details that I could easily have lost with the passage of time. I hope the people come alive as vitally as I remember them. I also hope this book can minister to people fighting bipolar disorder, as well as those who have loved ones battling the disease.

I am careful never to say that I *am* bipolar because I am much more than an illness. Bipolar disorder does not define me. I am Claire, a beloved child of God who happens to have trouble with an illness.

Bipolar disorder is not a death sentence but an affliction as complex as human beings. I am fearfully and wonderfully made (Psalm 139:14 NIV), and in the process of researching and writing this book, my respect and awe of my Creator, who designed each of us—body, soul, and spirit—has grown. I owe God my trust and love. He is everything to me. He has been with me through the years, through the good times and during the confusing manias, psychoses, and crippling bouts of depression. When friends fall away He remains with me. Without Him, I am nothing. I will forever praise Him and thank Him for His sustaining presence.

Chapter 1

Roots

Weeping may endure for a night, but joy comes in the morning.
Psalm 30:5 (NKJV)

Blessed are those who mourn for they shall be comforted.
Matthew 5:4 (NASB)

In 1927, when my parents were born, Calvin Coolidge presided over the nation while the economy roared with new inventions like cars that started with keys rather than cranks and refrigerators. In May of that year, aviator Charles Lindberg made the first transatlantic flight from New York to Paris. A revolt began brewing against the laws prohibiting the sale of alcohol. Rebels of all stripes perfected the crafting of liquor in their homes and barns and down in the holler. Hooch became available in speakeasies under the direction of thugs like Al Capone. Still looming were The Great Depression, the horrors of Adolf Hitler, and the atomic bomb. An upbeat song, "I'm Looking Over a Four-Leaf Clover," was popular on the radio at the time, while F. Scott Fitzgerald penned stories of dysfunctional love. Our nation still had a few years to go before Franklin Delano Roosevelt became a household name. However, the optimism that followed World War I soon faded into the dust of the "Dirty Thirties."

Dad

My dad, Joseph William Foltz, was born in a small hospital near Des Moines, Iowa. Upon his birth, he joined his parents and two older sisters, Evelyn and Margaret. Dad was eventually followed by two more sisters and a brother—Jeanie, Estelle and Sterling. Shortly after his birth, the young family relocated to a small town in Nebraska and later to a small farm in the Sandhills. Dad grew up poor, skinny, and often hungry. His dad worked for the Works Progress Administration and was away from home for long stretches of time. As the oldest boy, Dad took on man-sized responsibilities in helping his mother. The kids sometimes climbed into bed hungry, drinking water beforehand in order to have full tummies. On Christmas, an orange or a candy bar split six ways was the extent of their celebration. One year, Dad received a toy truck, a cast off from the banker's son.

During Dad's school days, the population of Page was nearly one thousand. The town boasted two grocery stores—a farmer's store and a general store, a movie theater, a hotel (which later burned to the ground), a bakery, five filling stations, two barber shops, two cafes, two hardware stores, a garage, and a creamery where farmers brought cream to be shipped elsewhere to make butter. Later, when Dad was in the service, his mother and sisters lived in the telephone office, where they ran the switchboard.

By the time I became aware of Dad's past, the population of his little town had dwindled to just over one hundred people. A town's proximity to a main Nebraska Highway played a big role in whether it thrived or began to shrink. The town where Dad grew up was just a little too far off the beaten path to continue to flourish.

The Foltzes attended a rather wild—to the point of being unruly—Wesleyan Methodist church in town. Members referred to as "Holy Rollers." One Sunday, things got so out of hand that people were running outside around the church building. A man who was still inside picked up a chair and began swinging it in a circle above his head. When he let go, the chair flew through a window and broke the neck of a man who was running outside. Shortly after that, Dad's family began attending the more sedate Methodist church in town.

More than once Auntie Evelyn told me, voice quivering, "Your father was a darling little boy. One Sunday, he had a shiny new penny, and when it came time for the offering, he walked to the front and put his penny in the basket."

Once, I asked Dad if he had ever accepted Jesus as his savior. He said, "Yes, many times."

He had walked down the center aisle over and over in response to altar calls. An altar call is the summons given by a preacher or evangelist to people who want to commit their lives to Jesus. In spite of his repeated commitment, his faith was unsure. As he grew older, it remained so, because he missed coming to a secure place of trust that God could keep him. He worried as a young man that he was going to hell because of certain trespasses from his young years.

After Mom died in 2008, Dad stopped by my house and told me he had a song he wanted me to hear. It was George Strait singing "Love Without End, Amen." I listened to the lyrics.

Let me tell you a secret about a father's love,
a secret that my daddy said was just between us.
Daddies don't just love their children every now and then.
It's a love without end, Amen.

As I listened, I knew he was telling me that he loved me. Those words were followed by the last verse, which I also found comforting.

One night I dreamed I died and stood outside those pearly gates,
When suddenly I realized there must be some mistake.
If they know half the things I've done, they'll never let me in.
Then somewhere from the other side, I heard those words again:
Let me tell you a secret …

Wow! I was stunned. As an earthly, imperfect father, Dad was telling me not only that he loved me but also that he believed in God's grace—all in one song. I had often worried that Dad was not spiritual enough, and here I was faced with the truth that Dad *believed* but felt unworthy. He knew he was flawed and admitted it. His unworthiness was a safer place to hang out than dwelling in an arrogant assurance that he could do no wrong.

As adults, Dad and his siblings were extremely cautious about church attendance. Three of his four sisters converted to Catholicism, while Dad and Uncle Gilbert chose the Methodist path in adulthood. They were also cautious about pious, self-righteous preachers. Dad's mom, Clara, had suffered at the words and opinions of 1920s Pharisees after she had gotten pregnant by a man she knew before she met Grandpa. Because of the pregnancy, she moved from her home in Nebraska to a small town near Des Moines, Iowa, where she met Samuel Foltz. She and Samuel were married in short order before the birth of her first child, Evelyn. Grandma Clara's oldest brother lorded her indiscretion over her, and Grandma suffered the rest of her days not only from the judgment of others but most likely from the judgment she placed on herself. She worked hard to put food on the table for her children. During the years I knew her, she worked as a waitress. She had her first heart attack at age sixty-five and survived because Samuel was there to massage the area around her heart. She died from another when she was seventy-four. At the time of her death, she was working for a family taking care of a lady who was older than she was. Was she still working away the shame she must have experienced as a young woman?

Dad's father Samuel had only a third-grade education and had been raised by his mother after his parents divorced. Samuel was gone for lengthy periods of time, working first for the WPA, making one dollar a *day*. When he found out he could make fifty cents an *hour*, he began working for Carlsen Brothers building culverts and bridges. When he was home, he managed to dig a basement and begin construction on the family home in a place they came to refer to as "Starvation Hill." For a time, Clara and her children lived in the basement while the rest of the house was being finished. When it rained, water gushed through their living quarters.

One day, the Foltz kids found a dog nearly dead in a ditch. They named him Sandy. Each of the siblings hovered over, hugged, and petted him until he was licking their faces in gratitude. He was a former circus dog, a mixed breed and black and white in color. Sandy could ride a horse, jump through hoops, and play tug-o-war. He also provided protection as a guard dog. Uncle Arthur had a great big dog, but Sandy was smarter and in a fight Sandy bested Arthur's dog.

The family also owned and loved Rex, a gelded stallion. To hear Dad tell it, Rex possessed mythical powers. He was big, deep brown and had a white star on his forehead. Dad rode him bareback holding onto his mane. Later in life, Dad's sister Evelyn wrote a poem about Rex, calling him her "gallant steed."

One summer day, Rex broke my Dad's heart. Under the direction of Dad and Evelyn, Rex pulled a hay rake over some ruts, causing the rake to flip and impale the beautiful horse. I don't know what happened next. I asked my oldest cousin, Evelyn's daughter what likely happened to Rex after the accident. Did they call a vet? She said that veterinarians weren't very available at that time. Did they shoot the horse themselves to put him out of his misery? If so where did they get the gun? I don't know. Dad and his siblings lived, worked, and played as adult children trying as best they could, to fill in for an absent father who couldn't help the distance because he was away doing everything he could to provide for his family.

In eighth grade, there were fifteen to twenty students in my father's class, but by ninth grade, the class of '44 swelled to thirty-six because country kids from one-room schoolhouses joined with the kids from town. Only a few survived the nearly inevitable early career choice of farming. Twenty-four of thirty-six graduated with Dad.

Dad loved sports of all kinds, and because of the small school size, He was able to take part in every sport offered by his school. He ran track, pole vaulted, dribbled as a basketball guard, and played six-man football. At the Holt County track tournament, Dad made the all-county team two years in a row. He was a little kid trying hard to be tough. With his dad gone so much, he needed to work to prove himself capable of being the man of the family.

When he was fourteen, Dad remembered hearing the news of the bombing of Pearl Harbor on the radio at a filling station on December 7, 1941. Once he heard that the Japanese had bombed the American fleet in Hawaii, he, like so many young men, could barely contain himself long enough to enlist to help protect and fight for our country. Dad yearned to be a fighter pilot.

Dad was the president of his senior class and graduated at age seventeen in 1944. After graduation, Dad showed up at a recruiting office to enlist in the air force. He was denied entry because a test revealed that he had albumin in his urine. I read that a healthy kidney doesn't allow the protein albumin pass into the urine. Albumin can indicate trouble in either the liver or the kidneys. In spite of the albumin, the Navy accepted Dad. He entered boot camp at Great Lakes near Chicago in the fall of 1944. From boot camp, he went to radio school in Indianapolis for five months.

On a chilling side note, according to the *Quad-City Times*, July 30,1945, the USS Indianapolis was torpedoed. It was a Portland class heavy cruiser and had just delivered components of the atomic bomb to Tinian Island near Saipan. Of the 1,199 men aboard, only 316 survived the exposure, dehydration and shark attacks." Dad said many of the guys he knew from boot camp were on that ship, where he would have been except for the fact that the Indianapolis had shipped out earlier than Dad. Dad was delayed because of the time he had spent at radio school in Indianapolis.

After completing radio school, Dad shipped out of San Francisco in March of 1945. As Dad's ship steamed into the North Pacific, preparations for the Enola Gay were being finalized. Virtually no one was aware at the time of the Manhattan Project. For all his family knew, Dad might be one of those who had no choice but to take part in the probable invasion of Japan.

The first bomb code-named "Little Boy," was dropped on Hiroshima August 6, 1945, followed by "Fat Boy," which was dropped on Nagasaki on August 9. These were the only atomic bombs that have ever been dropped in the history of the world partly because Harry Truman had the inner strength and courage to follow through, even though he hated to do it to "those kids" (Japanese children). While near Shanghai, Dad served aboard the USS Manikin (AOG-60). Japan formally surrendered on September 2, 1945. Dad then spent time in Shanghai. His ship refueled minesweepers near Okinawa, Japan.

A typhoon hit the area in October 1945. Dad told me he wasn't really scared, as the ship had a lot of ballast. In Shanghai, Dad and his buddies saw people living on houseboats, bodies floating in the river, and rickshaw runners on the streets.

In 1946, his ship was ordered back to Pearl Harbor. Dad got a three-hundred-dollar bonus for signing up for the atomic bomb test. He flew from Hawaii to Kwajalein Island in the Kwajalein Atoll of the Marshall Islands. There, he volunteered and was chosen to accompany Admiral Byrd to the South Pole. Even though that particular trip fell through, the group got to go to New Zealand instead. There, they were treated like kings, complete with tours and dinners. The two-engine plane they took back to Kwajalein was overloaded, and a tire blew during a stop on Wake Island which worried the pilot.

Back on Kwajalein, Dad was assigned to fly around the islands on a shuttle plane and deliver mail to the outposts. Later, while stationed in San Francisco, Dad was assigned to a flotilla of landing crafts. One day Dad was called into the commander's office. The commander wasn't a nice person. Dad did not like him.

Dad got out of the service in the fall of 1948 and spent part of the winter living and working on a ranch in Nebraska owned by his oldest sister, Evelyn, and her husband, Carl. The winter of 1948-1949 was the time of the Great Blizzard. Years later, that storm was dubbed the "Katrina of the Great Plains." A hay rack could not make it through the deep snow. They used bulldozers to open trails to the cattle.

Dad told me that he'd thought he'd probably be a truck driver, and he might have chosen that occupation if it hadn't been for the Servicemen's Readjustment Act of 1944, more commonly known as the GI Bill." Aunt Evelyn enrolled him at Wayne State Teacher's college in northeast Nebraska. It was there that he met Mom in 1949.

Mom

My mother, Emma Jean was born in December 1927 to William and Myrtle Schluensen in a farmhouse in northeast Nebraska. Emma joined her eighteen-month-old brother Herbert. Grandma Myrtle said her baby, my mom, cried a lot due to a birth defect that caused her pain. Mom was born with congenital hip dysplasia, a condition where the hip socket does not properly form around the head of the femur. She was treated by being placed in a cast. I do not know how early she learned to walk, but when she was little, she began riding a pony, which gave her a form of recreation and transportation that made her childhood more pleasurable than it might have been. I mention this because Mom's hip played a significant role in my life. It affected what Mom could do, influenced her mood, and limited our activities. When we went shopping together, she often took breaks to rest. As a little girl, I found the frequent stopping while shopping to be nearly unbearable and easily grew tired of standing in one place.

Mom was the second of six children and one of four who were born with birth defects. Each of her three brothers, Herbert, William and Peter had cleft lips and palates. William died in a hospital when he was nine months old. My grandmother and mom, who was only two at the time, were in the room with "Little Brother" when he drew his last breath after having surgery to patch his lip and palate. His death so traumatized my grandmother that she did not allow her next son, Peter, to have the surgery until he was much older.

Her decision, while protecting Peter's life, didn't do much for his ability to communicate. It proved difficult to decipher what Peter was saying, and he had to work hard as a little boy to make himself understood.

Mom cared for younger siblings. In addition to her brothers, she had two sisters—Sophie and Rosie. When Peter was born, Mom remembered overseeing little two-year-old Sophie. Unlike today, when getting up and moving around is recognized as an important part of post partem recovery, in Grandma's day, women spent at least a week in bed after giving birth. Even though Mom was probably seven at the time, she remembered running after Sophie, caring for and comforting her as best she could.

The congenital difficulties of the four babies got around through gossip. The young family felt the sting of being different. Mom said that there was a common belief at that time that people with defects were cursed. I now believe that a combination of genetics and poor nutrition led to the birth defects. Grandma didn't have prenatal vitamins. I also believe that we all have curses on us that can be broken by a knowledgeable healing counselor. Mom's family wasn't any worse than other families.

However, I believe these experiences with rejection from the community affected the way my mother later viewed our neighbors and my dad's coworkers. Outsiders could not be trusted. When I was a child, one of Dad's friends would occasionally dropped by unexpectedly. Mom suspected he was just collecting information to be used against us. Her paranoia may have had some grounds, but it also kept people away who could have been family friends. Whenever we did have company, substantial cleaning and food preparation always preceded the visit.

Mom's family lived on a rented farm and worked hard to make a living. Grandpa raised cattle, hogs, and chickens. They also owned several horses and ponies when Mom was little. The children took part in daily chores, which included milking cows both before and after school. Milking each cow took about fifteen minutes. Once the milk was collected, it was placed in a separator for extracting the cream from the milk. The cream would then be placed in a gallon-sized butter churn, with a crank that you turned until butter was made.

Grandma had an extensive vegetable garden of potatoes, cabbages, peas, green beans, tomatoes, and carrots. Sweet corn grew in a small field. Whatever the family didn't eat fresh, Grandma canned. On Saturdays they went into town, where they could buy flour and sugar in cotton sacks.

Mom's mother Myrtle came from a large family. When she was young, the family lived for a while in Washington state where her mother Maggie spent time in an asylum. Aunt Rosie recently supplied me with writings where Grandma Myrtle shared memories of her mother's illness. Grandma remembered her mother before they moved back to Nebraska. At times her mother was uncharacteristically, loud, abrupt and unkind. During, those periods she had trouble sleeping and kept her husband Henry awake as well. After they had returned home on a train and settled on a farm, the young family was relieved for a few years. However, under considerable stress from cooking, tending to her family and the boarders who lived with them in their house, Maggie had another breakdown. Her husband, my great grandpa did his best to tend to her, but soon, reluctantly took her to an asylum in Lincoln, known as Green Gables. Grandma Myrtle's much younger sister had to go live temporarily with another family. Was my trouble with bipolar disorder inherited through Great Grandma Maggie?

After she graduated from high school, Mom taught in a country school and saved her money so she could go to Wayne State Teacher's College. She was a junior working as a cashier in "the Caf" when my dad, whose college career had been delayed by service in World War II, walked in as a freshman. They got to know each other and began dating. Everything was fine, but then they each went their separate ways for the summer.

A few weeks later, Mom got a call from Dad. He told her he wanted to meet her in Norfolk because he had something to tell her.

Mom's older brother Herbert drove her into town. Dad announced that he wanted to break up with her. News of the Schluensens and their birth defects had travelled the seventy-five miles or so from Mom's section of Nebraska to the Sandhills, where Dad's mom, Clara, had heard about the birth defects. She advised Dad that my mom wasn't good marriage material. Mom, of course, was devastated, and she cried. "I knew no one would want to marry me," she told Dad. As a result of Dad's announcement, her plans for the future shifted. She decided she wanted to own and operate a movie theater.

However, in the fall at school, Mom and Dad resumed their romance as if nothing had happened. Mom graduated from college in 1950. That fall, she taught school in a town about fifty miles south of the college. In May 1951, Mom and Dad were married by a Presbyterian minister at Mom's home on the farm with family and close friends in attendance. After a brief honeymoon to Kansas City, they lived in an apartment.

Dad was called back into the service in the fall of '51, this time for the Korean War. In a photo taken before he left, Mom is smiling, but Dad has a melancholy, faraway look in his eye. He reluctantly left Mom and travelled to San Francisco to board the Fred C. Ainsworth U.S. N.S. on his way to Guam. On the way his ship harbored in Pearl, Hawaii for three or four hours. In the short time he requested and was able to see his little brother Sterling who was on another ship. I have a letter Dad sent to his mother that included a picture of Sterling standing in front of his ship.

Dad had to spend a year on Guam as a radio operator. He sent pictures to Mom of him climbing a coconut tree and one of him in a communications office. Upon his return, with another year of service under his belt, he began his junior year at the University of Northern Colorado in Greeley while Mom taught and worked part time at a hospital as a switchboard operator. Dad finally finished his degree in the summer of 1954. He and Mom then moved back to Nebraska.

Chapter 2

Soil—Nebraska and Iowa

Nebraska

By the time I was born, the United States had emerged as a superpower. World War II and the war in Korea were past tense, although a new war was brewing in Vietnam. Former Commanding General of the European Theater of Operations, Dwight David Eisenhower and the controversial Richard Nixon presided over our nation as President and Vice President. "Unchained Melody" played on the airwaves, and fourteen thousand girls swamped Elvis after a concert in Florida. Science rose like a god, as the race into outer space was about to begin. Two years later, Dr. Arvid Carlsson of Sweden discovered the neurotransmitter, dopamine. It wasn't until 2000, that he won the Nobel Peace Prize in Medicine/Physiology for his discovery.

My Birth

Mom and Dad got teaching jobs and rented a house in Oakdale, a town halfway between both sets of grandparents. I was born in May 1955 in a little hospital in nearby Tilden. I broke my mother's tailbone during the birth process. Of course, I didn't mean to, but her coccyx was in the way. I'm not sure what it did to my head, but I know I was separated from her for a few days after I was born, as she wasn't feeling very well. Many years later I was told about the tailbone incident. It made me wonder what that incident and separation may have done to my head, not to mention my sense of well-being.

The more I have learned about inner healing and epigenetic damage, the more I realized that the circumstances of my birth could very well have contributed to later difficulties with mental illness. Any number of things can cause trauma that damages our DNA. I have reason to believe that my DNA was harmed that day. In addition, the immediate infant-mother connection is essential for anyone who hopes to raise a healthy, well-adjusted child. To a newborn, minutes can seem like hours. I believe the time I spent isolated from Mom caused separation anxiety and abandonment fears that plagued me most of my life.

After I was born, Mom and Dad found teaching positions at a high school in southeast Nebraska in Hebron. Our little family lived in that town for two years. I spent my days with Mrs. Gordon and Helen. My caretakers were nice ladies. They reported to my parents that I would stand by the storm door, look out and say, "I love you, outdoors." Dad told me that one afternoon as the school was preparing to batten down for a possible tornado, he ran from the high school to Mrs. Gordon's house to make sure they were making plans to take me to the basement.

It was while we lived there that Mom experienced an ectopic pregnancy. One morning, Mom was not feeling well. Dad sensed there was something seriously wrong as he was getting ready to go to work. He lingered long enough to recognize that Mom was in trouble and got her to the hospital before she bled to death. Dad and I spent several days without her. Mom came home with a large scar on her belly and only one ovary. For a while after that experience, Mom held me back whenever I wanted a hug. Hugging would hurt her incision. The scar looked enormous to my little eyes. I needed a big "Mama" hug more than ever when she came home, but I had to make do with sitting by her side as she read me stories. Because Mom was in pain, a sideways, "good enough" hug had to suffice.

Eventually, Mom and Dad decided to find a bigger school that wasn't so subject to the soap opera drama of a small town. Apparently teaching jobs were scarce. Dad wrote to several schools, including one in the Quad Cities, which is made up of Davenport and Bettendorf, Iowa and Rock Island and Moline, Illinois. Each city is joined to the others by bridges crossing the Mississippi River. Dad was hoping for a job in Lincoln, Nebraska but the Quad Cities had a job opening at a new junior high. He met with administrators for an interview and was taken for a visit to the new school to get a feel for the "tone" of the building. The personnel director offered Dad a job that day to teach physical education, science and typing. He also could potentially coach football, wrestling, and track. Dad waited for about a week before letting them know he would take the job. I was two years old.

Quad Cities

By the time we arrived in the Quad Cities, we had moved twice since my birth. Almost immediately, Dad was caught up in the whirlwind of a new job plus invitations for golf outings on the weekends. I remember my parents exchanging angry words about Dad leaving on Saturdays to go golfing while Mom was left alone, as she had been all week. Mom was still adjusting to a "big" city and lots of time alone with me. She grew up in the country where the nearest neighbor was at least half a mile away.

Mom kept life regular. She included me in chores like folding and "sprinkling" freshly clean clothes. She'd spend hours at the ironing board toiling over stiff shirts and pants. Mom remained sane by exchanging letters with her mother at home on the farm. In the summers and at Christmastime, in the days before Interstate 80 was completed, we travelled the old Highway 6. It took us twelve hours to drive four hundred miles. We had to slow down to a lower speed limit in every town along the way. There were no public facilities in rest areas. It was challenging to take little people just learning to use the toilet into less-than-sterile gas station restrooms.

Mom was complicated. I knew her well. She needled me, confused me, and cared for me, in spite of her own complexities and contradictions. In her later years, she almost obsessively tried to understand me. I love her for her attempts but coming to a place where I could accept and truly love her took more than I was able to completely manage in her lifetime.

I believe I knew Mom better than my sisters did, or at least I knew her in different ways. As a little girl, I felt secure in her presence but also smothered at times. An ongoing feeling for me in childhood was an almost physical sensation of not having enough air to breathe. Mom always knew what was best for me and for everyone else. In the presence of others, she usually spoke for me, which didn't do much to build confidence in my own ability to speak for myself. There was an unarticulated expectation that I needed to be perfect. It was only in my adult years, starting around age thirty as I pursued emotional and spiritual healing, that I began to understand what Mom had unwittingly done to hamper my growth and stability. Her unaddressed, unhealed hurts had affected me fundamentally.

As her oldest child I felt her pain, disappointments, fears, and sorrows. She was real and open when things bothered her. She was not one to retreat to the bedroom and sob quietly into her pillow. She had trouble hiding her true feelings when she sensed injustice or felt threatened. Mom was touchy and often negative and irritable. Arguments between Mom and Dad easily got loud. Apparently, they had no idea that their words might be disturbing to their young children. I dreaded their arguments. I got so I could sense the tension rising. I became alert and would often hurry to see what I could do to ease any simmering unrest. I could clear the table or straighten a mess in the living room. I knew the signs—Mom's discontent followed by Dad's frustration.

Mom had a bright and sunny side to her also. Her praise resounded, and she delighted in real triumph. I believe her ability to enjoy and remark on what was good increased as she aged and lived with my dad, who often praised her sincerely. "Emma, this is the best chocolate cake I've ever eaten." Time and again I would hear him exclaim with genuine surprise and delight after tasting some morsel of her excellent cooking.

When I was young, Mom was in the habit of keeping the wolf from the door. Her fears often filled the air in the form of warning, criticism, or discrimination about who or what might be allowed to enter our sacred family grounds. When I was little, newly transplanted to the Quad Cities from small-town Nebraska, the nights without Dad while he worked at Sears or coached wrestling or football, proved to be frightening. Mom and I would often scuttle from room to room together.

When I was about four years old, I remember going to Baumgartner's house, where neighbors had gathered to discuss a "peeping Tom" in our area. I doubt that such a person had ever even been mentioned in small-town Nebraska. To Mom, the Quad Cities area was big. It had not one but many junior and senior high schools. There were people of color just down the street from our house. This was good—simply different. African Americans were a novelty for those coming from sparsely populated places like rural Nebraska. There was never denigrating talk of "people of color" in our house. Mom eventually taught at a high school that had a substantial number of African American students.

Back in 1957, '58 and early '59, it was just Mom and me during the day. We shared breakfast, and I usually watched Captain Kangaroo and Mr. Green Jeans, who I imagined was my uncle Herbert who also wore overalls. Mom included me in chores as much as I was able. On winter mornings, she hung clothes on a line in the basement. After they dried, together we sprinkled water to soften them making them easier to iron. Mom ironed while I rode a little tricycle around and around on the basement floor.

At lunchtime, we watched *As the World Turns* and made lunches, like tomato soup with Velveeta cheese on grilled white bread. Mom and I often watched *Queen for a Day.* For each episode, three women shared their stories of hardship and heartache. An applause meter determined which of the three distraught women won the title "Queen for a Day." Mom cried along with the chosen queen as she received a crown, a robe, appropriate prizes, and encouragement to keep going despite her difficulties. Stories of trouble always softened Mom.

I was a rather fussy child. It seemed that little things bothered me, like tight or scratchy clothing. I tried hard to be good but was often dissatisfied with the way things were. I did well with the rather strict schedule that Mom kept.

During those years, Mom took me to a pediatrician who was located in a brick building near the center of town. It was during those visits that my mistrust of doctors began. This guy had the authority to prescribe medicine and shots. I still remember when he came in the room for my examination. I don't remember that he either introduced himself or brought himself down to eye level with me.

I modestly clutched my undershirt in front of me. Irritated, he grabbed it and cast it to the side. After listening to my heart and taking my temperature, he left and a nurse came in with a shot. I hid behind my mother while the nurse got a hold of me and held the syringe up to my skinny little arm. She promised me a sucker if I would hold still. I held still as she injected the needle and then swiped my wound. I got the sucker. I hated suckers! I don't remember going to see that doctor as a teenager.

Mom spanked me to keep me in line. When I fidgeted, frustrated by the limitations her broken hip placed on her mobility, she let me know of her disapproval. As a young child I tried to always tell the truth—even tell on myself. That habit seemed to mitigate any reprimand.

My sisters didn't come under the same scrutiny that I did because Mom was outnumbered after they were born. Sometimes they were actually able to climb the stairs before she could catch them.

After lunch, Mom usually read to me. I learned a collection of nursery rhymes by heart from a supplemental book to the *World Book Encyclopedia* that sat on a bookshelf. We had a complimentary set because Dad had been a *World Book Encyclopedia* salesman for a while. Mom read and reread books like *Heidi, Goldilocks, Dr. Dan the Bandage Man, The Little Engine That Could*, and *Little Black, a Pony*. Books became a delightful way to escape from life for a little while.

After reading, we would take a nap. Usually, I woke up to find Mom downstairs, sewing or preparing food for supper. In the late afternoon, Dad returned to eat with us but was often right out the door again on his way to a job in the men's clothing department at Sears.

For toys, I had a doll, a yellow stuffed chicken, and a blue, '57 Chevy pickup- a gift from my Uncle Herbert. I didn't have many toys so I used my imagination. I remember having a plastic nail that I pretended was a little person. The bottom of the wooden television stand could be a stage, a porch or a house—whatever my imagination required.

When I was little, there were a lot of movies and television shows about the old west. On Saturday nights I was allowed to stay up late—until nine o'clock to watch a popular western which started at 8:00. Fresh from a bath, I loved sitting on the couch next to Mom and Dad, as the theme song that evoked galloping horses came on the air. A map of the Ponderosa caught fire while Adam, Hoss, Little Joe and Pa came riding onto the scene. It was both exciting and cozy to tune into the adventures of Ben and his sons as they directed operations at the Ponderosa Ranch in Nevada. As soon as the show was over I had to go to bed so I could get up in time for church the next morning.

During those preschool years, The Roy Rogers Show caught my fancy. It was set in the 1950's and ran until 1957. I must have caught the reruns which were available on Saturday mornings. In addition to Roy, the show featured his wife Dale Evans, Trigger the palomino and a German shepherd, named Bullet. The show offered a lot of cowboy related merchandise. Maybe that's how I got my cowgirl skirt, hat and a stick horse. I often pretended to be like the cowgirls I'd seen on TV.

I missed Dad and wished I could see him more often. I remember one rare evening when he was home sitting on the couch singing. I lay next to him with my head in his lap. Dad had a mellow voice. A lonely melody accompanied the words about leaving on a train. "If you miss the train I'm on, you will know that I am gone, you can hear the whistle blow a hundred miles." I cried as he sang. I loved him so. His frequent absence made my longing for him more intense.

Eventually, we acquired a stereo. Dad often came home, stretched out between the speakers and listened to the Kingston Trio or Marty Robbins. Mom liked Frankie Lane, and of course, given Dad's more recent history in the Navy, we had an album with Mary Martin and Mario Puzzo on the cover containing the beautiful music from *South Pacific*.

In the warmer months, Mom and I got to know some of the neighbors. A pair of sisters, Catherine and Frances lived next door. I often rode my tricycle down the block and stopped to talk with Frances. She might be out digging up dandelions from her lawn.

"Why are you digging up the pretty flowers?" I asked.

"They are weeds and if I don't dig them up now, they will take over my yard."

I still didn't understand, but I liked Frances. One day she invited me into her house. I loved looking at her house from the inside until there came a knock at the door. It was my mother. She had looked outside and noticed my abandoned tricycle. Sure enough, she found me!

Across the street, Mom found a neighbor about her age. Mrs. Aiken lived in the brick house with her husband and little boy Joey. Mr. Aiken just happened to be a dentist. Someone we needed! So, we all got to know Dr. Aiken as patients. His office was about three blocks down the street and around the corner. After I had lost my baby teeth, he noticed my permanent bottom teeth were crowded and overlapping. He told my parents that if I would just push on the teeth with my tongue, I could avoid braces. Unfortunately, my tongue mostly forgot to push on my teeth.

February 1959

Late one evening in February 1959, I was taken across the street to the Aikin's house and placed on a twin bed in Joey's room. Joey was my buddy, and I spent the night with him while our baby was being born. My sister entered the world on Valentine's Day at five o'clock in the morning. I woke up that day to get dressed and have oatmeal in a way I never had before. It was crispier and crunchier than the kind Mom made. As I was attempting to adjust to our neighbors and their strange ways, Joey actually got back into his pajamas for our naps in the afternoon!

Meanwhile, Grandma Myrtle was on a Greyhound bus coming to be with us for a while. After our naps, Mrs. Aikin thought Joey and I could have fun pouring maple syrup on the newly fallen snow and then scooping it into cereal bowls for an ice cream–like snack. Joey and I sat in their backyard in our little snow suits while Mrs. Aikin poured syrup on the snow. She helped us scoop the syrup-snow mixture into our bowls. *Hmm, weirdly OK, but why?* I wondered. Didn't these people know about ice cream?

Fortunately, my dad went to the bus station to pick up my more familiar grandma who had arrived from Norfolk, Nebraska. She was a welcome addition to the family to help with our new member while Dad was at school. Her presence brought calm and helped us all get used to caring for the baby they were calling Megan. Dad, in his enthusiastic way, giggled about Megan and how sturdy she was. When he lifted her an inch above the crib and dropped her, she got mad. He seemed pleased with her robust manner. His apparent joy with Megan made me uneasy, and I began to doubt my importance to him. A rival had entered my life. How would I cope?

One day Mom and Grandma were in the only bathroom at the top of the stairs bathing Megan in a little tub placed on a card table. Feeling neglected, I deliberately wet my pants. I knew what I was doing. My rival was getting all the attention, and I needed some. Mom and Grandma were kind and made excuses for me. It was so nice to have Grandma nearby, if only for a little while.

After Grandma went home, Mom carried on and lived beyond expectations in taking care of Megan and me. Despite her bum hip, she managed to keep me busy while tending to the baby and climbing the stairs to the only bathroom.

As Megan began to get around, Mom had to watch so she wouldn't climb the stairs by herself. Sometimes, I helped watch over the toddler. I remember sitting next to my little sister at the top of the staircase, while Mom was in the bathroom. For no reason, Megan, who must have been teething, bit into my upper arm. "Mom!" Her new little teeth were sharp!

The Tangle That Kept Me Bound

Mom had allowed a tangle of perfectionism to grow inside her as a form of protection to keep away the pain of trauma as a result of distance from family and the shame of a birth defect, not only her own but the hare lips of her brothers. Perfectionism coupled with control became a way of way of coping and blocking out the horror of the sexual abuse that she had suffered at the hands of Floyd, a hired man, when she was only seven years old. Surely, no one needed to know of that particular childhood trauma, and I only found out from Dad toward the very end of her life.

After Mom's death in 2008, in shuffling through pages, letters, and clippings from her writings, I came across a mention of Floyd.

Mom wrote, "Floyd turned out to be quite a pedophile. He liked to capture me in the cave or the hay mow and fondle me. I kept telling him he should smell his hands and then he would not do that anymore. My parents were not apprised of this. I am sure he told me not to tell. I certainly never would have." That was all she wrote. She never mentioned it to me.

Although my dad did say something about Floyd before Mom died, I never heard or understood any more than those six sentences she left behind. Questions remained. Did her hip problem make it hard for her to get away from him? Did he take advantage of her because she was obviously damaged? How much had this groping confused and dirtied Mom's spirit?

Those few sentences said so much, and I am sure they at least partially explained the undercurrent of anger that I felt in day-to-day life with her. There was a spirit of heaviness hovering over her daily labor, whether cooking, cleaning, or tending to the needs of her children. My mother often seemed to be under a cloud that I did not understand. I could not figure out how to blow it away so she could see and feel the warmth of the sun. Mom kept a keen eye on me whenever I had friends in our house. We were not allowed to play doctor or have the bedroom door closed. I am thankful for her watchfulness.

Perhaps it was the perfectionism that forced a wedge between Mom and me—that made what could have been an easy, trusting relationship into one that was more formal and less fulfilling. I wanted Mom to just hold me and cuddle me, but there was often a distance. Perhaps it was something more.

Maybe perfectionism divided us, but what kept us together? Mom was driven to be the mother of perfect children, but she also had a college degree and a drive to make something more of herself than just a perfect mother and housewife. Mom went to great lengths to prepare wholesome meals, based partly on the knowledge of cooking she had gained from working alongside her mother.

Every fall, just as Grandpa William had helped him, neighbor men showed up to help my grandpa bring in the harvest. Mom and her sisters helped my grandmother make large, from-scratch meals to satisfy the gathered farmers. Potatoes from the garden were mashed with milk from the cows that my mom, Herbert, and their younger siblings had milked that morning. Butter had been churned just days before. Grandma and daughters filled their table with garden vegetables, like green beans and cabbage, rolls, some form of beef, chicken, or pork and always pies or cakes. They worked hard enough when it was just grandpa and his sons, but the work multiplied when the extras gathered around their dining room table during that season.

Country kids who worked hard in the morning before breakfast were hungry and ready to eat when breakfast rolled around. But we lived in the city. Even so, in the mornings, Mom would coax, "Claire, eat your Cream of Wheat. It will warm your tummy."

"My tummy isn't cold."

"You need something that will stick to your ribs."

"My ribs?"

"Yes, so you don't get hungry later."

"But I'm not even hungry now."

One night after supper, Mom was getting Megan ready for bed, and Dad took me into the kitchen and speared a couple of slices of roast beef from a pan of leftovers in the refrigerator. He chewed a piece of the beef and spit it out onto a spoon and offered it to me. He wanted me to have some beef in a more palatable way. L-salivarius is a probiotic found in human saliva. Had dad learned this from his mother? It seemed odd to me, and I don't remember him ever feeding me in that way again. Surely my mother would have scolded him for it. Dad wasn't as rigid as Mom in regard to food and cleanliness. He seemed more apt to follow his instincts, which were telling him that his little girl needed the protein, fat, and zinc that roast beef provides.

As a young father, Dad was often impatient. One morning I went into the bathroom to watch him shave, brush his teeth, and gargle. I showed some interest in the gargling business. He put some mouthwash in my mouth. I played dumb, hoping he'd give instructions, but he didn't have time for my games. Sheepishly I spit it into the sink. Dad would go down to breakfast, eat his cereal, and then pour his coffee into the cereal bowl so it would cool quickly. He could finish it before heading out the door.

On days when before I started school Mom prodded Megan and me to pretend we were characters from a book or animals we had read about—like Peter Rabbit of Chicken Little. Mom had directed plays for high school kids when she taught school. So it was *in* Mom to encourage us to pretend—to act and to use our imaginations. I loved pretending.

In warm weather, I played in the backyard. I loved playing dress-up. One afternoon, I had on one of Mom's long dresses with high heels. I carried a curtain rod as a pretend cane. As I neared the top of the stairs, the heel of my shoe caught in the hem of the dress, and I tumbled backward, cracking the back of my head. My head bled so much that Mom called Dad, who came home from school. Eventually my head stopped bleeding.

On summer evenings, Mom put Megan in a stroller and we walked down our side of the block, crossed the street and came back up the other. On one such evening we met Mrs. Warnken. She was sitting on her porch and invited us to sit with her and talk. So, I climbed the five steps to her porch, and Mom carried Megan who was placed in her lap. I wasn't particularly paying attention to what Mom and Mrs. Warnken talked about, but I do remember Mrs. Warnken had a candy dish. On her porch, I got to taste chocolate covered raisins for the first time.

Wyoming

In late May of 1960, our little family prepared to spend the season at the University of Wyoming in Laramie. Dad was going to school again. Congress had passed legislation in 1958 to help the

U.S. keep up with the Soviet Union in space. President Eisenhower signed the bill into the law called the National Defense Education Act, which provided financial support for teachers who wished to further their education in the sciences. After World War II, science was highly revered and offered a way to keep our status as a world superpower.

We packed up the 1957 Pontiac. The car had a large interior. The night before we left, Mom and Dad managed to fill the trunk and interior of the car with all the clothes and items we might need for the summer. Early the next morning we headed west along Highway 6.

Grandma and Grandpa's little hilltop farm in Nebraska was our first overnight stop. We spent a day there, and I sat for the first and only time atop my mother's twenty-eight-year-old pony. Buster was frail and bony. He was the same pony that had made it possible for my mother to get around as a young girl. I'm glad that, though he was feeble, I got a chance to experience the remaining bit of Buster. He broke his leg while we were in Wyoming. Grandpa and Uncle Herbert had no choice but to shoot and bury him on the farm.

In Laramie, Wyoming, we lived in furnished student housing. I wasn't aware at the time that Mom was pregnant again with my youngest sister, Annie. Mom made a home for us in the little two-bedroom house on a street with identical dwellings that went on for several blocks. Hampered though she was by her hip, she shepherded Megan and me through walks around the block. Megan climbed onto every tricycle in every yard, and the walks seemed to take forever. At the house, Mom did allow me to visit two or three houses away by myself, but I wasn't permitted to cross the street alone.

One afternoon, our little family prepared to go shopping. Dad and Mom got Megan and me ready. Dad took us to the car to wait for Mom. Dad fidgeted as we waited, talking about how slow Mom was. In some ways Dad was like a little kid and I could convince him to act on some of my little girl ideas.

"Daddy?"

"What?"

"Let's drive around the block while we wait."

"Okay. She'll probably be ready by the time we get back."

I wasn't prepared to find Mom outside crying when we returned. Did she really think we were going to leave her? I felt bad for her. Dad apologized when she got in.

"Oh Emma, we weren't going to leave you," he said, soothingly.

That summer in Laramie was colder than my parents expected. We had little shorts and tops designed for hot, humid Iowa weather. One Saturday, our family joined other families from student housing, in a forested area for a cookout. Even though I had an earache, I went along but spent most of the time lying on the back seat of the car.

In Laramie, I caught more than one bout of fever and sniffles. One night, Dad drove me to a clinic where I was given a shot and Dad received instructions to feed me 7UP. I had earaches and ongoing sinus troubles. My summer afflictions foreshadowed a difficult year in kindergarten.

Somehow, that summer with two children and another on the way, Dad managed to study and gain credits that could move him up the salary scale. He also learned more about science related issues that would help him in teaching junior high students.

Chapter 3

Grade School - 1960-1967

My year in kindergarten disappointed me in more ways than one. I had longed for and dreamed of kindergarten—sitting at desks and being a big kid. That dream never materialized. We sat at round tables. Our kindergarten room was large, with a fishpond and a second-floor loft that overlooked the main floor. The loft housed a make-believe house with tables, chairs, stove, refrigerator, dolls, and a doll bed—a dream come true for little girls. I rarely got to ascend the stairs to that magical place.

Our class was filled with forty-two children. Baby Boomers, the children of World War II veterans overwhelmed the schools. I cannot imagine teaching a kindergarten class, much less one with forty-two kids. We spent a lot of time with our heads down on a table.

Every day around ten o'clock, a couple of crates filled with bottles of milk arrived in our room, and each child was required to have a snack of lukewarm milk. Even thinking about the milk now makes me feel slightly nauseated. Conventional wisdom at the time told us that American children needed a lot of milk from two-thousand-pound animals so that we could have sturdy bones and muscles and grow big and strong. I have no doubt that the "snack" at school, combined with all the milk I drank at home, contributed greatly to my ongoing earaches and sore throats.

In college, Mom had minored in home economics and learned about the four food groups, which in those days consisted of 1) meat, 2) dairy, 3) fruits and vegetables, and 4) breads and cereals. There was no fiber in the first two food groups. Mom fed us according to the existing standards. For a while we owned a milk box which sat near our front door. The milk man would stop by and put a bottle of milk in our insulated box. After we moved to another house, we made regular trips to a nearby milk store. I believe my streak of sickness in kindergarten was fed by the substantial emphasis on animal products.

That year, I missed six weeks of school with measles, chickenpox, and scarlet fever. My diet, heavy in milk, meat, and cooked vegetables, contributed greatly to my malaise. Most of the grains were in the form of processed white bread and worthless cereals, like puffed rice or sugar-puffed wheat. Shredded wheat was probably the healthiest form of cereal that we ate. Occasionally, I ate part of an apple or a piece of banana, but mostly fruit came in the form of orange juice which contains very little, or canned fruit, peaches or pears in syrup. We ate a lot of beef, chicken, corn, potatoes, and canned green beans, peas and wonder bread.

We also drank a lot of milk. Later in life, when I realized that I had an intolerance to milk, and gave it up, at least some of my problems began to clear. Stuffiness, earaches and headaches disappeared.

"Salads" usually consisted of cabbage with a mayonnaise dressing or fruit swimming in sweet, colored gelatin. Sometimes, Mom added nuts, celery or carrots to the Jell-o. Our diet was very sweet. We believed Mary Poppins when she sang "a spoonful of sugar helps the medicine go down." If something like grapefruit or cottage cheese wasn't sweet enough, a teaspoon of sugar, made the sour morsels acceptable. I survived, but I cannot say that I was super healthy. In those days, the meat and dairy lobbyists worked hard and found much favor in Washington D.C.

Annie

Annie, who was supposed to be a boy, entered our lives a few days before Christmas in 1960. She was dark haired, long, and skinny. Because of the timing of her birth, Grandma didn't come to be with us. Christmas was near and Dad would soon be home from school for a break. In the days leading up to Christmas, my little rival, Megan grew in her ability to entertain. She learned Christmas carols and unabashedly sang for us and neighbors.

While Mom was in the hospital, Frances, our next-door neighbor, watched Megan and me during the day. Megan experimented with her skills at being bossy. Frances humbly obeyed when Megan pointed to the table and told her to put the ketchup "right there." Pleased with her newfound power, Megan regularly practiced being bossy. We were both so glad to see Mom when she came home shortly before Christmas.

In June, we moved to a new three-bedroom ranch in a developing area in the west part of town. The outside of the house was covered with charcoal gray brushed cedar shingle siding. Dad had arranged with the developer to have our house built $15,000. Lots of nearly identical houses began filling the lots in our neighborhood. Ours was one of the first on the block. We had an attached one-car garage and a relatively big backyard that was lined with poplar trees. Megan and I shared a bedroom. Annie had the little room, being the baby and all.

In the fall of 1961, I entered a new school, which was across the street from the junior high where Dad taught. I was a first grader. On my first day of school, I forgot my lunch box on the playground. I told the teacher and cried like I was bound for certain death. My teacher quieted me, and soon the lunch box was found.

When I saw the actual lunchroom, new fear entered my heart, as I was to join other kids sitting at a long table on a bench in the basement of the school. Five children joined me on the bench, and we sat across from six kids. The noise, smells, and the close proximity to other noisy children was overwhelming. I froze and couldn't eat. Until I became accustomed to my fate in the windowless lunchroom, I was so distressed that I wound up in the principal's office more than once calling my mother to come to school and take me home. She came several times in the first few weeks, but eventually I came to a reluctant acceptance of that rather grim lunchtime reality.

In first grade, I did learn to read and print my letters. My teacher was young. She was born with a missing hand and part of her forearm. Miss Betty played the class piano with one hand and carried her purse on the special crook created by her unique arm. I liked her. After school, before supper, I played school by myself in my bedroom pretending to be Miss Betty. I bent my left arm, stuffing it into the sleeve in my shirt to better imitate her.

That year, I took ballet lessons along with four other little girls at a dance studio on Saturdays. I wore a leotard, tights and ballet slippers. I loved the lessons. After one year and a recital at a theater which required the purchase of a tutu, Mom and Dad decided on no more lessons. I believe the expense of the lessons, and extra attire figured into their decision. I was disappointed.

Second grade was perhaps my best grade school year. We had a teacher who took a rather unique, experimental approach to teaching. We were allowed more freedom to explore and learn on our own. My friend Lori and I used our seven-year-old imaginations to make up games and stories while under the supervision of that kindly teacher. Lori's dad was the man who hired my dad to teach in the district. She and I became best friends in the second grade. She was the youngest of four daughters. I often spent time with her at her house. We played in her bedroom in the upstairs of their small house with dormer windows. She had a "Clue" game. We didn't know the rules, so we made up our own.

Lori had a pet hamster. One day the hamster bit my finger and drew blood. I felt guilty like I had done something wrong. I quickly wiped up the blood and hid my wound from Lori's parents as well as my own. For a while after that day, I worried that I might have rabies. I was greatly relieved that rabies never materialized.

I was never again in a class with Lori in elementary school, junior high or high school. I totally lost track of her and in fact I didn't even think to look for her in high school. Her father was a great friend to education in the school district. Eventually, a new junior high was named after him. The larger school system in Davenport may have provided less soap opera drama for the teachers, but constant shuffling from class to class for me was unsettling. I became attached to one "best friend" never to see her again. Less drama for them, more trauma for me.

In my second and third grade years, I belonged to a Brownie troop. It was there that I met Michelle Solomon for the first time. I didn't even remember seeing Michelle much. Only recently did I open up an old scrap book to a page with a picture of my old Brownie troop. There Michelle was standing near me. We didn't get to know each other very well until my sophomore year in high school when we rode a school bus to high school together.

My Other Grandma

Dad's mom, Grandma Clara had more grandchildren than Grandma Myrtle. Yet, she loved us and tried to be with us as often as she could. Understandably, in the days before cell phones, she'd just show up at our door. One day, when I got home, there she was! While Megan and I were at school, she had taken Annie to Kresge's dime store and allowed her to pick out whatever she wanted.

After we got home, from school it was time for Megan and me to go with Grandma to pick out something of our choosing. I have a picture of Grandma sitting in the kitchen, with the three of us girls standing with the gifts she had bought us. Annie is standing next to her ironing board and iron. Megan has a brown purse shaped like a barrel and I have I have a velvet, flat purse with a zipper. I have a faraway look in my eyes.

At that visit I remember Grandma pointing out to mom that my royal blue sweater didn't exactly match the royal blue skirt I was wearing. And I thought Mom was a perfectionist! I guess my dad's mom was too.

In the summer before third grade while running through a sprinkler in our front yard, I slipped and fell, breaking my left arm. As I cried, Dad pulled me aside and tested my arm.

"I'm afraid its broken," he said. "We'll have to go to the doctor to get it fixed."

I worried as Dad called to find a place to take me. I wanted to change into shorts, but Mom and Dad insisted I remain in my swimming suit. I felt embarrassed as we walked into the doctor's office, but Dad stayed with me as the doctor adjusted my arm and proceeded to place a cast on it. That summer I learned just how much I used my left hand. Little things like tearing off a piece of toilet paper became more difficult. When the cast was removed eight weeks later, I was surprised by the smell coming from my unwashed arm. As the doctor removed the cast my arm floated up toward the ceiling.

It was upon settling into my third-grade classroom, I discovered my best friend, Lori had been placed in a different class. My third-grade teacher, Mrs. Powell scared me. One day she talked about "My Country, 'Tis of Thee." I took it upon myself to look up the song and find the rest of the verses in our encyclopedia at home. If I had known Mrs. Powell would have me sing all the verses to the entire class by myself, I never would have done the unnecessary homework. I learned more than one lesson that year.

I learned cursive writing with curvy blue pens provided by the school. Our teacher informed us that we needed to learn how to write in such a way that our fingers wouldn't get cramped from holding the pen improperly. After all, many of us might become secretaries and we would have to be writing all day, so I'd better learn to glide with the pen, moving my whole hand. I worked hard to achieve the flow.

On Friday, November 22nd, shortly after lunch our principle, Mr. Culver came into our class room and pulled Mrs. Powell aside. They talked in hushed tones and then Mr. Culver solemnly informed us that the president of the United States had been shot by an assassin. He also announced that school was out. We could go home.

Stunned, I along with the other kids, gathered my things and began my mile long walk home. When I got there, Mom was just getting up from a nap with Megan and Annie. She was bewildered by my sudden appearance. I told her what I had heard at school about President Kennedy. She turned on the tv and was soon in tears as she watched the real-life drama unfold on national television. And thus began a weekend of horror as we learned of the suspect Lee Harvey Oswald and Jack Ruby who shot Oswald right in front of cameras and reporters. Somehow life went on after that awful weekend.

That spring, I also came to understand that teachers are unpredictable and rather random in their use of anger. One spring day, Mrs. Powell yelled at us for leaving our jackets and sweaters in the coat closet rather than wearing them outdoors for recess on a warm afternoon.

"Your parents sent you to school in these jackets for you to wear," she scolded as she opened the closet doors and picked at the sweaters and jackets left on the hooks. "You wear what your mothers sent for you to wear!"

None of us dared to reason with her or remind her of how much warmer the afternoon had turned out to be than the morning. Obedience without questioning was taught and expected.

A Violin and a Piano

In June 1963, my folks rented a three-quarter-size violin so that I could begin lessons during summer school. I met several children that summer who eventually became fellow orchestra members in junior high and high school. Our family went on a one-week vacation while the little beginners orchestra continued to meet. When I returned, I had lost my place amongst the violins, and was moved back several seats. Even at my tender age the competition was stiff.

Dad asked me to teach him how to play. I instructed him to hold the violin with his left hand while positioning the chin rest up to his neck. I explained the four strings---a high E, A. D and G. Next came the correct positioning of his fingers on the bow with his right hand- thumb at the front, the rest of the fingers atop the bow. Pretty soon Dad was playing! Open A, third, second and first fingers on the D string and 2nd finger on the A string--"Mary Had a Little Lamb." I would have happily taught him more but he seemed satisfied with that humble accomplishment.

During the school year, our elementary school provided a half-hour lesson a week. In fourth grade, during my allotted time, I slipped out of class to meet Mr. Glenn in the basement. He was a nice person, but I remember being afraid of him. He had dark hair, black-rimmed glasses and wore dark suits. He also did not play the violin. He taught band at the local junior high. Nevertheless, he was able to keep me on target regarding counting out the quarter notes, eighth notes, and half notes. He had some sort of tuner to help me tune the four strings on my violin.

In 1964 Dad found and bought an upright piano for $25.00. He bought it and hired movers who would move it to our place for $10.00. I still remember how much I worried as the movers jockeyed the piano into place, placing straps around it in order to lower it safely down the basement stairs. There simply wasn't room on the main floor of our one story, three-bedroom house for such a large instrument.

Because of that purchase, I had the privilege to take piano lessons for $2.50 per half hour from a lady who lived about six blocks from our home. Most of the time I walked to Mrs. Philip's house after school. When I entered the living room, I could smell supper in the oven. For some reason she had a dining room table right in the middle of the room, covered with books, mail, lunch boxes and assorted other items from family life.

She was an excellent teacher. She taught me scales for both major and minor keys. My parents bought the recommended books and a stenographer's notebook to keep track of my assignments. Mrs. Phillips would write out the fingering for the scale of the week. First, I learned the C major scale for the right hand 1-2-3-thumb under 1-2-3-4-5. Then back with the third finger over the thumb on the way down. Easy. Then the left. Progressively with the addition of sharps and flats, the scales became more complicated.

She introduced me to the piano books of John W. Schaum. I loved the lessons and I loved her in spite of her cluttered ways. Eventually, she asked me to baby sit her children. I remember being with the kids in their basement family room but most of all I remember trying to frantically straighten up all the bottles, jars and tubes scattered across the bathroom counter.

Eventually, Mrs. Phillips announced that she could no longer give me lessons but recommended a new teacher-- Mrs. Michaels, wife of the director of a high school orchestra. Mrs. Philips helped me prepare several songs I could play for Mrs. Michaels so she could understand the level I needed in ordering piano books. She lived a few miles away, so the convenience of a ten-minute walk to my piano teacher, vanished. Dad took Megan and me to lessons after school and both of us waited for the other one to finish. One day, Mrs. Michaels pulled out a pair of fingernail clippers so Megan could cut her nails. I didn't get that shaming treatment because I regularly trimmed my fingernails with my teeth.

Fights

One of the things I absolutely hated about my childhood was the quarreling of my parents. I have distinct memories of more than one fight. Although I can't remember the words that were exchanged, I do remember the build up to Dad's explosions. Mom would be needling him about something until Dad's anger built up and he'd act in a frightening manner.

One summer after a weekend camping trip, Mom and Dad were unpacking food and various items in the kitchen. I don't remember much of that incident except that after angry words, Dad grabbed some raw hamburger and flung it at the ceiling.

Another time, Mom was picking at Dad and he became so enraged that he reached up with his left arm and swooped the hard plastic drinking glasses off the top of the refrigerator. They clattered to the floor. More than once after such an altercation, Dad stormed out to the garage, got into the car, backed into the street and roared away. Other times he went to the basement to sulk. He never struck Mom or us girls. There was no drinking involved because Mom and Dad didn't keep alcohol in the house.

Each time during their fights, Megan, Annie and I huddled together like little birds in a nest waiting for the storm to pass. From what I know now, I'd guess that Dad had pyrrole disorder which is linked to anxiety, depression and anger. It is best treated with zinc and vitamin B-6.

Summers

Summers in our neighborhood were filled with kids and lots of hours outdoors. For a long time, Dad always had a summer job either working for the Park Board to watch over the children who showed up for the summer programming and later as a manager of a local swimming pool. Dad managed the pool for four summers and on those summers Megan, Annie and I took lessons. Near the end of every swimming season, Dad and Mom hosted a party for the guards. I remember Mom making a delicious picnic of fried chicken, potato salad and cake. We all got to have the large swimming pool to ourselves. It felt like a royal privilege.

Mom, though, grew restless in our neighborhood. Unlike the other mothers, who watched soap operas and tanned in their backyards, Mom had more ambitious plans. She wanted to return to teaching and began taking refresher courses at college so she could go back to teaching after Annie started to school. As time drew near for her career to continue, Dad began taking summers off.

As the oldest elementary student in the neighborhood, I often hatched projects for the little kids to partake in. One summer we had a bike parade. We decorated our bicycles by weaving crepe paper through the spokes of our tires. We also tried to sell rocks and later potholders from door to door. To our surprise, the handwoven potholders were more popular than rocks with our customers.

One day when I was especially exercising my authority over the younger children, Dad quietly drew me aside and suggested that I refrain from being so bossy. "People will like you better," he told me. I wanted to be liked, so I appreciated and tried to follow his guidance.

Summers always included a trip to Nebraska to see both sets of grandparents. We enjoyed being at Grandma and Grandpa's farm so much. The first farmhouse I remember was small two story with a two-part staircase accessed through a door in the dining room. Upstairs were two bedrooms—one for Mom, Sophie and Rosie and the other for Peter and Herbert.

There was no bathroom on either floor. We accessed the primitive toilet by walking on wooden planks from the back door to a wooden shed which had a wooden seat with two holes in it. Underneath the seats was a big hole dug into the earth. There were no windows in it, but two people could do their business at the same time. Before entering we checked for spiders. It was dark and smelly. I hated going to the outhouse and I definitely never wanted to go in there alone or at night.

Once back inside the house, we washed our hands in the sink with a pump for water. For dishes, Grandma had to pump water which she then heated on her stove. I don't remember the stove. It must have been gas. I believe she had a refrigerator, although she also kept canned goods in a place she called the cave which was an outdoor cellar that also served as a place to hide in case of tornadoes.

We didn't own a dog but loved to play with Grandma's dogs. The first dog I knew was a little black dog named Prunes who may have been a Pekingese. When I was about four, I thought that I might try to ride him. Dogs have a way of teaching small children and Prunes was no exception. Prunes snapped at me letting me know quickly that sitting on his back wasn't a good idea.

Uncle Herbert lived and worked on the farm with his folks. He was a kindly uncle. He taught us about the farm animals and one summer fashioned a swing out of straw and a burlap bag. He also made a toy out of a dish soap bottle and a long string that he knotted and stuffed into the base. When we squeezed the bottle, the string would come hurtling out the small hole in the nozzle.

In my younger years, Aunt Rosie also lived on the farm. She was only eleven when I was born. At first, I was afraid of her. After we arrived for a visit, she would take me into the main floor bedroom where there was a bed and an upright piano. It was there that she tickled me until I laughed so hard that I was gasped for air and pleaded with her to stop. Hearing my laughter, the adults in the kitchen assumed we were having fun.

After our renewed acquaintance was complete, Rosie invited me to sit on the piano bench beside her. She played and taught me songs. She loved to sing, and I loved to listen.

> "Bill Grogan's goat, was feeling fine
> Ate three red shirts from off the line.
> Bill took a stick, gave him a whack and tied him to
> the railroad track.
> The whistle blew, the train drew nigh,

Bill Grogan's goat was doomed to die.
He gave three groans of awful pain,
Coughed up the shirts and flagged the train."

She also sang, "Get along home Cindy, Cindy, I'll marry you someday," as well as one about the old lady who "swallowed a spider that wiggled and jiggled and tickled inside her." Singing with Rosie was the best and it sure beat tickling.

I loved my grandma and always felt safe and welcome at her house. I was happy because my mom was happy. Mom was always so thrilled and relieved, after many months apart, to be able to share with her mother all the details of our lives. I loved to just sit and listen to the grownups talk.

As I got older Grandma would give me a pair of scissors and permission to gather a bouquet of the flowers in her garden. She'd pull a pretty vase out of her hutch for me to use for an arrangement. I brought in the flowers for her table. Then she'd send me down the long lane to get the mail from their large mailbox.

Usually on one of our five days in Nebraska, my dad would drive back to his hometown which was about seventy-five miles west of the farm. There, he visited his mother Clara and whatever other relatives might be hanging around. Dad's dad wasn't there because summers are a busy time for people who repair highways and construct bridges. Usually, Megan, Annie and I went with Dad although I hated tearing myself away from Grandma Myrtle. But, seeing Grandma Clara and nearby cousins made the trip worthwhile. Grandma Clara would make us a meal that included garden vegetables, homemade bread, some sort of meat, usually followed up by angel food cake.

One summer she was living in the larger town of O'Neill in a rental for the summer. After we arrived in the early afternoon, we went shopping in O'Neill to buy all of our favorite junk food. That evening, we had a slumber party for the five of us.

Grandma Clara was a mystery to me. She was little and dark haired. I thought of her just as Grandma. I loved her because I loved my dad. Sometimes we'd stop in to see my dad's oldest sister on her ranch near Clearwater.

Leaving Nebraska, especially the farm was always traumatic. We'd linger as long as possible over breakfast and get pictures of everyone. Grandma, Grandpa and Uncle Herbert would follow us to the car. Grandma always put together a lunch for us to eat on the road. As we drove back up the lane, we waved as hard as we could, and the tears would start. Mom cried and I did too. It was so hard to leave knowing that it would be months before we would see those humble people again.

All my life I felt like a part of me was missing. I hungered for family and kept trying to make friends into people who would never leave me. It never seemed to work very well. After I became a Christian, I slowly began to realize that Jesus is the only one who is able to keep a promise to remain. Friends come and go. Family members and neighbors may die or move away. The Bible does tell us refrain from putting our trust in man. Only Jesus promised to never leave us.

Sundays

On Saturday evenings, after our baths and before bed we reviewed colorful Sunday school pages we had received as we left our classrooms the week before. We would sit on the couch with Mom or Dad and read a review of our lessons. On Sunday mornings, we went to church. Dad had grown up going to church, and Mom, who had not, told me that she wanted us to go because as a kid, she had felt inferior to people who *did* go to church. She wanted us to have the status and confidence that goes with church attendance.

Megan, Annie and I went to Sunday school and were always a part of a choir. In preschool, I was in the cherub choir and in a choir all the way through high school. Before she began teaching school, Mom went to the church during the day to help iron choir robes. She also helped with vacation Bible school in the summer.

I had a variety of teachers for Sunday School. I don't remember my first or second grade teachers, but I particularly remember Mrs. Sauer in third grade. During her reign, each child received their very own Revised Standard Version Bible in a church ceremony. I remember the twin girls who rarely came to church showed up that day so they too could receive a Bible. Mrs. Sauer put her little old foot down. If they did not care enough to come every Sunday, they certainly did not deserve a Bible.

At the time, I was rather amazed at her hardened attitude. In the first place, if the twins weren't regular attenders, was that their fault? They were too young to drive to church. Secondly, wasn't it possible that they may have been in greater need of a Bible than those who came every week? Even though I had not given much thought to what it meant to be a Christian, it seemed to me that Mrs. Sauer's attitude was not in keeping with the "Jesus loves me" we had been taught to know.

Once we had our Bibles, we were to bring them to church every week, and under no circumstances were we to place them on the floor or allow another book to be placed on top of the Bible. I wonder if Mrs. Sauer was all rules or if she had a real relationship with God tucked away somewhere.

School

Back at school, fourth grade was relatively unremarkable. I had finally adjusted quite well. Our family had acquired a Puma pop-up camper trailer which was parked in our one car garage. Dad assembled the tent part of the trailer and on warmer evenings after supper, he took me out to the camper and read. Together we read a book about a racehorse called *Come on Seabiscuit!* by Ralph Moody. Dad remembered listening on the radio to the famous match race between Seabiscuit and War Admiral in 1938 when he was eleven. Years later in 2003, Dad and I were thrilled when a full-length motion picture came out. As a late bloomer, I identify with Seabiscuit.

In August, after 5th grade, our family drove the short distance to West Branch, Iowa to join with others in a posthumous birthday party for President Herbert Hoover who had died in October 1964. Mom and Dad at the time were Eisenhower Republicans. Viet Nam War protesters wandered the grounds carrying signs. Both President Eisenhower and his former vice president, Richard Nixon were there. I remember sitting in the crowd with my family behind a lady in a puffy polka dot red dress. Two days later, President Lyndon Johnson signed legislation creating the 200 acre National Historic Site at West Branch. My mom loved politics and government and shared that love with us kids. Years later, I studied the Great Depression and Herbert Hoover and was greatly saddened that he became the scapegoat for the Depression.

In 1966, by the time I was eleven, thanks to President Eisenhower, most of Interstate 80 across Iowa had been completed. That meant faster travel and easier access restrooms on the way to see our grandparents, aunts, uncles and cousins. About the same time, Grandma Myrtle and Grandpa William were able to purchase a farm with a large, beautiful house.

The "new" house had a large kitchen complete with running water, room for a washer and drier, and a pantry large enough for a "deep freeze." Just off the kitchen was a big bathroom with everything but a shower. Outside the bathroom door, the hallway held a staircase leading to the upstairs bedrooms, more stairs leading to the back yard and basement and a place to keep shoes and hang jackets. Grandma and Grandpa's bedroom was at the end of the hall. They had a large dining room, living room, a small room just off the front door where the old upright piano fit perfectly.

Best of all, were the upstairs bedrooms! Uncle Herbert's room at the top of the stairs, was flanked by four other rooms. All of the rooms had beds. There was room for all of us to have a bedroom. Two rooms at the end of the hallway had three double beds between them. Mom and Dad slept in one room. An adjoining door separated us. We three girls took turns having a bed to ourselves or sharing. It was just like a motel only lots better, because Grandma and Grandpa were under the same roof.

The only drawback according to thinking today, was the lack of a bathroom in the upstairs. In the middle of the night, I had to make my way down the wide wooden staircase to the bathroom. I didn't care because I no longer had to worry about going outside to an outhouse.

In my sixth grade classroom, we were divided into groups. Each group took turns entertaining the whole class on Friday afternoons. I had written a play about Eliza, a runaway slave girl who made it to safety via the Underground Railroad. All the kids in my class were white, but our group agreed we could use our imaginations. My friend Suzie agreed to take the role of Eliza, but one of the boys balked.

"You want me to be in a play about runaway slaves?" he scoffed. "You've gotta be kidding." His remark caused us to lose our enthusiasm for the play, so we dropped the idea.

I believe it was in 6th grade that I first read the *Diary of Anne Frank*. I don't now know if I read it during library time at school or if it was part of the curriculum. More information concerning the horrors of World War II were yet to come in in 8th Grade.

I greatly admired my dad and longed for his approval. Sometimes when we were out in the northwest part of the city, teenaged boys would call out, "Hey Mr. Foltz!" Being with Dad was like being with a local celebrity. Even certain boys in my elementary school classes knew who my dad was. He was the junior high football and track coach. He also taught science, typing and boys physical education. Those subjects were all good, but it was the coaching that impressed them.

That summer Suzie and I staged a play about Cinderella in our basement, much to my mother's approval. Dad hung curtains. Suzie was to play Cinderella, while I doubled as both the wicked stepmother and the fairy godmother. Two neighbor girls agreed to the stepsisters' roles, and one of Suzie's brothers was innocent enough to agree to play the handsome prince. My mother played the piano.

On the day of the premier, we charged five cents for kids and ten cents for adults. Several mothers and neighbor kids showed up and sat on our kitchen chairs to watch. At one point they heard me, in my most authoritative voice, command Suzie's little brothers to "close the curtains, you idiots!" The little guys sheepishly obeyed, and of course I was in trouble and regretted my words.

In our neighborhood, I got to know Steven Grady. When I first became aware of him, he seemed reluctant to join in and play with the other kids. So I worked up the courage to get to know him. He was a year younger than I was, but I got so I loved him. He eventually came and joined the other kids in the dead end at the base of our block. There, we played "kick soccer" -- a game like baseball only with a larger ball and without a bat. We also frequently lined up with other kids in our backyard for relay races and often played a board game called "Life" in our garage.

One afternoon I sat on the stoop in front of Steven's house to learn to play poker with him and some other boys. When his mother peeked out the front door to check on things, she clucked her tongue. "A girl playing poker?" she asked. I felt ashamed and headed home.

Steven got in trouble one day as he and I sat in front of my house. He was sitting on a lawn chair and I was on the cement stoop when a policeman drove by in his squad car. Steven raised his hand to wave and shouted, "Hi yah Fuzz!" I cringed, thinking he had made a big mistake.

Sure enough. To his surprise, the policeman stopped his cruiser, backed up and got out. By the time the patrolman walked up to our house, Steven had disappeared.

The officer didn't chase him but gave me a stern warning. "No one should ever run from a policeman."

"Yes Sir," I agreed."

"And do not call us names! We are here to protect you. Remember, we are your friends."

Still in shock, all I could manage to do was nod at the gentleman. I also silently hoped that Steven would soon return. I had been so enjoying the conversation with a boy I liked.

As I remember, Steven had run into the back yard and jumped over the fence into the corn field that bordered the backyards on our side of the street. When enough time had passed, he felt safe to jump into his own back yard. I doubt that he ever told his mother what had transpired, but I think he was sufficiently frightened to refrain from disrespecting the law ever again.

One evening in the summer before 7th grade, I experienced possibly the most damaging event of my childhood. I was out for an evening walk with my family. Leading the group, I overheard my dad speak disparagingly of me, to my mother.

"Look at her. She's pigeon-toed. What will ever become of her?"

"Claire, point your toes out," Mom instructed.

I couldn't believe my ears. Oh, Daddy, how could you? My heart ached.

I swung around and said angrily. "I'll be the first woman president! You just wait and see!"

Years later, as I followed instructions from a "Counseled by God" online class, I invited Jesus into that memory in order to understand from God's perspective. In that exercise, I "saw" not only my dad's criticism but also understood his concern. I was enabled to forgive him from my heart.

As I thought about the memory, I also became aware that even as a toddler learning to walk, I had modeled myself after Mom whose ability to walk had been hampered by her defective hip. When the original hurt from Dad's comments solidified, tendencies to strive for perfection became set into my personality. I erected a wall in my heart to protect myself from criticism and rejection. The healing of that scene began the breakup of the protective wall and destructive cycle as I increasingly became enabled to believe I am loved and accepted apart from imperfections. I also began to understand and feel more deeply for my mother. However, I still wasn't completely healed from that wound. I believe logically and I understood why Dad may have talked to me that way, but God only knows what it takes to heal our hearts.

The second Saturday night in January 2022, I had a night mare. I only remember the last part: I was standing at one end of our upstairs hallway and my dad who in real life died in 2011 was at the other end about 10 feet away. He was facing me and had a gun. I was hysterical and woke up saying, "Please Dad! Don't shoot me. Don't shoot me." My husband Bill awoke and heard my distress. It was so real. I told Bill the dream and expressed my fear that I wouldn't be able to get back to sleep. He prayed with me and I was able to sleep again but for only one more hour.

That morning at church, I told my dream to the people in the class who were learning how to pray like Jesus did—for healing of body, mind, heart and spirit. I got some prayer and good advice and agreed with one lady that I should pray over my old house so that any demonic entities were bound and had to leave. After all, our house is over 100 years old and who knows what may have happened there. So that evening, Bill and I went through the entire house anointing doors and windows and asking God to show us anything that might give demons a right to hang out. That took us a while, but I was determined to get it done before we went to bed. I didn't want another nightmare like I had the night before.

Mission accomplished. I slept well that night, however I still didn't understand what Holy Spirit was showing me in the dream. As I had time to think and remind myself of some of the principles of inner healing, I remembered how important a father is in calling forth his daughter during her adolescent years. A father's approval and endorsement enable both teenaged sons and daughters to confidently take hold of life. That was it! At a time when I so needed Dad's approval, he delivered to me the opposite—disapproval and doubt. That particular incident cut me to the core. Yes, there were other aspects of my malaise, but Dad's treatment of me was a root of ongoing hurt.

In that same summer I was playing with the younger neighbor kids. A couple of us older, taller ones decided it would be fun to give the younger kids rides on our backs. Bad idea. I was carrying little Cathy in that lofty position when I tripped and fell hitting my chin on a crack in the neighbor's sloped driveway. Because my hands were behind me holding the little girl's legs, I couldn't break my fall. Cathy, unhurt, quickly climbed off me as I became aware of blood coming from my chin. Of course, I ran to Dad crying.

He took me in the bathroom to get a wet washcloth. Inspecting the gap in my chin he gave me the bad news.

"You're going to have to have stitches."

"Oh, no!" I groaned and worried, silently wishing I could go back and change my stupid idea to carry little Cathy on my shoulders. How could this possibly be good? Dad's presence gave me the courage to go along.

Dad drove me to the doctor. He stayed right by me as the doctor poked me with a local anesthetic and stitched up my wound. In the following days, I learned to wash my face carefully to avoid that tender area. I entered junior high with a scar on my chin. Unfortunately, I think I also developed a habit of feeling sorry for myself.

Horses

Mom and Dad made it a point to enrich us with a variety of experiences. They both had fond memories of lives in the country. As I was growing up, they gave us the opportunity to ride horses on three different occasions. The first time we went to a hilly farm about twenty miles from the city. Dad procured three horses. As I recall we didn't have a guide. We mounted the horses in a big ted barn. I needed help getting my foot into the stirrup and onto the saddle. Megan and Annie each found a safe place behind either Mom or Dad.

The first part of the ride wasn't bad as we climbed a hill across the highway from the barn. From there we rode in a meadow and had a fairly easy time of it. It was the trip down the hill and back to the barn that terrified me. My horse followed the other horses to the hill and I, looking down from the large beast assessed the situation, while imagining all that could possibly go wrong. I had to trust that he was surefooted enough to make it down the hill with me still astride. He did it, but that experience had caused my stress levels to skyrocket.

A year later, we found horses to ride at a ranch in Colorado. As we gathered with the owner and other cowboy wannabes, I asked for a gentle horse. I was introduced to Walter and advised that if I wanted a tamer horse, I'd have to put a quarter in it. Walter and I became the best of friends on the first part of the ride. We followed behind the other horses, bringing up the rear. It seemed that Walter understood that I needed him to be careful with me. At the time, I didn't realize that Walter was still a young horse at heart.

It was on the return to the barn that good old Walter turned on me and morphed into Seabiscuit racing for the finish. I must have missed the class on how to gallop gracefully. All I could do was hang on for dear life. The horse and saddle went down as I rose up. As I came down, the saddle and I met in the middle with a thump each time. There was a flow to the process I simply didn't understand. I was miserable but I survived. No one had given me riding lessons. Once again, I was learning that a fantasy (my stick horse, cowgirl hat and skirt) was a far cry from the reality of a real horse. Dale Evans, I wasn't.

The next summer, my third and last horseback ride was a simple, slow moving trail ride in South Dakota. We had camped our foldout Puma near the clearest stream I had ever seen. Our pop cans stored under the icy cold water near the bank just steps from our camper were refreshing when we returned. As I recall, trail rides were available in that park. I don't remember any trauma with that simple out and back ride.

Books

During that time of adolescence, I read several memorable books. One was *My Shadow Ran Fast* by Bill Sands. It was a memoir of Sands, a man who by the age of nineteen was serving three life terms in San Quentin. I don't remember much of the book except his horrifying description of how his mother punished him. She made Bill go outside to her rose bush and cut a long thorny stem so she could make a switch for his bare back. After whipping him, she got out the rubbing alcohol to make sure his back would sting in pain. That scene left a lasting impression and something I never wanted to repeat in raising my own children.

I also read *The Diary of Anne Frank* a tragic yet tender and hopeful story of young Anne. She and her family hid in the back upper part of a warehouse connected to her father's business as the German army was bearing down on Jewish people in Europe during WWII. This book was my introduction to the many horrific events of that war.

Chapter 4

Junior High

After a ten-year hiatus, Mom resumed her teaching career at the high school level on the same day I began seventh grade, Megan third, and Annie first. Dad took over breakfast duty and the before-school preparations. At first, we really missed Mom in the mornings. Dad struggled in helping us with our hair, but we adjusted reasonably well.

Like most of my friends, I wanted to sign up for Spanish. My mother had insisted I study French. After all, I belonged to her, didn't I? Her will was my command. She had taken French in college and hoped that our shared French experience would help us connect. Despite my initial frustration with Mom's control, I loved French class and was amused by the teacher. She not only had visited Paris but told us fantastic stories about touring the sewers of that enchanting old city.

I don't remember her name, but she was one of my all-time favorite teachers. She rarely sat behind her desk but would move around the room from student to student speaking in French expecting us to repeat in order to check our pronunciation.

We memorized dialogues: I still remember the first one:

"Bonjour Jean. Comment va tu?"

"Tres bien, merci. Et toi?

"Pas mal, merci.

"Qui est-ce?"

"C'est un ami. Il s'appelle Paul"

And so on. As a result of my French teacher's influence, Paris moved to the top of my list of foreign cities I'd most like to visit someday.

Acne emerged as an unwelcome part of my life, adding doubt to my already shaky sense of self. Dad showed me how to apply rubbing alcohol to pimples on my face. He told me that he too had acne when he was a kid.

My seventh-grade chorus class became the stage for a scene of cruelty. Our teacher Mrs. Kohler wore her hair in tight curls and chose old songs for us to sing in preparation for upcoming programs. She did not seem to have a clue as to what songs junior high kids might find enjoyable. I especially remember "rocking" with "Rockin' Red Wing," a song that was written in 1907.

There was a boy in the class who took it upon himself to make life miserable for Mrs. Kohler. One day he was throwing boogers at the girls around him. Mrs. Kohler stopped us all mid-song.

"Terry! What are you doing this time?"

"Nothing."

"Terry Crandall, why can't you be more like Claire Foltz?"

I gasped. The worst! Why did she have to say that? None of the kids respected Mrs. Kohler, and now here I was being selected as her favorite. Terry wasted no time singling me out to pick on. The very next day, as kids were making their way to assigned seats, Terry stopped in front of me and posed like a monkey.

"What's this? What's this?" he pranced, laughing and scratching at his chin.

I knew he was pointing out the rash of acne that had sprouted on my chin where I had to have several stitches just a couple of months before.

"Oh, Terry, you're bad," giggled Shelley, the girl sitting next to me.

Thanks a lot, Shelley. How would I ever live that down?

By that stage in my life, Dad was helping me as best he knew with my acne problem. He told me that he too had pimples when he was a teenager. Dad taught me how to use rubbing alcohol to dry up the unwanted blemishes. After washing my face, I'd apply the alcohol. It didn't seem to help much.

In our junior high orchestra, however, for the first time in three years, I had a director and teacher, Miss Vitale, who actually played the violin. Under her guidance, I began getting A's on my yearly solos. I spent many stuffy, sweaty hours with her in a practice room. Orchestra was the one class where I felt most like I belonged.

At church I took part in confirmation class. That class was designed to prepare us to officially join the church. I don't remember the content of our lessons, but I do remember the associate pastor walking into the room and saying, "Let there be light," before flicking the switch on the wall. There was no mention of asking Jesus to be our Savior from sin and giving our lives to him. If we did talk about being born again or how to receive eternal life, I don't remember. It was only later that the passage in John 3 where a Pharisee named Nicodemus came to talk to Jesus about whether or not he was the Messiah, stood out to me. The truth about the Holy Spirit being instrumental in the lives of people in the church seemed to be missing.

One Sunday evening after UMYF (United Methodist Youth Fellowship), during our Junior High choir practice, the young choir director had a meltdown. He was playing the piano and apparently, our singing didn't live up to his satisfaction because he suddenly stood up, grabbed the wooden music rack and slammed it to the floor. I was horrified. I think there was another adult in the room but I don't remember what was said or what we all did after that. I don't recall any discussion about the incident at home or at church, but the troubled director was soon replaced by a mild-mannered man.

In my English class in 8th Grade, Mr. Hahn was my English teacher. I didn't like him. He seemed a bit angry and shifty. More than once I had to give a speech in his class. That was torturous. During that year, we read a book about the atomic bombing of Hiroshima. I believe it was simply called *Hiroshima*. And thus, I had more WW II horror stories to add to my collection which had begun with Anne Frank.

During that year, I was placed in a small group of girls and we were to select a novel to read, discuss and report on. Mr. Hahn gave us a choice of books. Our group chose a novel called *Five Smooth Stones* by Ann Fairbairn. It was the story of the love between a black man and white woman during the thirties. One girl in my group was forbidden by her single mom to read the book. The cover itself suggested explicit sexuality. I felt sorry for my friend who came back to report her mother's reaction. I don't remember what we did as a group, but I think we chose another book.

At the time I felt for my friend. I think her mom, concerned about the protecting her daughter in the absence of a father was doing the best she could in trying to guard her from thinking sex outside of marriage was okay. If she didn't like the racial aspect of the book, I don't know. Having raised a daughter myself, I understand her mother's concern. Mr. Hahn was young. I doubt that he had teenage children. My teachers were not always very wise in what they expected from the children under their tutelage.

Vacation to Washington and the Pacific Ocean

Because Mom had returned to teaching, our family could afford to take longer vacations to places other than Nebraska and neighboring states. One summer we visited Seattle and the Space Needle which had been part of the World's Fair in 1962. While in Washington, we also visited the beach and the Pacific Ocean.

I still remember that particular visit. Dad was driving. For Mom's sake he wanted to get us as close to the water as possible without getting out of the car. So, we were literally driving on the beach. Mom and Dad seemed oblivious to the signs which warned us not drive on the clam beds. I was stunned but spoke up.

"It says, don't drive on the clam beds." I said insistently.

Frantically, I repeated, "Don't drive on the clam beds!"

It was too late. Our car got stuck in the sand and the tide was coming in! Disgusted with my parents, I got out of the car and furiously began digging the sand away from the back tire. It was hopeless, not unlike getting stuck in the snow. The whole family got out to help. Within a few minutes a tow truck drove near us but stayed far enough away to avoid our dilemma. The driver attached a giant hook to the bumper and pulled our car from the forbidden area of the beach. Of course, they charged us. I don't remember how much but we were all greatly relieved.

My favorite part of that vacation was the international food court near the Space Needle. We got to choose a nationality and I chose Thai. That was the first but definitely not last time I ate Thai food. It was surprisingly delicious.

Another Move

The summer before ninth grade, we moved to a brand-new two-story house in a new housing development. It was hard for me to say goodbye to my old neighborhood friends--the kids I had played and squabbled with. I was especially going to miss Steven Grady. Mom and Dad allowed Steven to come with us one evening to help when we loaded our car to carry incidentals that were not included in the moving van. That was a nice gesture, but I didn't have much further contact with either Steven or the others. I was really going to miss all those kids.

In those days, apart from the deaths of loved ones, people didn't very well understand loss and grieving. I grieved, even though I might see those kids again at school or in passing at a store, it just wasn't the same. I couldn't drive. There wasn't a good way to get back to the neighborhood by bicycle. There was at least a mile, a creek and a highway between us. It was hopeless.

During my junior high and high school days, fashion for young girls was difficult for those who wished to dress modestly. During those years there were mini skirts and dresses with a dress code that demanded feminine clothing for girls. And so in seventh grade I learned how to wear nylon stockings which required a garter belt. Just try keeping your garter belt from showing beneath your mini skirt while sitting in a little desk in class. Thankfully, panty hose soon because available. Even better, after I got to high school, some brave senior girls wore pants to school one day. They were kicked out of school, but soon, pants were allowed for all the girls.

That fall, I began walking to my junior high from a different direction. I walked with Patty who was easily the most negative person I had ever met. Fortunately, Patty and I crossed a bridge over the creek and walked about four more blocks to catch up with Valerie and Connie. From there we divided up. Valerie and I walked the rest of the way to school together.

I really liked Valerie. She became one of my best friends. She had long strawberry blonde hair, was sympathetic and easy to talk to. Her mother was a nurse and one of the kindest adults I knew. She was Catholic.

At school, in spite of the move, I still had some girlfriends. There was Rita and Sarah in orchestra. In the ninth-grade study hall, I was seated one chair away from Valerie. To pass the time, Val and I worked on a story that included us as characters, along with Glen Campbell and Jerry Reid. Valerie particularly liked Glen Campbell. We passed our story back and forth, making up silly dialogue and situations for our characters. In our imaginations and on paper, we eventually launched into space with Glen and Jerry.

In that same study hall, I sat across from Carol, who told me about her father. He had a drinking problem and was mean to her. Unfortunately, one day Carol found out that my dad was her typing teacher. In no time, Carol began venting pent-up anger and shame onto me daily in study hall. I was baffled. She became relentless in unloading her rage.

One day she got me so riled up that I raised my purse over my head as though I would strike her with it. The next day she grabbed my purse and told the guy next to her to pass it on. I watched helplessly as my purse passed from person to person down the long set of study hall tables. I realized I had to get up and walk down the aisle between tables in order to retrieve it. I kept the purse out of her reach from then on.

At the supper table, I complained about Carol, and Dad eventually took her aside and told her to leave me alone. I don't know specifically what he said to her. The next day she promised me she would get me when we got to high school. That never happened. I hoped and imagined that my dad was kind to her. He had known rough times when he was a kid, and I hope he was gentle with her. A year later in high school, Carol and I happened to run into each other in a restroom. She silently eyed me, and I braced for a beating. She walked out of the bathroom.

My ancient history class nearly challenged me beyond my capabilities. I sat next to a tall, red-haired, raw boned Canadian. He was nice. He and all the boys in the class were extra smart and seemed to relish the class discussions with the teacher who happened to be a friend of my dad's. I don't think I ever said a word in that class, although I took it all in—and learned about ancient Greece— Socrates, Plato and Aristotle. I wrote a poem about Socrates and suffered a day-long trip to Chicago with my teacher and class to visit a museum complete with mummies.

Acne and Bullies

At school, there were other incidents related to my "pizza face." Unfortunately, my algebra teacher, Mr. Romney, also had acne. The kids in my class were incredibly cruel. On the lowest day, some of the boys began lobbing chalk board erasers at him. The boys apparently lacked empathy and enough imagination to be able to put themselves in his shoes. Mr. Romney looked at me forlornly. I felt bad for him, but what could I say or do? I had my own battles. Sometimes the teachers seemed to expect more of me because of my dad.

One day, two girls I had known in elementary school stopped by my locker.

"What's that on your face?" asked one.

"Yeah, what *is* that?" said the other.

"Um, I don't know," I replied, astounded at their audacity.

"Yes, you do." They laughed.

I took it all in while becoming increasingly disgusted with all of humankind.

Eventually, I visited a dermatologist who prescribed tetracycline—an antibiotic which I believe had a negative effect on my microbiome which contains the enteric nervous system. The large intestine is sometimes referred to as the second brain because it manufactures all important neurotransmitters such as dopamine and serotonin.

Later, after my breakdown, Dad and Mom correctly surmised that the antibiotic given for acne affected me in a negative way. I now know that antibiotics affect the gut biome where neurotransmitters are created. Antibiotics destroy all the flora both the harmful *and* the beneficial. Antibiotics also play a role in eradicating Dopamine, a neurotransmitter known to be a factor in bipolar disorder. Too much dopamine can lead to mania and sleeplessness, while too little can contribute to depression and lethargy. Serotonin on the other hand creates feelings of well-being and stability.

One day in the summer, with the approval of our parents, Valerie who liked me in spite of my zits, took a long bike ride with me. We decided to ride our bikes downtown to eat at a buffet restaurant. It was quite a trip from the northwest part of the city to the shopping area in the downtown, within blocks of the Mississippi. We had on our short shorts, and I wore a tube top. I think we had shirts in a bag to put on in the restaurant. I don't remember warnings about wearing sunscreen at that time. The first part of our journey was mostly downhill.

After we finished eating, we began the long trek home. We wound up pushing our bikes uphill for about sixteen blooks until we were at the top of the river valley. By the time I got home I was tired and had a major, blistering sunburn, but I had experienced an adventure on my own without my family.

Flirting with the Occult

It was during my junior high years that my mom's dad was hospitalized. She bought little gifts to send to him—usually something she could tuck into an envelope and send for a few cents more. One time she picked up a small astrology book from a rack at the checkout lane in the grocery store. According to astrology, Grandpa was a Scorpio. Before Mom sent the book, I had a chance to read from it. Intrigued, I began to wonder about my sign. On my next opportunity, I purchased a book about Taurus, the bull. It wasn't long before I discovered that I was not only a Taurus but was born on the cusp, which made me a Taurus/Gemini. I found more books on the subject as I could.

I didn't know the dangers of my misguided involvement in the occult. I believe that my "dabbling" in astrology was one of the factors leading to the breakdown I experienced as a sophomore in high school. No one at church had informed us of the many scriptural warnings against such things. The chance to understand what makes people "tick" intrigued me. It's no wonder astrology is often referred to as parapsychology.

That spring, a muscular man wearing a bull mask appeared on the cover of *Life Magazine*. The accompanying article was about astrology. The magazine displayed colorful pictures to illustrate each sign of the zodiac.

I was intrigued and soon decided to have an astrology slumber party for my birthday. I went all out. I decorated the wall above the fireplace in the family room with cutouts of the twelve signs from the astrology article. In the living room, I set up a round lamp as a crystal ball and playfully told each friend her future. We played with a Ouija board and attempted to lift each other with just our fingers, curiously experimenting with the paranormal. I did not have a clue about the scriptural warnings concerning involvement with occult practices.

At the time, I thought my experimenting with the occult was all in fun. I didn't know that I was opening a door to the devil. I opened it not only for myself but also unintentionally defiled the friends who came to my party. It didn't matter that I wasn't interested in the astrology to predict the future. I was hungry for the supernatural and hadn't yet really caught the supernatural aspects of the Bible. Plus, I mostly wanted to understand people so I could get along with them. I was lonely. I missed my friends from our old neighborhood. I missed my grandparents and cousins. I wanted real relationships and I had long held a fascination in personality and psychology. There is a reason that astrology is often referred to as parapsychology.

When my ninth-grade year ended, I was more than ready for a new experience in high school. As spring turned to summer, I eagerly anticipated a new school and new classes.

High School

By the time I entered high school, we had been living in the new two-story, four-bedroom house for a year. We seemed to be running as fast as we could from the poverty my dad had known as a child to the American cultural symbols of affluence. The new home was in a neighborhood where the houses were spaced at greater distances than in our previous one. I never really made a close friend near the new house; however, I did ride the bus with Valerie and Michelle, girls from junior high who lived in a neighborhood across the creek.

I remember sitting near Michelle on the bus. She had long dark hair and was the first Jewish person I had ever met. Getting to know

Michelle, eventually led me to a fascination with all things Jewish. Because of her, I got to attend her brother's bar mitzvah as well as her own bat mitzvah. Never had I tasted such delicate appetizers and sweet little cakey desserts. Even though I didn't hang out with the popular kids at high school, I was invited to Michelle's house where we gathered to eat, play games and learn to dance the hora in a circle in her living room.

And so, it was in my sophomore year that I began to shed the humiliation of junior high. I loved several of my teachers and new classes. My biology teacher made a profound impression. She talked about pollution and encouraged us to let our parents know that pastel-colored tissues and toilet paper were bad for the environment. I remember one day she wanted us to poke our fingers with a pointed tool to draw blood. I couldn't do it and refused to cooperate. I don't think that affected my grade for the class.

Geometry was difficult. I had a kindly male teacher but there seemed to be a disconnect for me in understanding geometry the way he taught it. One day we had a substitute teacher—a woman. The day she taught our class explaining equations, it finally made sense. Geometry made sense! Do men and women differ in the way they process math?

I loved my English class where we studied Shakespeare's *Julius Caesar*. I still remember the lines of Caesar to Anthony: "Let me have men about me that are fat. Sleek headed men and such as sleep at night. Yond Cassius has a lean and hungry look. He thinks too much. Such men are dangerous."

French was fun. My tenth-grade French class was led by a grey-haired gentleman who gave us lectures in French. Michelle shared the class with me. Our friendship grew as a result.

Mrs. Michaels, my piano teacher was the wife of the orchestra director. She insisted that because I was a first born, I was a natural leader. I don't know how much influence Mrs. Michaels had with her husband, but I was allowed to be first chair second violin in orchestra for a time, until Rita, my stand partner challenged me.

High school was turning out to be a much better experience than junior high.

As my understanding of the world grew, I read as much as I could about a variety of issues. Often, I'd go to my dad showing him something I had just read-- something perplexing or scary. I can't remember any of the details of what I showed him but I do remember his frequent response. "Aayah," he would say in a guttural voice, "You don't believe everything you read, do ya?" His skeptical reaction was just what I needed. I did, in fact, tend to believe anything that was in print-whether in a newspaper, book, or magazine.

This is the same father who told me one of the theories about how the human life on earth began--people from another planet landed here to dump their crazy citizens, purposely leaving them behind when they lifted off to return to their own cosmic home. I can imagine how Dad might have entertained that idea. Having lived through the World War II he'd seen firsthand the horrors and crazy leaders of that terrible time. Yes, we were living here on earth with a lot of insane people.

As a busy father, school teacher and coach, Dad equipped me for life as best he could. Mom was there also. When she got home from a long day at school, she planned and made meals with help from Dad and us girls. Our parents tried various ways to fit their professional lives in with family life. At first, they prepared lunches on Sunday evenings by making sandwiches and putting them in the freezer, so each of us could bag a sandwich and an apple before heading out the door to school. The frozen sandwiches idea didn't last for long. The texture of the sandwiches wasn't quite right.

On Fridays after school, Dad gladly prepared cheese burgers while Mom, Megan, Annie and I cleaned our rooms, dusted our dressers with dust rags and wooden floors with a dust mop. Each of us were assigned part of the bathroom to clean. I cleaned the bath tub along with the nasty, slime ridden sliding glass door with a track on the bottom. Attempting to clean the track for the door was an ongoing challenge. I don't remember who cleaned the toilet or sink.

On Saturday mornings, we girls took turns alternating between cleaning the kitchen, family room and living room. Mom wanted our house to be clean so we could enjoy the weekend. I understood, and appreciated her insistence on chores, except when cleaning interfered with events like football games or time with friends. Like many moms, my mom had a hard time letting go of us as we grew up.

Mom usually cooked while we cleaned. She often made a cake in a 9X13 pan and cut it into pieces small enough so that we could each have a piece of cake for dessert after supper during the week. She was teaching us to be disciplined about our eating.

None of us knew at the time or were prepared for a major wrench that was about to be thrown into workings of family life.

Chapter 5

Amarillo

Spring, 1971

At first, I hardly noticed him. Mark was the timpani player in third period orchestra, sixteen and a junior. I was merely a second violin sophomore, too wrapped up in my own affairs to notice much of anything. But he noticed.

Mark was friendly with Rita, my buddy. In March, Mr. Michaels arranged for the pianist Van Cliburn to be guest artist in a concert with the orchestra. In 1958, Van had been greeted in New York City with a ticker-tape parade after winning the International Tchaikovsky competition in Moscow. The very same musician played that night in our high school auditorium with our orchestra. In the lunchroom at Cliburn's reception after the concert, Mark and his friend Frank seated themselves at the same table as Rita and me.

Frank, who was never at a loss for words, did the talking while I studied Mark for the first time. I noticed a certain sparkle about him that made him appear to be even more handsome than he actually was. He had smooth, shiny, light-brown hair and a silver tooth that showed when he smiled. He was attractively slim in his spring-colored suit and shirt, and I liked him vaguely yet wondered why he had bothered to sit with Rita and me.

Rita, too, took notice of the unexpected attention. I liked Rita, whom I had known since junior high. Because we took turns challenging each other for the first chair position, we liked to say that we were "best enemies." An extrovert and flirt, Rita was not shy but quite sure of herself. That evening, she was particularly vivacious, her laughter filling the air. After all, she and I both knew that Mark was not someone to ignore.

We sat at a round table exchanging ideas and impressions about the concert. Our voices lilted with laughter. We were in a special mood happy to be together outside of school hours.

"Did you see that guy? Those hands!" exclaimed Rita, spreading out her own hands in disbelief.

"They were extremely large," I agreed.

"Well," said Frank in an authoritative voice, "all it really takes is exercise to develop the muscles in the fingers." He held up his own hands for us to admire.

"Yup, ole Frank Van Cliburn here," Mark chuckled, clapping Frank on the shoulder.

"All right, wise guy," said Frank, making a wrinkly face and clenching his upheld fingers into a fist.

"Everything about him was big," agreed Mark with a swift change in mood.

"Including his piano!" Rita observed, and we all laughed.

Our conversation continued as Frank and I discussed the fact that our fathers had taught phys ed together at the same junior high school I had attended. As we talked, I noticed my dad motioning in my direction.

"I've got to go now," I said, standing up. I turned to Mark. "It was nice to meet you. And you, Frank, well..." I smiled.

At home, Mother asked about the boy that Rita and I had been sitting with. I asked if she meant the one with the light hair.

"Yes, the good-looking one."

"I guess his name is Mark."

"Oh? Mark who?"

"I don't know. I don't really know him."

"He's kind of cute."

"Yes." I couldn't deny that.

As the days passed, Mark tried to talk with Rita more often. She became a link that helped strengthen the bond between him and me. Occasionally, Mark threw in questions asking what I thought of him. When Rita reported that to me, I replied that I thought nothing of him, as I really didn't know him. My reply failed to discourage him. I was but one of many girls in whom he had interest.

As for me, I had a secret admiration for someone else—a friend of Mark's named Dan Culver, a cellist. Dan's dad was the principal at the elementary school I had attended. At a school skating party when I was eight, I had even skated with Mr. Culver holding my hand. Mr. Culver had played a part in my growing ability to enjoy roller skating. How could I help but have a crush on the son of the man who helped me learn to skate?

Another charming fellow played bass. Rick had a moustache and twinkly eyes. Best of all, he was a senior. Rita had said in reference to him, "What a bod!" Sometimes he would wink at me. I knew it wasn't serious. He was just teasing me.

These half-baked love affairs were a minor part of my school life. There was still geometry—an incessant plague—and biology, which, though interesting, required much patience and homework. I fondly remember French class and the teacher, a gray-haired master. He gained my respect through his part-English, part-French lectures, which were like dessert after a satisfying meal. Compared to junior high, this first year of high school was mostly happy and surprisingly fulfilling. But the school year ended with a tornado of confusion.

The twisting began with the orchestra's trip to Amarillo, Texas, for a music contest with other high school orchestras. In November, six months prior to our trip, our orchestra, had raised money by selling Texas oranges and grapefruit to friends and neighbors. I don't remember how much I raised, but the time had finally arrived for us to actually travel to Amarillo for the contest.

Something happens to a group of teenagers after twenty hours on a bus with only a few chaperones. It was especially difficult for someone like me who had been so sheltered from the ways of the world. It put me in a position where I had to learn quickly or fail at the attempt.

Set to leave on a Wednesday evening after a full day at school, we would pull into a motel in Amarillo on the afternoon of the next day. The bus ride proved to be very cozy. Out of the three busses headed toward Amarillo, Mark and Dan somehow managed to ride the same bus as Rita and me.

As the three tour buses were preparing to leave from the school parking lot, I got on my assigned bus, holding tightly to a cosmetics bag. I made my way down the aisle to where Rita was sitting. My jaw dropped when I saw her shirt. In bold, white letters against a navy-blue background were the words *Think Sex*. Not knowing what to say, I said nothing.

Reaching up, I put the bag on the overhead rack and noticed Rick Kern staring at me with those twinkly eyes. He had a guitar and I judged him for bringing something so impractical. Still eyeing me, Rick ran his thumb across the strings and sang in a low voice, "I'm in love with Claire."

"What?" I asked almost harshly. His unexpected attention made me nervous.

He just smiled that huge, toothy grin. Not able to fight it, I smiled back and slid abruptly into my assigned seat, which was directly in front of his. Suddenly, my seat jerked back, and I heard a low chuckle. Looking around, I found myself face to face with Rick.

"Hey, I thought I had control over this seat."

"Oh, you do," he assured me, rather surprised at my reaction.

I smiled apologetically, wishing to remain friendly. Still, I was not sure I liked his tactics. He scared me. What was I going to do if he continued acting so familiar with me? I had no grid or understanding of how to maintain my boundaries and yet have fun in this sudden proximity to boys older than I.

All this nearly overwhelming attention, and our bus had not yet rolled out of the parking lot! There was further delay: students disembarking to say goodbye to parents, give hugs to girlfriends and boyfriends. Then, we were off to impress Texas with our fantastic orchestra. We were a boisterous, happy group setting out on a romantic adventure. The atmosphere was warm and homelike. Rita asked me what I thought of her "Think Sex" shirt. Irritated, I told her I thought it was interesting. She laughed, and I settled back into my seat.

A few minutes later, I noticed that Rick and his friend had moved back a few seats. Rick was sitting with an attractive brunette who played in the first violin section. Within moments, as deftly as panthers, Mark and Dan moved into their vacated seats. Rita pounced immediately.

"Hi there," she said in her Mae West voice. "I'm glad you could come and see us."

"So are we," said Dan.

"We've got to do something," said Mark.

Dan whispered words in Mark's ear, and they both laughed. I shifted in my seat uncomfortably, half-wishing they would find other seats. I noticed Dan reaching for Rita's hand.

"Ooh, warm hands," she purred appreciatively.

"Mine are cold and clammy," I said, setting my own trap. Surely clammy would be a turnoff.

"Mark can take care of that," Dan insisted. He guided my hand in Mark's direction. Mark was waiting.

"But," I protested, "I don't know Mark." I choked on his name. Mark didn't seem to notice.

He took my hand and held it in his. I looked at him. Though his hand was warm, his blue eyes shone cold. He ran his thumb along my forefinger, and I shivered.

"You *are* cold," he replied, feigning concern while taking both of my hands and rubbing them together.

Feeling insecure, I withdrew my hands carefully, placing them in my lap. Mark looked in my direction. "Do you have any cards?"

I shrugged my shoulders. "No, but Rita might have some."

When she replied in the negative, he left, muttering that he would find some cards. He returned with a deck and Mr. Michaels, our director. I liked Mr. Michaels. He was young and enthusiastic, always willing to try something new. His manner was direct and precise. I always knew where I stood with him.

"What are you going to play?" he asked.

"How about hearts?" Dan suggested.

"Fine." Mr. Michaels smiled.

"I don't know how to play hearts," I sighed, wishing not to play.

"You could sit this one out," Dan suggested.

"We'll teach her," Mark growled.

We settled down to Hearts. With Mark's help, I won two of four games. Dan howled in disbelief both times I won. Mr. Michaels enjoyed himself and said so. He then moved on to chat with a chaperone.

The game changed to five-card stud. Rita already knew how to play. After suffering through two games, I left Rita to her own cunning and got up to sit with Lynn Werner, who in the pre-trip shuffle for seats had ended up without a seat partner. I felt sorry that she didn't have someone to sit with, so I decided to spend part of my time with her, thinking Rita and the others would do the same.

Lynn was a tall, sensitive person, and she joked that she was five foot twelve. Seven inches separated us, and she would lower her head to attend to our conversations as we walked the halls between classes at school. For Lynn, geometry was a piece of cake. I envied her ability. Although we looked at most of life through different lenses, we enjoyed each other's company. Together, she and I had sold oranges and grapefruit in November, raising money for this trip.

That day, Lynn told me about the book she was reading, written by some science fiction author. I listened politely, wondering what she could possibly see in that "stuff." We talked about the problem of pollution. Lynn was and remains an avid environmentalist.

Her often wry comments about men and inequality intrigued me and made me wonder about her relationship with her brother and her dad. My parents had three daughters, and we grew up feeling that we were just as important as boys. The only "boy" I really knew was my dad.

Upon returning to my seat, I saw that Mark, Dan, and Rita had finished another boring game and were gathering the cards as I sat down. At the time, I was still fascinated by astrology and how people of various signs interacted with one another.

Trying not to be too obvious, I decided to approach Dan first.

"Er, Dan, when is your birthday?"

"April." He looked up quizzically.

"Ah, Aries," I said with a smile and a nod. Inside I thought, *not bad*, but all this time I had suspected and hoped he was Capricorn.

"What are you, Mark?" I ventured.

"I don't know."

"Well, when is your birthday?"

"August sixteenth."

I gulped. My mouth felt dry. "Oh, Leo." That was the worst.

"Why, what are you?

"Me?" I asked, still shocked. "I'm Taurus."

"Yeah, she's a bull," Rita laughed.

About this time, Mr. Michaels told us to quiet down because we would be stopping at 5:00 a.m. to stretch our legs. Rita and I decided to try to sleep. I noticed Mark slip into the seat in front of me next to Gloria Richards. I was curious as to what they were doing but fell asleep before I could knew it.

When I awoke at 4:30, I felt tingly and warm. I looked over at Rita, who was wide awake.

"I was beginning to wonder if you were dead. I've never seen anyone sleep so much." She looked at me seriously.

"I can't help it. Just tired, I guess." I yawned, stretching my arms.

Margaret looked up from across the aisle. "You'll never guess what Mark was doing," she whispered mysteriously.

"No, I guess not."

"He was tickling your ankles," she said.

"What? I didn't feel anything."

"He was."

"I don't believe it."

"He was, wasn't he, Faye?" vowed Margaret, looking for backup.

Faye piped in. "He sure was. I'm surprised you didn't feel it."

I didn't know what to say. What right did he have to tickle my ankles? Especially when I was asleep and defenseless? By this time, Mark had turned around and was looking at me. Those blue eyes held a look of merriment.

"What were you doing?" I demanded to know.

"You mean this?" he asked, coolly reaching for my foot.

I shuddered. "I guess, but I didn't feel a thing." I pulled my foot away. His audacity made me nervous.

For an instant he looked hurt but recovered quickly.

"Didn't feel a thing, huh?" Mark grinned. "When you sleep, you really die."

I nodded.

It was nearing five o'clock as we began to gather jackets and purses, eager to get out of the bus. We stopped at a bus station in Kansas. The early morning air was cool, and although the sun was beginning to peek above the horizon, streetlights still blazed overhead, setting an eerie mood. Exhaust from the busses settled on us.

We entered a small diner. The aroma of fried eggs, bacon, and coffee reached and repelled me. We walked about, found restrooms, and drank water from a drinking fountain. I noticed Rita tagging along behind Dan. *Wow*, I thought. *She's braver than I am.* Dan soon lost her, and she came back to me.

"Ooooh, what a bod!" she gushed.

"Who?" I pretended innocence.

"Dan! Who else?"

"Oh, I don't know about that."

"I see you have your eye on Mark."

"I don't have my eye on anyone," I retorted indignantly.

"I'll bet you do. Oh ho, Claire!"

I couldn't keep from grinning.

It was nine o'clock before we stopped for a real breakfast in a rich-looking restaurant. We began to gather while Mr. Michaels went to see if they were ready for us. While we waited, a siren could be heard in the distance.

Several of the kids yelled, "They're coming for you, McCarthy."

"Yeah, Mark! What have you done this time?"

Mark stood up and grinned. "They can't get me. I haven't done anything … yet."

The *"yet"* bothered me. Although it was a perfectly harmless exchange of words, it seemed that people expected the worst from Mark, and I was afraid they would get it. He would only be living up to expectations.

Once inside, we had to wait again. I can still see the interior of the restaurant. The color scheme was black and red, and the lighting was what I would call poor. Rita and I stood on shaky feet, speculating as to what we might be having for breakfast. Mark approached me and casually laid his head on my shoulder.

"I'm tired," he explained, yawning.

"I've got bony shoulders," I apologized, feeling uncomfortable.

"So do I."

I felt uneasy and pulled away from him. He snorted and patted his stomach.

"I'm hungry. They'd better have something decent."

"I'll bet we're having scrambled eggs. I can smell them."

"Yeah, probably. They're easiest."

I sat with Lynn and Trudy, who never failed to make me laugh. We had toast, grapes, pineapple, hash browns, some breakfast meats, and what indeed appeared to be scrambled eggs, which I found tolerable. Trudy began her assessment of the powdered eggs and greasy bacon as we broke into fits of laughter. Once again, she was doing what she did best, turning an everyday event into fun. We giggled about cold hash browns and soggy toast, trying our best to choke down what we could.

I fail to recall the rest of the morning. Perhaps I slept until we arrived in Amarillo at 1:00 p.m. After arriving at the motel, we were told to meet at the pool for further instructions. The pool was set in a jungle-like atmosphere. Palm trees lined the room, and smaller potted palms served as centerpieces on each table. Our room was directly across from the pool. The whole group gathered at the pool, and Mr. Michaels told us that we could use the afternoon as we wished: swimming, bowling, or sleeping. In the evening we would board a bus again to take in a local amusement park. He passed out the room keys, and we went our separate ways. Most returned for swimming.

Rita, Trudy, a chaperone, and I were assigned to the same room. Rita eagerly slipped into her bikini. I wasn't nearly so eager and for good reason. In the first place, I didn't want to get my hair wet, but even more worrisome was the acne on my back. With a little coaxing from my friends, however, I agreed to take a dip. Rita was dressed and out the door within five minutes. Then I heard Trudy giggling.

"I can't go out there in this," she laughed. "Just look."

"Well, Miss Glamour," I said, "you think you're beautiful? Just look at my suit."

Together we laughed nervously.

"Well," I said bravely, "I'll go if you will. We don't even have to get in."

"OK," she agreed shakily.

We ventured out slowly. Screams of laughter and delight reached our ears. The pool was filled predominantly with boys and Rita.

"Let's go back while we still have a chance," Trudy whispered.

"Aw, come on."

"But I can't swim," she faltered.

"You don't have to, Trude," I assured her. "You can just get in the shallow part."

"Well, all right."

Near the pool, we found a cluster of chairs. I adjusted my eyes to the pale-green light. Rita seemed to be directly in the middle of the boys. I smiled just to watch her. My smile changed to alert concern when I noticed Dan and Mark walking in our direction.

"Uh-oh!" I poked Trudy.

Whew! They walked past us. Before I could feel much relief, I felt a pair of hands around my waist. Mark was behind me and Dan behind Trudy.

"We'll just have to throw them in, since they won't get in themselves," Dan said in a threatening tone.

"Now, wait a minute!" Fear and a sense of injustice fueled my sudden courage. I turned around to face them. "You can't throw Trudy in; she can't swim … *And* you're *not* throwing me in, because I'll get in by myself."

"Humph! Have it your way," Dan gave in. "We'll be waiting."

They walked off, and I shuddered.

"Whew! That was close." Trudy wiped her brow.

"We'd better get in before they come back. Come on, Trudy."

"I think I'll go back to the room."

"Oh, Trudy, don't leave me now," I pleaded.

She was already grabbing her towel.

"Oh, please, just the shallow end?"

She relented.

Why I felt I had to get in, I don't know. Perhaps I was trying to prove to myself that I was just as fun loving as anyone else. I made my way cautiously along the length of the pool, trying to exude an assurance I did not feel. I got into the water slowly, shivering at the change in temperature. I heard a masculine voice. I think it was Dan.

"Go get her, Mark!"

Mark came over to me.

"What are you going to do?"

"Throw you in."

"But I'm in."

"Not all the way, you're not."

In an attempt to keep my hair dry, I had drawn it back and fastened it with a barrette. This did not go unnoticed, and I realized the futility of my hope—to stay dry in a pool with boys in it.

"You'll have to let her hair down."

I looked up, startled by Rick's voice. I gave him one of my slit-eyed stares. He only winked. After Mark had removed the barrette from my hair, he moved behind me, slipping his arms about my waist. I decided to put up a fight.

"Hey, hey, you're going to hurt somebody," was all he said.

But he held me there for ten seconds. It seemed like hours. It didn't take much for me to guess that he was looking at the pimples on my back. I felt ashamed and wanted to get away from him.

"Please, Mark," I begged for mercy.

Finally, he lifted me into the air, and I dropped into the water. Quickly, I swam toward the deep end. When I looked around, Rick was laughing. Margaret was at the other end. I made attempts at sounding disgusted about the ill-mannered boys, but honestly, I felt good. I was hoping that Mark really did like me.

Margaret and I swam about, practicing the various strokes we had learned in swimming classes at school. I was slightly disappointed to see Mark go to his room without any further attempt in my direction. After a short while, we decided to go back to our rooms too.

Once in the privacy of the room, I could barely contain myself.

"That Mark got my hair all wet. I might as well wash it now. You know, though," I said pensively, "I wouldn't have had any fun if I hadn't gotten it wet."

"I think they are going to throw Michaels in tonight," Rita reported.

"With all his clothes on?" gasped Trudy.

"Of course. It wouldn't be any fun if he didn't have his clothes on," Rita said matter-of-factly.

"Boy, I'd like to see that," Trudy replied.

"Does anyone object if I use the shower?" I asked, not interested in their conversation.

"No, go ahead." Rita wrinkled her brow. "I think I'll take one when you're done."

"Oh, and ..." I said absently. "I brought a hair dryer in case any of you want to use it."

"Good, I might use it tomorrow," said Rita.

I took a shower and set my hair. Then I settled under the hair dryer to scan a journal article I had to read for biology.

By five o'clock, my hair was sufficiently dry. The four of us—Rita, Trudy, Mrs. Benson, and I—decided to have supper so we would be ready to go with the group to the amusement park at six thirty. While we were having hamburgers at the motel restaurant, one of the chaperones told us that it was very chilly outside and advised us to dress warmly.

"All I've got is shorts," Trudy wailed.

"Wear knee socks with them?" I suggested.

"I guess I'll have to."

By 6:00, we were bundled as warmly as possible. Standing outside our door, waiting for the others, we chatted about various encounters we'd had so far. Lynn joined us. I noticed she was wearing a pheasant feather in her hair. I thought it was rather strange.

"You're wearing a feather in your hair!" I laughed.

"Sure, she is!" Mrs. Benson piped up. "She's just doing her own thing."

"Er ... I didn't ... I just meant ..."

"If she wants to wear a feather, she can wear a feather. That is her business. It makes her an individual. I could ask you why you're wearing a blue jacket. That would be the same thing. She has just as much right to wear a feather as you have to wear that blue jacket." She took a breath.

"I guess you're right," I said, defeated.

"Now as for me, feathers aren't my bag. I go for gaudy hats. I've got to show you this new hat of mine. It's red. I got it at Petersen's for half price. I'm always on the lookout for bargains, you know. I've got it somewhere here in my purse." She paused as she peered into her large, over-the-shoulder bag. "Do you like my hat? Wait a minute, I'll put it on for you."

She withdrew a red, knit fedora from her purse and placed it pertly on her head.

"Well, what do you think?" she asked. "Do you like it, huh?"

"Oh, yes," I answered quickly for fear that if I did not, she'd continue to talk about how wonderful it was. She did anyway.

"I think it's kind of cute, myself," she purred as she took it off, fondling it in her hands. "I've always liked hats—better than a purse or a scarf. A hat really has personality. Now, Trudy doesn't agree with me. I can't get her to wear a hat. Not even in the coldest weather. She claims her head never gets cold. Mine sure does. How about yours? I guess it depends on the person. Some people really don't have to wear hats. Mr. Benson never wears one—no, never. I do not think he has had a cold a day in his life. Of course, I have not had too many either, because I really know how to take care of myself. I always say that if you dress properly, eat properly, and get enough sleep, you can always have good health. That's a pretty good philosophy. Don't you think, huh?"

I nodded, vowing privately never to comment on a person's appearance again. As Mrs. Benson continued talking with as few pauses as possible, we walked out to the bus and got on. I sat with Rita. Rick and his friend sat behind us. After roll call, we set out for the park.

On the way, Rita and Rick had a lively conversation. Rick had gone bowling that afternoon and was pleased with his score. I added an occasional comment. As we neared our destination, Rick said something that made me glow and feel warmly toward him.

"Claire," he said with that twinkle in his eye, "you've got good-looking legs, and don't let anybody tell you different."

Feeling generous, I smiled and said, "Rick, you're a nice guy, and don't let anybody tell *you* different."

I sat back and thought about my legs. It was funny, but I had never really thought about them. I guess maybe they did have a nice shape, but I had never really analyzed them.

At the park, though it was cold, we were in a joyous mood. I, along with a group of girls, decided to ride the merry-go-round just for fun. So, after buying a roll of tickets, we climbed onto the painted horses, reliving the fun of earlier days when it was acceptable to be childish. The ticket taker, no older than we were, smiled at our joviality and obliged us when we requested to ride just a little longer. Mr. Michaels watched, smiling at us silly girls. When that pleasure had ended, we went off to buy caramel corn and ride some of the scarier rides.

Many chose to slide down a mammoth slippery slide located at one end of the park. Because of rumors about people breaking their legs on such things, I decided not to try it. Instead, Trudy and I nearly lost the contents of our stomachs on a ride in which the seats were attached only to the top of the great arms of the machine. After I had endured that, I wondered if maybe the slide might have been safer.

Near the center of the park was the "Bullet," which was without a doubt the most frightening ride of all. There were two small capsules at each end of a huge rotating arm. At times, the passengers in the capsule were upside down. I did not even consider it until Mark approached me.

"Would you like to go for a ride in it with me? I've taken Margaret and the student teacher already."

"Well, just how many times have you been up there?" I asked, looking up.

"Oh, three or four."

"And you want to do it again?"

"Sure! Come on," he coaxed, taking my arm.

"Wait a minute. Not so fast." I pulled away. "I'm not so sure I want to do this."

"Aw, there's nothing to it! It's really not bad at all," he said. However, his tone seemed to change once we were seated in the capsule. As the ticket taker clasped the skinny bar in front of us, I felt an impulse to jump up and run away before it was too late.

"Should I put on my scarf?" I asked.

"No, it will blow away," he said seriously. "Here, I'll stick it in my pocket."

"Now, all you've got to do is hold on," he directed.

I was a little annoyed and wondered vaguely why he didn't put his arm around me. Once the Bullet began to move, I wondered no more. As we rose in the air, I held my breath and clutched my purse tightly. At the top, there was a frightening yet almost delicious feeling of weightlessness.

"You're not screaming." He sounded surprised.

"Why? Do you want me to?"

"No, it's just that Margaret screamed the whole time. So did the student teacher."

"I just don't see what good it would do," I said reasonably.

"No good at all."

I was too inhibited to scream and reverted to analyzing rather than spontaneously letting go of nervous tension. I bottled the tension, which later worked against me.

At the top a second time, I asked, "Is this what it feels like to be in space?"

"You mean the weightless feeling?"

"Yeah."

"Exactly!" he replied. "No gravity."

I giggled, pleased with the new thought. He seemed to feel my sudden pleasure at the idea.

After about ten times around, I had had enough.

"Will it never stop?" I worried aloud.

"A couple more times around," Mark replied. He had the entire ride down to a science.

The ride began to slow. Finally, my torment was over. Mark jumped up, full of life. I felt like an old woman. He was halfway down the walk as I carefully climbed from the still swinging capsule. Holding tightly to my purse, I staggered slowly after Mark.

I looked up to see Mr. Michaels laughing heartily.

"What's the matter, Claire?" he called. "Too much for you?"

"Yes," I huffed, "I'll never do that again."

By this time, Mark had turned around. Noticing my condition, he chuckled. He then walked back and placed his arm around my shoulders.

"That bad, huh?" he asked.

"Yes." I shivered.

"Now, how about a roller coaster ride for dessert?"

"Well …"

"Oh, come on!"

Before I could even protest, he was dragging me by the arm in the direction of the Mad Mouse. I sat in the front of the car, and as he seated himself behind me, he did something that made me mad. Deftly, like an artist, he smoothly slid his hands to my waist. I gasped, not knowing what to do. Perhaps, I should have said something, but I chose not to mention it.

Mercifully, the Mouse was a short ride, and after its completion, I went for a final ride with Rick Kern on the Scrambler. He was quiet though appreciative of my laughter.

When we got off, Mark was quick to snatch me away, enveloping me with his long arm. Quickly, I slipped out of his grasp while picking up his hand, swinging it as we walked out of the park.

"Did you have fun?" he asked dutifully.

"Yes, did you?" I looked up at him.

"Aw, it was OK."

We sat together on the way back to the motel, and Mark suggested, "Stay by me, OK?"

I nodded, pinching myself at my good fortune of having a boy so interested in me. Once at the motel, Lynn asked if we would sit with her while she had dinner. Lynn ordered tacos with hot sauce, and Mark helped her eat the tortilla chips that came with the meal. Watching them eat, I looked away so I wouldn't get sick. For the rest of the trip, my appetite was nearly nonexistent. When another member of the orchestra joined us, Mark and I took the opportunity to slip away. Holding hands, we walked out of the restaurant and into the pool area.

Splashes and laughter could be heard from the pool as Mark led the way to the cigarette machine. Feeling giddy, I insisted in a babyish way on pushing the button to release the pack. Mark looked at me curiously, discovering a new side of my personality. It seemed he didn't care for my silliness, but he shrugged it off.

The jungle atmosphere around the pool was created by huge palm trees, the balmy air, and lawn chairs arranged haphazardly about the edges of the pool. I felt warm but uncomfortable with this boy I scarcely knew. Yet, as we walked along the pool, I felt a certain pride, strange and unknown to me, just from being seen with a guy older and more popular than I. Carefully, Mark steered us clear of Rick and several girls who had gathered about to sing and listen while he played his guitar. Mark suggested that we inspect the ice machine. I wanted to join the others, but wishing for harmony with Mark, I agreed to his idea.

The ice machine proved to be like other ice machines, humming and full of ice. Mark reached for a few cubes and placed one in my mouth and one in his. I rolled the cube around with my tongue and then decided to tease Mark by slipping one down his back. I failed to accomplish my mission but enjoyed every moment of the struggle. I gave up with a giggle. He laughed too and said, "Let's go."

"Just a second, one more cube," I called as he opened the poolside door.

Hurriedly, I reached for a cube, knocking the entire bucket of ice onto the floor. Only a few cubes had fallen out, but the bucket was too heavy for me to lift. I stood helplessly, the fallen bucket of cubes at my feet. Having heard the clatter, Mark returned and laughed when he saw my dilemma.

"Oh, Mark, look how clumsy I am," I moaned. "I can't even lift this dumb thing."

"Well, let's see," he grabbed the bucket. "Lift the lid, will you?"

I obeyed shaking my head.

"How could I do such a silly thing?"

"Forget it," he said, replacing the bucket. We re-entered the pool area. "How about some ice cream? I'm starved."

"Oh, not for me."

"Will you come along?"

"Sure."

The restaurant was deserted except for two chaperones sitting at the counter eating chocolate sundaes. One of them was my new friend Mrs. Benson. Seeing her, I felt relief knowing that she would carry the burden of the conversation, which I found weighty at times.

After the proper hellos, we seated ourselves beside them, and Mrs. Benson took over.

"I didn't have any supper before going to the amusement park," she said, explaining her sundae. "How are things? Did you enjoy yourselves?"

"Oh, yes, it was a nice place."

"I thought so too. A very nice place. I think everyone had a good time. Aren't you going to order? This sundae is quite good, except the sauce is too thick. That can nearly ruin a sundae. A strawberry one might be good."

"Well—"

"Trudy said she liked their malts. That pie in the window doesn't look bad either, now does it? Do you like apple pie?"

"Oh ... I'm not having anything," I faltered," but Mark's having ice cream."

"Not having anything?" Mrs. Benson raised her brows. "Aw, you ought to have some ice cream."

"Yeah, have some ice cream!" Mark joined in.

Giving him a slit-eyed glance, I tried, "Well, those rides were kind of hard on the stomach."

"Oh, do you have a queasy feeling?" Mrs. Benson asked. "I know how you feel. We wouldn't want you to get sick now."

By this time, a scraggly haired waitress was standing in front of us with a pencil cocked over a pad of paper and that dull "I wish I were somewhere else" look in her eye.

"Ahem." She looked at me.

I shrugged and looked at Mark.

"Uh, a dish of ice cream and some water," he said.

"Vanilla?"

He nodded.

"Will that be all?" Her gum clicked between her teeth.

"Yeah, oh, and thank you." Mark smiled and winked.

"Why, you're very welcome." She beamed.

"The water's for you," Mark noted.

"Always thinking of me, aren't you?"

"Of course," he yawned.

The waitress was humming when she returned with the ice cream. Handing the dish to Mark, she gave him a broad smile and clicked her gum, which I thought might drop from her mouth at any moment. I was amazed at the change in her attitude. I attributed it to Mark's inborn charm.

"Oh, did you forget the water?" Mark asked gently.

"Oh, I did," she giggled. "Sorry."

"'S' OK." Mark got up, heading for the restroom.

Mrs. Benson, just finishing her sundae, cleared her throat. "You know what I always say?" she asked, wiping her mouth with a napkin.

"No, what?" Mark returned, pretending interest.

"You hear kids these days saying they never have any fun. Me? I always have a good time, and that's because I take the good times with me. That is what you must do. You can't expect fun to just happen. You have got to make it yourself. What do you think?"

Mark smiled, I nodded, agreeing totally, and he said, "That's true."

"Last winter, I went on my first ski trip in Colorado. I had never been skiing before in my life. Do you think that stopped me? Of course not. And I had a great time, too! Just ask Trudy."

"OK," I said, knowing that I wouldn't.

"Really, it's all in a person's attitude. If you go somewhere expecting a good time, you're bound to have it."

"Uh-huh."

"It was in Colorado. We had such a good time riding horses. Did Trudy ever tell you about that? Why, I had the time of my life. I hadn't ridden in quite a long time, but that summer—it was last summer, you know—we went riding nearly every day. They had trail rides with great scenery. I think Trudy liked the guide. I'll have to admit, he wasn't bad looking." She chuckled and slapped her knee. "Do you see what I mean? Have a good time, and don't forget it."

"Oh, I won't."

"Have you had a good time so far?"

"Oh, yes, the amusement park was nice."

"Well, Claire." She rose from the stool and whispered in my ear, "Take it easy." I think she was referring to Mark.

"I will, Mrs. Benson."

"Bye."

"Bye."

She and the other chaperone walked out, leaving me, Mark, and the waitress to ourselves. The waitress walked over and planted herself in front of Mark. She rubbed her arm before speaking.

"Uh, are y'all from around here?" she asked.

"No," said Mark with distant politeness. "We're from Iowa."

"Oh? What are you doin' down here?"

"Aw, nothing special," Mark said flippantly. Then he laughed. "No, really we're here for the music festival."

"You're with a band?"

"No, orchestra."

"Oh, I see." She moved away, grabbing a dish rag from behind the counter.

"Dumb broad," Mark muttered to me.

"You know how to handle 'em," I whispered.

Mark looked pleased. "It's easy."

"If you're a guy."

"You're probably right."

We rose, and while Mark paid the bill, I looked out at the pool area. After viewing some rowdiness, I walked nervously back to Mark.

"Mark,"—I tugged at his sleeve— "they're throwing people in."

"Just a minute." He counted his change.

"How are we going to get out of here?"

I had no desire to be thrown into the pool. Some of the kids—boys especially—liked to catch their "friends" off guard and toss them in, clothes and all. One girl had been thrown in twice already, though I was sure she liked the attention. Unsympathetic, I was certain she could have avoided the second dunking.

"They're throwing people in, huh?" Mark asked, stuffing his money into his pocket.

"Yes, I don't see how we can avoid them unless we just stay here."

"Let me see … I've got it. Let's go outside. There's a side door right over there."

"Good thinking."

Mark grabbed my hand, and we walked to the door. Once outside, we ran beside the parked cars until we were about halfway to the next door. Mark stopped abruptly.

"What's the matter?"

"Here, feel this." He took my hand and placed it on his chin. "Feel anything?"

For a moment I was not sure what he expected for a reply, but then I suddenly realized he was worried about having hair on his face. I encouraged him by responding enthusiastically.

"Hey, yes! Yes, I do!"

He smiled.

"Here, let me look." I pulled his chin down to my eye level. "Why, I can even see some whiskers poking through."

"Oh, you." He laughed and took my arm as we trotted down to the other door.

Inside, I convinced Mark to go with me over to the pool where a small group was gathered. I quickly found a lounge chair, and Mark stood beside me, looking uncomfortable. Selfishly, I remained seated, wishing to listen to the music even though I sensed his uneasiness.

"Why don't you sit down?"

"Nah, I'll stand," he replied, still looking at Rick, who was basking in the allure his guitar seemed to generate.

Rita looked up from where she was sitting. Seeing me, she walked over and sat in a chair next to mine. By this time, Mark was talking to some other kids. Rita bent close and asked, "What did you do?"

"Oh, we went to get ice cream."

"I saw you holding hands."

"Yeah." I fell silent.

The next thing I knew, there was a splash and laughter. Mark had been thrown into the pool. Watching him swim slowly, carefully to the side, I marveled at his dignity. It was something I grew to expect and recognize. I believe to this day that Mark would maintain his pride if mud were splattered on his face. In situations where I would be red and flustered, Mark remained cool and calm. Though I respected his dignity, I found it difficult to climb behind that royal reserve. Somehow, if he could have shown a human dependency or awkwardness, I would have been relieved and more comfortable in his presence.

He climbed slowly, almost gracefully from the pool, giving me a look that said, *well, it happened.* Someone threw him a towel as he walked to the spot where Rita and I were sitting.

"Mark, you're soaked," I giggled.

He rubbed his head with the towel.

"You'd better take your shirt off," suggested Rita.

"Yeah, I'd better,"

Handing the shirt to me and rising to his feet, Mark said, "Look for a comb, would ya? It's in one of the pockets."

"OK," I said, taking the brown shirt with the thin orange stripes. He left me sitting with his wet shirt in my lap as he joked with some other guys.

Picking through his pockets, I found some matches, a comb, and a razor blade. Rita raised an eyebrow at the sight of the razor blade and whispered something to the effect that I should be careful, as if Mark were some sort of Jack the Ripper. I disregarded her warning and sat holding the shirt, which smelled pleasantly of cigarettes, aftershave, and Mark. Clutching his shirt, I memorized its scent.

After three or four minutes, Mark returned, still wet, and asked if I wished to go with him to his room and wait outside the door (of course) while he changed. I declined, desiring to soak in the tropical atmosphere and ponder the warnings given by Mrs. Benson and Rita. Their warnings puzzled me, making me feel suspicious of Mark.

Mark changed quickly and was soon beside me again with neatly combed hair and a fresh shirt and pair of jeans. Still feeling the glow of a happy evening, we walked slowly in the direction of my room. I savored every step.

"Tell me about myself," Mark prompted.

"Do you mean astrologically?"

"Yeah, tell me about Leos," he purred.

"Well." Although this was my field, I still found it hard to give off-the-cuff dissertations on the subject. "You're proud and brave and, um, let me see …"

"That sounds good," he said, cocking his head.

"And you've very royal—uh, you know, proud and majestic."

"Uh, huh!"

"And, oh yeah! Leos are often quite jealous, with fiery tempers."

"Oh?"

"Well, according to the horoscope books."

"I see."

By this time, we had reached my door. I sat down about five feet away, awkwardly crisscrossing my legs. Mark sat down smoothly, and as if it were the customary way for any girl and boy to sit, he placed his head on my lap. After recovering from the shock of this foreign position, I rather liked holding his head, feeling his silky hair, and looking into his blue eyes. He seemed comfortably content to rest.

Shyly, I asked Mark what he thought of astrology and if he thought there could possibly be something to it. Also, I told him that according to the stars, he, a Leo, and I, a Taurus, were incompatible. Quietly, he said that he didn't believe in it and that it only scared people. Though I valued his opinion, I told him that I was convinced that there is indeed something to astrology. He did not try to change my mind but talked of other things.

Soon, I grew quiet, feeling overwhelmed by so many sudden changes in my normally calm, boring life. Mark sat up after I told him he was cutting off my circulation. Finally, after I had yawned for nearly the fifteenth time, he looked at his watch.

"I bet if I let you go in now, you'd be out in five minutes."

I nodded, relieved at the signal for my release. We rose, and Mark stood behind me with his nose in my hair.

"I love long hair," he murmured.

Feeling uncomfortable, I pulled away, saying, "Mark, how can you stand to even touch it? It's so dirty." My tendency to self-criticize became glaringly apparent.

"Oh."

"Well, I've really got to go in."

"All right. Goodnight." He squeezed my hand.

"Good night." I slipped inside to be swallowed up by Trudy and Rita.

"Well, how was it?" Rita asked.

"What?"

"Oh, you know," Trudy giggled, clasping her hands together.

"Were you guys watching the whole time?" I asked, trying to sound disgusted.

Trudy giggled again and shook her head no.

"I thought I saw someone peeking through the curtain."

"Well," confessed Trudy, "we were looking just a little."

Amarillo, Day Two

The next morning, after poolside scrambled eggs, bacon, and toast, we boarded the busses and drove to a local high school for practice. Rain trickled down the windows of the bus. Though the air was chilly, our holiday mood remained unaffected.

When the two hours of mandatory practice ended, we picked up our stands and cases to reload the buses. Mark helped me with my coat and offered to carry my violin. As we stepped into the rain, Rick caught up with us.

Noticing Mark with my case he asked, laughing, "What's wrong, Claire? Are you too weak to carry it?"

"I guess so."

Because I didn't feel hungry, I got a piece of chicken and a dish of watermelon at the cafeteria where we went for lunch. Mark ate heartily, sitting at a table with Lynn and me. I noticed Rick sitting at a nearby table. I am afraid Mark's lunch was miserable, though I rather enjoyed mine. Between bites, I would look up to catch Rick's eye. After one of Rick's winks, I smiled broadly. Mark looked up and stopped talking mid-sentence. Dutifully, I resumed the conversation, and Mark seemed bewildered. Even though he said nothing, I know that Mark was uncomfortable with my flirting. I pretended not to care and assured myself that winking at Rick was harmless. Mark, though, seemed eager to leave the table.

Upon our departure from the cafeteria, Mark started to help me with my coat. Still hearing Rick's words about me being "too weak," however, I pulled away, saying I could put on my own coat.

Rick sidled up to Mark, his hand to the side of his lips. "A liberated woman," he muttered.

Mark said nothing. I was furious—furious with Rick, but mostly with myself. Inside, I knew that I should not treat Mark so nastily, and I vowed silently to do better. Besides, I really liked him helping me with my coat. I scarcely glanced at Rick for the rest of the trip.

In the early part of the afternoon, we took a train ride through a canyon among the sage while a grizzled old man bellowed over a loudspeaker about the marvelous scenery. I was chilled even with Mark's arm around my shoulders. We said little, though Mark did comment that living as the old man did might be a nice way to retire. I agreed.

We walked to a gift shop after the ride. Upon entering the shop, I inhaled the air, disliking the atmosphere immediately. Something about such places—almost any store, really—makes me want to run in the opposite direction. Nevertheless, I purchased a copper roadrunner pin for my mother and a tiny shot glass with a map of Texas thinking of my dad.

Noticing some master-slave sweatshirts, Mark said they would be ideal for us. I agreed, providing he wore the shirt marked *slave*. His pretended desire for the shirts faded quickly. We also saw some green, rubbery snakes, which looked chillingly real. Mark seemed fascinated with the things, and although I didn't realize it at the time, he bought one. As we walked back to the bus, he firmly refused to show the contents of his bag, telling me I would find out soon enough.

When our bus returned to the motel, Mr. Michaels informed us that we had the rest of the afternoon to use as we wished if we stayed within a few blocks of the motel and in groups. Several of us walked together to a movie theater just four blocks away. We settled into our seats to watch the latest remake of *Wuthering Heights*, which tells the tale of Heathcliff. Taken into the family of Mr. Earnshaw, Heathcliff, an orphan, grew up with Catherine Earnshaw and her brother Hindley on the moors of northern England. When Mr. Earnshaw dies, Catherine's brother makes life miserable for Heathcliff. Catherine eventually marries a man with money, and Heathcliff becomes increasingly bitter and jealous. I can't remember the details of the story very well, but I do remember holding hands with Mark during the movie. His hand eventually rested on my knee. I was wearing a homemade brown, cotton, fitted dress. Although I enjoyed it, I felt slightly guilty being in such close proximity to Mark.

Back at the motel, as we prepared for the concert, a knock came at the door. Trudy answered and said that Susan Willers wanted to see me. I was a bit surprised to think that Susan would ever want to see me. I went to the door, and Susan looked up and said, "Er, Mark wants you."

"He does? Well, where is he?"

"Up there." She pointed to the balcony of the second floor, which was directly above my head.

"Thanks, Susan."

I stepped out the door under the balcony. As I turned around to look up, I saw a wiggly object dangling from above. Startled and annoyed, I jumped.

"Oh, Mark! Boy! You sure know how to scare a person," I said.

Mark peered down over the railing, rubber snake in hand. "That's why I bought it."

"Can I see it?"

"Not now."

"Wow! It looks real."

"Yup."

"Come on, let me see it."

"Later …"

"Well, all right. I've got to get ready. Aren't you getting ready?"

"No hurry."

"We have to leave in half an hour."

"I know."

I went back inside the room. Rita looked up from the bed where she was putting on a pair of nylons.

"What did he want?" she asked, running a finger smoothly along her leg.

"Oh, that Mark!" I paused. "He has some dumb rubber snake, and he's trying to scare everybody with it."

With that, the phone rang. Trudy answered it eagerly.

"Hello? Yes, she is." Handing the phone to me, Trudy whispered excitedly, "It's him!"

"Mark?" I asked.

She nodded, handing me the phone.

"Hello?" I sat on the chair by the desk.

"Hi, it's me."

"Well, I kinda figured that."

"Who's laughing?"

"Oh, just Trudy and Rita. They're always that way," I explained.

"Yeah? Well, you know that snake?"

"Uh-huh?"

"I'm going to put it in the bathtub tonight and really scare these guys."

"That'll be fun to see what they do."

"Yeah, I don't think Gregory even knows I have it."

"Boy, will he be surprised."

"Are you ready?"

"No, you'd better let me go so I can be."

"OK, I'll see you in a few minutes."

"OK."

"Bye."

I hung up the phone. "OK, now how do I get rid of him?" I asked. I did not mean it. The feeling was so delicious that I just wanted to play with it a bit.

"Well," Trudy said, looking at me sympathetically, "it may not be easy."

"Oh, you don't want to get rid of him," Rita assured us all. "What color is your dress, Claire?"

"It's pink with green and yellow bumble bees."

"Oh, perfect! I've got some green eyeshadow you can wear."

"I don't know about eye shadow."

"A little will look nice." Rita held the pencil for me to inspect.

"Well, OK. Thanks"

We got ready for the concert and proceeded to the bus. The concert was OK. We marveled at the strange way Texans had of talking. Lynn sat between me and Mark at the concert. That upset me a little, but Mark was good natured about it. We returned to the hotel, promising to get to bed early, since we would be playing for the judges in the morning.

The next day dawned bright as the mood among us grew more serious. This was the day we were to prove that we were not a rinky-dink group but an orchestra to be seriously considered. We ended up doing quite well. Every one of the judges gave us the highest possible score. We were elated at the outcome. The effort seemed worth it. We would have to wait until evening to hear the final results as to the grand winner of the festival. Then, immediately after the award program, the orchestra was to climb aboard our buses and head back home.

The evening was a bit disappointing. Even though a Texas orchestra won the grand prize, ours received the top score in every category. We consoled ourselves by agreeing that the judges were biased. We climbed back into the buses, beginning the long ride home. There was no more question as to my seat partner. Mark remained by my side all the way. We slept side by side.

I didn't feel much like eating. I remember trying to choke down some chicken at a restaurant. Mile after weary mile, the constant jiggle and roar of the motor began to wear out the best of us. I remember kids standing in line near the restroom waiting to vomit.

"Do you feel sick?" I asked Mark.

"Not really. How about you?"

"Not the greatest, but I'm OK."

"What's with these guys?"

Everyone was asking around, and they seemed to agree that the vomiters had all ordered the same ham dinner a few hours earlier. I was so glad I hadn't eaten much.

"I can't imagine waiting in line to barf. For me, there is pretty much no choice left when it comes time. It just happens," I said, trying not to think the worst.

We settled in for one last haul from Kansas City through Des Moines and then home. Somewhere between Iowa City and the Quad Cities, Mr. Michaels began to make the rounds. By that time, Mark was asleep on my shoulder, and I felt embarrassed. I was both tired and wired. When Mr. Michaels stopped to give last-minute instructions, I shifted in my seat, and Mark began to wake up. Mr. Michaels only seemed amused.

My parents were waiting when our bus pulled in. I was in one piece but felt like I had been to the far side of the moon and back. Mom made casual talk in the car, and though I had never felt particularly comfortable sharing certain things with either of my parents, it felt like the list of unbreachable topics had grown by miles.

Life went on, and I went to school on Monday. Mark appeared almost immediately after I got off the bus with my friend Michelle. He insisted on walking to my locker with me, and Michelle, who had always walked with me in the mornings. She suddenly became tagalong. Adjustments! I was not sure how to handle this new dilemma. Yet, we had fun in the next couple of weeks.

I was growing quite fond of Mark. However, I remarked to Rita that he was "too fast" for me. I meant it seriously, and when he heard of my assessment, he took it to heart. He began coming over to see me during his supper breaks from his job at the local grocery store on a street near our home. In doing so, he also got to know my mom and dad a little. He treated me with respect and seemed to have a protective attitude toward me. We made a habit of meeting before school. After school, he walked with me to my bus. He tried more than once to get me to ride home in his car, but I refused, because I knew my dad would not approve.

One day before orchestra, I couldn't find my violin. Mark helped me "search" for it, knowing all along that it would turn up right where he had hidden it, inexplicably in the section among the cases of saxophones. Another time, I saw him coming down the hall and looked at the ceiling and in every other direction but his, pretending not to see him. We laughed together.

On a Friday, Dad agreed that I could ride home with Mark in his car after a music rehearsal at school. Mark drove me home in his convertible, and I sat rather shyly in the front seat with my legs crisscrossed. I had planned to tell Mark what I thought of him.

"I've met a boy that I like a lot," I began. I saw him stiffen. "He's tall and good looking, with light-brown hair, blue eyes, and a nice personality." He listened, and I kept talking. "And he happens to be in the orchestra." I paused dramatically. "He's in the percussion section"—Mark began to smile— "and he just happens to be playing timpani in the festival tomorrow." He seemed relieved and pleased at my description of himself.

I arrived home safely and promised to see Mark the following day at the Tri-City Music Festival. In excited anticipation of the day at school with Mark and some of my favorite people, I couldn't sleep. Time flew by in the middle of the night, but I finally slept and woke up without feeling fatigued or worn out. I was floating on a cloud.

The last real day with Mark came on Saturday, just a bit over a week before my sixteenth birthday. We spent the day at school along with hundreds of other kids from area bands, orchestras, and choirs. The atmosphere was electric. Buoyed by the music and time with Mark and friends, I was nearly over the top with excitement. I called my parents from school and tried to convince them of how wonderful it was. I insisted they should consider coming for the concert that evening.

Mark and I ate lunch together and sat in the sun by the goal posts on the practice football field at the back of the school. I was in love with the spring day, the music, and this boy who wanted to be with me. At four o'clock, we were dismissed for supper, and I went home to eat with my family. I was so nervous and giddy with anticipation as Mom helped me get dressed. Then I returned to school for the evening concert wearing a dress.

Little did I know that Saturday would be one of my last days spent in normalcy as a regular teenager. As I sat in the large, assembled orchestra, I noticed a man who seemed to be looking in my direction. I couldn't shake the feeling that this stranger kept looking at me. He may have been watching his child. I think my dad showed up for a short time, although I once again rode home with Mark. Frank and Rita followed. We gathered in the living room at my house. Rita and I went to the kitchen to prepare "mixed drinks" for the boys.

"What mix do you prefer, Mountain Dew with Orange Crush, Pepsi, or 7-Up?" we asked.

We talked about the festival and gossiped. We talked about how prissy a certain girl was. Mark mimicked her, and we laughed. I really, truly liked her, and she had been very nice to me, but I was thrilled that Mark had caught on to some of my prejudices.

Getting serious, Mark said, "I feel like a loser compared to my brother."

I leaned in to listen carefully.

"Actually, I think I was an accident."

I was sipping some pop and choked unintentionally when he said *accident*. We all laughed, and Mark looked at me warmly.

"I would rather believe that 'it' happened one warm December evening in 1953."

We laughed and agreed.

All too soon the evening was over, even though I wished it would never end. After slipping into bed, high on music, Mountain Dew, love, and my unbelievable good fortune to suddenly have such a perfect life, I lay awake for the entire night.

Chapter 6

Breakdown and Mercy

Saturday Night

Once I got in bed, thoughts came rapidly.

How happy I am, and how good life is! Mark loves me, and I love him. Now I know what heaven must be like. The evening has been perfect. Mark's so loving with his endearing looks. Can I ask for anything more? Surely this is too good to be real. Something evil must be lurking. But I must not think of that. Instead, all the joys of the evening must fill my mind. I never realized how much we have in common. He dislikes prissy Beverly as much as I do. He imitates her with perfection. When Mark impersonates Bev, his pursing of tight lips and batting lashes are synchronized exactly with the swinging of his (her) legs. Oh, Mark, how much I love you! The way you face life fills me with admiration. So, you like lumpy cereal! That's the spirit. You take life lumps and all. What a great guy you are! Oh, I know he smokes too much and likes to drink, but that will pass. I will help him over it. Though Mark may hate me helping him at the time, how he will love me when he is cured of those habits. I will convince Mark that he must stop to preserve his health. It may be a struggle, but with love we can make it. I know that we were truly meant for each other. How could I ever have doubted that?

At first, I was so unsure of Mark, but now with his encouragement, I am convinced he is the one. Though we may have to wait a few years for a solidified relationship, I know now that the future is meant for us with each other. I'm glad to know that Mark likes Burt Bacharach's music too. That's another thing we have in common—a love for music. Though his taste leans a little more toward rock, the basic bond is there. Right now, only one thing bothers me. Mark can be so fiery, so wild. How strange. He told me he wants to die a violent death. That is the difference between us, for when I die, I wish to be asleep. Perhaps his fierceness will mellow. He certainly does have great energy if he wishes to use it. Maybe I can curb his wildness …

Thoughts like these kept coming rapidly as the minutes ticked by. I wasn't aware of feeling tired, yet I did feel wired. I lacked any sense of sleepiness. I couldn't shut off my thoughts. My brain was stuck in high gear, but I could not figure out how to shift to a slower one.

This happiness, this love is a gift from Heaven. Thank You, God, but how can it be so simple? There must be a catch. Love cannot be so uncomplicated, so beautiful. Or can it? I don't know, but oh well… Oh, no, no! I know, I know, I now know the awful truth. Oh, God, no! I won't believe it. But You want me to die, don't You? You had it planned—yes, planned for us to meet and share part of our lives. Oh, I thank you for that, but God, I don't understand. Why do you want me to die? How long will it be? I mean, how will I die? I guess I must accept your will, and I will accept it bravely. But, oh— I mustn't cry. Why am I crying? Dear God, you must know that it is just difficult for me to accept this idea. But I can face it if that is what you wish. Our happiness will flourish to the end. Mark will understand. I will try to make it easy for him. We can do things together as usual. Now I understand that this is just like Love Story. *My happiness is temporary. Oh—gulp—I can take it. Dear God, I can take it.*

I turned resolutely in my bed with tears streaming. On my back, I lifted my chin toward heaven and pulled my fingers through my hair. My heart, aching and sincere, could not cope with my out-of-control imagination. Suddenly, I brightened. Tears dried and were forgotten, replaced by a giggle that rippled through me. I clasped my hands smiling to myself in the still dark room.

Oh, God, what is beautiful is now. *I must not think of my death but of Mark. Our love is* now. *I will live for today. Oh, God, thank you for that love. Thank you, thank you!*

I sighed and settled into my pillow. Now I was content and ready to sleep, if only I could. As the clock ticked into morning, my contentment faded. Again, the dreaded thought of an imagined death crept into my mind. I sighed heavily and turned on my side as tears began to fall more freely than before. What began as a boy-likes-girl affair had become a love tragedy.

Surely some good will come of this. My death will not be in vain. I'll give Mark all my love. Surely some good will come—surely.

Sunday

My family began to stir, so I got up and told Mom I hadn't slept. I cannot remember if we went to church. We had some breakfast and drove to a local park to walk around as a family. That afternoon, I sank into Mom's bed and we started to talk.

"Did you have fun last night?"

"Oh, yes, I really like Mark."

"I never had a boyfriend until I met Dad." The introduction of a boyfriend into my life apparently raised my status from daughter to confidant in my mother's eyes.

"Did you like Dad right away?"

"Yes, but I thought he was too short. Joan, my roommate, thought Dad was so cute. She thought he looked like Gene Kelly."

I had seen the movie *An American in Paris* and watched as Gene Kelly danced to "Singin' in the Rain." I smiled. I could imagine my dad looking like the actor when he was younger and still had hair.

As Mom talked, she began to recount in great detail all the ways she had been hurt by Dad's family. "Your dad's sisters were a force to be reckoned with when we first got married," Mom said. "They were a unit. I remember right after we were married, we went to Evelyn and Carl's ranch for Thanksgiving, and we never really sat down as a family to eat. Dad brought bites of turkey and mashed potatoes from the kitchen, but we didn't eat together at the table. I couldn't understand and wished we were at the folk's house." Mom always referred to her parents and family as *the folks*. At their house, Grandpa would have been seated at the head of the table, with the rest of the family all around.

I was baffled by my mother's description of Thanksgiving with my dad's "folks," and years later, I wondered if perhaps they had all gotten into the habit of eating on the run when food was scarce and Grandpa was often gone working for the Works Progress Administration.

Mom went on to list other ways she had felt excluded and snubbed by his family. Dad's sisters sent letters addressing Dad first. She took great offense at something they had probably not even considered. There were other minor, probably unintended slights that a more secure, robust individual would have easily dismissed or not even noticed.

Her memories did not help me calm down. Instead, I began revving again with worry and distress about Mom's attitudes. This kind of talk disturbed me, as I did not know how to process her ingrained bitterness and sense of injustice.

I barely slept again Sunday night if at all. I talked to Mom early Monday morning and explained that uncontrollable thoughts were still racing through my head. She decided that I should go to school because then I would get tired enough to sleep that night. I do not remember much of that Monday. I remember seeing Mark in the hallway; he offered me a book about a teen romance or something. I told myself that the kids in the orchestra were crying with joy because they had conspired to bring Mark and me together. Margaret, who had known Mark in junior high, had told me that Mark was a nice boy. I just knew the orchestra kids were seeing what a gift I was and what a great couple we were. The story I told myself was grandiose and was certainly a mark of how great a longing I had to matter, to belong, and to be accepted by my peers.

At home after school, I may have dozed off for a few minutes. I don't remember for sure. Later, I began looking everywhere for Mark. Mom became alarmed when she heard what I was telling them that evening, and she began to worry that I was on drugs. LSD was in the news a lot in the late sixties and early seventies, and she had attended workshops for teachers at the school where she taught. She recorded in her journal that she called the police in the evening and described my behavior. They confirmed her fears, based on her description of my behavior, it sounded like a drug-induced reaction, and they advised that I sleep it off and possibly see a doctor. Unfortunately, sleeping it off was not a possibility.

I got into bed with both Mom and Dad that night. Dad grasped my wrist. They were afraid of what I might do, as I had suggested I could fly and land on a wire outside just like the birds I could see from my window. I kept smelling custard pudding, which may have been the smell of Dad's aftershave multiplied by ten. Smells and sounds were so intense.

Tuesday

Mom and I both stayed home on Tuesday. She thought I would sleep, but my behavior became increasingly manic. Her journal states that I randomly ran and shouted. I looked everywhere for Mark and believed that television characters were my teachers and various people I knew. I pulled everything from my closet and lined up shoes, dresses, skirts, and blouses in front of my bedroom door.

Mom climbed the stairs and looked into my room. "What are you doing?"

"I'm leaving," I announced matter-of-factly.

"What?" she choked out. "Where do you think you are going?"

"Mark and I are getting married. That's what people do when they love each other."

My extreme fatigue upset the normal family routine and took its toll on my parents and sisters. Fear and confusion reigned for a while. I ended up in the hands of a general practitioner, whom my mother came to consider a sensationalist. As we drove to the doctor that day, I rambled on in the back seat about taking mom to the doctor. Deep down, I must have been upset with Mom for burdening me with her woes, and I remember thinking that we were taking her for treatment.

Mom told me later that I was in the back seat muttering, "Poor Mom! Don't be sad. It will be OK. They know what they are doing. You'll feel better in no time."

Later in the exam room, Dr. Ziegler came in. He had a large head. "Well, young lady. How are you? I hear that you have been having a hard time."

I shook my head. "No, I'm doing fine."

"Doctor," Dad said, "Claire just hasn't been herself. She hasn't been eating or sleeping. She has both Emma and me very worried."

"I'm so afraid for her," Mom said. "She talks about flying and getting onto a telephone wire like a bird."

The doctor thought and scratched his ear. "Hmm." He walked over and stood in front of me. "Have you been smoking weed? What about cactus buttons? Popping some uppers? Tell us, Claire. How about acid? Have you been tripping?"

I sat on the table and protested. "I haven't been doing *anything*. I do not even know what you are talking about. I'm fine!" I pointed to Mom and said, "She's the one who's lost it!"

"Oh, I see." He clicked his pen and made a note.

Dad, Mom, and the doctor all looked at me with sad eyes, shaking their heads in pity at how mixed up I was. They talked in quiet voices, and he convinced my parents that he couldn't prescribe *anything* because a mix of a drug with a prescription medication could kill me or fry my brain. He convinced my parents that someone had slipped me some LSD, which had induced a psychotic reaction. By this time, my parents were scared. The doctor recommended hospitalization. We left to go home and pack for the hospital.

Even though we had lived in the Quad Cities for thirteen years, Mom and Dad had few real friends and certainly none that they could call on in times of need. On the way home from the doctor's office, my dad sobbed, "Maybe there are people who care."

The Merciful Hospital

After stopping at home to gather my things, we headed to the psychiatric wing of the hospital. I remember believing that I was going to be married. We were led to a small room with a nun inside. My delusions continued to unfold. In my feverish mind, the nun was there to perform the wedding ceremony for me and Mark, who was sure to be arriving at any moment. He never did arrive, but I found many other things to distract me.

I was placed in a room with a roommate. All my inhibitions and boundaries were gone. Shortly after I arrived in the room, I noticed my roommate's makeup. I gave no thought to the idea that the makeup might be hers. I was like a curious toddler, touching, tasting, sniffing. I was running on very little sleep, and it was as though I were sleepwalking—living in a dream.

Mom and Dad remained haunted by the notion that someone had slipped me an illegal drug. Mom felt helpless and confused. She spoke to a nurse who suggested that she stay away for five days or even a week. She talked to the mothers of my two best friends, Michelle and Valerie, who called often. Rita's mom called too and said, "If Claire's on drugs, all the kids are."

Mom was also influenced by the scary warnings coming from Dr. Ziegler's mouth. At the time, LSD was one of the most frightening of all illegal drugs, and there were stories of people slipping LSD into the drinks of unsuspecting acquaintances.

I do have memories of that hospitalization. Because of the doctors' fear of mixing medication with the supposed drugs in my system, I lived through an extended psychotic episode. Until I started to come down, the psychosis I experienced in the hospital was for the most part very liberating and oddly enjoyable. I was normally quite shy and unsure of myself, but during that short period, I felt free to express myself.

I know that mania can be a great experience for the one who is manic but difficult for those around the person who are trying to help. To me, it was like being two years old again. Life was an adventure, and I could do or say anything I wished with no consequences. If I tried something dangerous, someone would be there to stop me or catch me. I did not have to be good or guard what I said, because I had no responsibility. All the controls were off. For that brief period, everything was good! I could sing, dance, shout, and speak my mind, and in those few days, I did some of all of that. All my inhibitions and all the hedges that had kept me in "good girl mode" had eroded.

I ended up in a room with a single bed that was low to the floor. The bed came with a belt to keep me in bed, but I do not remember being upset by it. I must have had a catheter, because I don't remember trips to the bathroom being an issue. I acted out fantasies and movies I had seen and books I had read. Everything and everyone seemed to fit in like props and actors in a play. I was assigned to a male nurse with dark hair and a mustache. He fed me, and in my delusional thinking, he became Rhett Butler. I, of course, was Scarlett O'Hara. In my best Georgia accent, I told him how scared I was.

"Oh, Rhett, you don't know how afraid and tired and hungry I've been …"

"Eat your meatloaf," he said gently. "The more you sleep and eat, the better you'll feel."

I obeyed.

"Now your beans." He lifted the fork to my mouth.

I truly was tired and did need coaxing to eat. Mania has a way of sapping your appetite. The sleeplessness only adds to the dream like state.

For two or three days, I was in the same room, tied to the bed. One afternoon my girlfriend Valerie, showed up with her mother who was a nurse. Having been advised to stay away for a while, Mom asked them to check on me. I was so surprised and happy to see Valerie.

"Oh, Val, I'm so glad you're here! Where have you been? I have been looking for you everywhere. I've missed you."

"We thought we'd come to see how you're doing."

"Oh, I've been so lonely. Please sit down."

After looking around, Valerie's mom said, "We can stand."

"Sorry, there's no place to sit," I said worriedly.

"That's OK. We can't stay very long."

"Oh, please don't go yet," I pleaded. "Just get in bed with me."

Valerie lowered herself to my level, got in bed and hugged me.

"You can just stay here with me, can't you?" I asked. "We can live here together."

Valerie and her mom reported back to my parents that I looked clean and fed but that my behavior was highly inappropriate. I was told later that my geometry teacher from school also stopped by. I have no memory of his visit. By that time, I must have been given some sort of tranquilizing medication.

I was also preoccupied with being born again, even though at that time I had no understanding of the Biblical reference in John 3:16. In 1971, the phrase "*born again*" was in the atmosphere; there was a spiritual awakening known as the "Jesus People Revival" that had coincided with the hippie movement of the late sixties and early seventies. More than once, Mom saw me in what she called a "birthing pose," lying on my back like someone about to give birth. To me, the birthing pose meant that I was giving birth to myself. For most of my life, I had been trying so hard to be pleasing to my parents, teachers, and anyone else in authority that I had lost a sense of my true self. Now, I thought that I was waking up, finally free to be myself. I had noticed a woman on the hallway floor in a similar position—on her back groaning as if in labor. I told myself that she was giving birth to herself, just like I had been.

While in the hospital, I turned sixteen. It passed by without notice. Mom saved cards from my grandmothers, and there were flowers from my friends Michelle and Valerie waiting for me later when I returned home. Flowers are not allowed in the rooms of people in a looney bin.

After a few days I was moved into a regular room with an older roommate. I do not recall the woman herself except that her snoring made it difficult to sleep. During that time, I was no longer tied down and was free to roam the halls and take part in meals, occupational and recreational therapy. I got to know several other patients, and I recall a young guy named Joe who had long hair and was good looking in a hippie sort of way. I remember sitting with him and some others at the end of a long hallway and being uncharacteristically loud and acting out.

At one point, in fantasy mode, I took on the voice of a railroad conductor and said, "All aboard! Everyone on board who's coming aboard." I "choo-choo-chooed," and Joe whistled. Later we waited for the train to come into the station. It appeared and began slowing down as it approached. I announced "Dav—en—poooort!" just as the train pulled into the station. We cheered.

One day in the lunchroom, as I was entering a more reality-based state, my imaginary Rhett Butler showed up to take my blood pressure.

"Are you going to bother me again?" I asked.

"I can't always do what I'd like to do," he said.

Wow, I wondered, *did he really just say that? To me?*

My delusional daytime dreams continued. They seemed to be centered around a theme of my being special. It was while I was there that President Nixon's daughter Tricia got married in the White House. In my imagination, as I watched the coverage on the day-room television, I was Tricia herself, beautiful and getting married. Somehow, I could be in two places at once. Did I mention I was delusional?

There were other kooky things during my stay in the hospital. One day I played like I was Dorothy from *The Wizard of Oz*. A group of us gathered in a lounge at the end of the wing where my room was. From my fellow inmates, I gathered castmates. I knocked on Joe's shoe to see if he was made of tin.

He played along. "If I only had a heart!"

An elderly gentleman agreed to be the lion. As a nurse walked by, I pulled the lion close and cried, "Stop scaring the lion, you wicked old witch!"

I grabbed Joe with my right arm, we scooped up the lion, and together we skipped through the halls singing, "Follow the yellow brick road! Follow, follow, follow, follow, follow the yellow brick road."

We stopped to free the "scarecrow," who was strapped to the same bed that had held me captive just days before. Untying his restraining belt, we freed him and helped him to come along with us on shaky legs, leery of "lions and tigers and bears, oh my." The staff was amused by our antics but did stop to intervene before we got far with our scarecrow, a young African American man who seemed perfectly willing to enter our collective psychoses and play along. Maybe his psychosis was intertwined with ours.

A day or two later, I found a fellow patient who was more than willing to accommodate my incarnations of Scarlett O'Hara. Somehow this lady obtained a wide, red ribbon. She combed my hair into a ponytail and completed my hairdo with the scarlet ribbon tied into a bow. When she finished, she exclaimed how great I looked and suggested I go check out my image in the mirror. I ran eagerly to my room, expecting the image of Vivien Leigh, only to be reintroduced to my own anxious face. I felt greatly let down by the reality.

My mother later reminded me of another incident that did not seem particularly important at the time but that served to reveal some deep-seated resentment toward my father. I believe I was still hurt by his comments to Mom when we were out for a walk in the summer when I was twelve. I picked up a phone on the ward one day, called my dad, and gave him a piece of my mind. It seems he may have been giving me some advice, and during the conversation, I angrily told him to back off. I do not recall consciously feeling angry with him before or after that, but in retrospect, I am guessing my outburst came from a subconscious suspicion that I was a disappointment in his eyes.

Still, underneath the surface, I had a sense that Dad would love me no matter what I said or did. In later years, I came to terms with the hurt he had caused me and my resultant restlessness, which has impelled me toward endless, anxious searching for approval from men in positions of authority. I later married a man who, despite many wonderful qualities, was not particularly confident or able to express to me in words the affirmation and encouragement I so longed to hear. It was hard for both my dad and my husband to give me affirmation freely when they themselves had not received much approval from their fathers or teachers either.

Before the conclusion of my hospital stay, I took the Rorschach inkblot test with a psychologist who had been assigned to me. It cost eighty dollars to administer, and my parents were told that the test would help the doctors come to a diagnosis. I had no awareness of the cost, but I took the test administered by the psychologist. I remember talking in a roundabout way about my relationship with my mother. Dad and Mom expected to hear about the findings of the test, and when Mom finally asked, she learned that I had some major psychological problems.

According to my mother's account, communication between my parents and the doctors was sketchy. They were led to believe that my mania had been triggered by a drug overdose. It was only later that they learned from a friend who worked as a nurse that I had experienced a nervous breakdown or psychotic break, not an overdose. However, mania can be triggered by certain drugs like

LSD, and although I highly doubt that someone had slipped me LSD. Knowing what I know now, I think among other things, that the caffein in Mountain Dew and cola products contributed to my sleeplessness.

Three or four days before I was freed to leave, I was placed in a room with a roommate who appeared to be pregnant. She was young and sweet. One day she was teary eyed, and I asked about her baby. She grabbed my hand and placed it on her distended belly.

"Does this feel like a baby to you?"

Her abdomen was hard. I had never felt a pregnant woman's belly, but apparently hers was not the real thing.

"I want to have a baby," she said sadly, "but this isn't a baby." I knew next to nothing about pregnancy, so I kept my questions to myself and only wondered about her predicament.

A day before I went home, a lab technician came into my room to draw blood.

"Please state your name."

"Claire Foltz"

"I don't trust her," the tech said to her companion. "Check her arm band."

She sounded angry, like she was holding a grudge toward me. I felt no guilt. What had I done? I was astonished by her wariness of me and felt somewhat bewildered that she didn't trust me.

The next day, my parents came to take me home to the reality of my own bed, my own house—minus the excitement, the people, and the fantasies—where the harshness of regular life and a summer without much going on would soon bowl me over into a depression deep and wide.

Chapter 7

An Account of the 1971 Breakdown by Emma Foltz

Three weeks before school was out, all my illusions about our wonderful life were shattered. We had been thankful and happy with our family and had pinched ourselves that the kids were healthy. Joe and I had good jobs that promised security, something neither of us had when we were growing up. After I adjusted to it, I felt privileged to have my job. As our savings grew, we had hope that we would have financial security and be able to cover the girls' schooling.

Claire's complexion problems were less impactful at that time, and she was happy and achieving well in high school compared to those sad junior high days. Then one sunny Sunday, that all changed as we became aware that something was a little different with Claire. That morning, I was awakened early by Claire calling. She had not been asleep. I now vaguely remember that she had been up late Saturday night at a music festival at school and that I had insisted she get up and eat and go to church. "If you have ambition to celebrate at night, you can surely get up for church." Going to church would ensure that she would sleep that night. This tact would have come straight from the logic of my dad.

That afternoon, our family took a walk in a city park. As we walked, I realized that Claire had an unusual and removed aura. She would sometimes look right at me as if she were puzzling over who I was. Otherwise, we just kind of ambled along through the park before driving home again. We did not know what the aura meant. I sensed in that fleeting moment something malevolent was being foreshadowed.

Claire went to school on Monday. She was tired, but she could come home and sleep. That evening, she was behaving pretty normally, but she said some outlandish things. She had spoken up in study hall, people had been crying, and other inappropriate ramblings. I called the police and asked to talk to someone in their drug division to get symptoms of a person under the influence of drugs. At the high school where I taught, police had come for an after-school program to give a workshop on drugs. They had brought samples of many different kinds, and we smelled them. LSD was the most feared drug at that time. I described Claire's behavior, though I have no hard-and-fast memory of any of this conversation. The person who spoke to me more or less confirmed our fear that Claire's behavior sounded like a drug-induced reaction. He advised that she sleep it off and said we should see a doctor.

But how could such a thing occur? The jump, for me, left little doubt, as Claire had had a mild connection with Mark since the Texas orchestra trip in April. He had a wild reputation, which I suppose meant he drank beer; lots of decent high school kids I knew did, so I decided not to judge him for that. With this new development, however, I immediately thought Mark may have slipped drugs into her food or water or something. Claire and I talked about it later and decided it was not fair to believe gossip. I do not remember her going on an actual date.

That night, sleep was totally disrupted for Joseph, Claire, and me. That guaranteed neither she nor I would be in school the next day. Since she had slept no more than an hour, max, I thought Claire might sleep during the day and then surely this drug would wear off. It didn't. She imagined constantly that TV characters were her teachers and other people she knew.

She wanted me to cuddle her and sleep by her, and she often got into a kind of pose like she was giving birth as she talked about being born again. We never used that terminology at home, and I had never heard her use it before. I knew that being born again did not mean physically being born, and I wondered how she could even imitate the labor process in the first place. Someone suggested that she and Valerie had probably talked about it, as Valerie's sister had a baby recently and Valerie's mom was a nurse. At that time, watching a birth on TV was not nearly as graphic and frequent as it is nowadays. For example, I watched *ER* on TV last night and saw eleven births within the hour.

The preoccupation with birth went on, and I thought maybe Mark had forced her into a sexual encounter after slipping her the drug. I even thought a friend might have been his accomplice. I thought something may have happened at the big multi-school music festival the previous Friday and Saturday, since it meant things at school were less structured for the musicians.

It was a challenge to get through that day Monday with Claire's random running and shouting. I think she may have dozed in the afternoon. She was looking everywhere for Mark. That night I took some food up to her. The rest of us tried to eat downstairs, but we kept hearing outbursts. We finally ran upstairs to find her in her room. She was standing in front of the east bedroom window with the screen and glass raised saying that she would like to sit on the wire with those birds and that she was sure she could fly. The reality of what we were up against now had turned serious. We had to watch her constantly. Her vision and hearing were extraordinarily acute. She looked out her window and pointed out Michelle's house. She was very drawn to the upstairs windows. She searched for Mark everywhere.

After several tries of going through bedtime rituals, Joe and I finally teamed up and lay on either side of her on our bed. Joe would doze off with his hand clamped around her wrist. There was very little sleeping for any of us, however.

Once she rubbed Joe's hairy arm and said, "You are Mark, aren't you?"

Joe took her hand and ran it across his bald head and said, "Now, does that feel like Mark?"

She laughed appropriately. Then she heard a bug or some sound we couldn't hear and called as if Mark were coming. I think Joe may have gone to her room at some point, as he had school in a few hours, but I do not remember the rest of the night alone with her. It was a great strain to be with her all day because she never could be left alone. This was now at least three days with no sleep. I recall that Joe came home between classes to help.

That morning, Tuesday, Claire took all the things from her closet shelves—even things from her dresser—and lined them up in rows in front of her door. She was moving out. I had just cleaned up spilled food and was trying to pick up the stuff she continued to strew all over the house. Thinking she might have been going for some shock value, I started picking the clothes up and ranting about being sick of this game. I tried to make loud noises to shock her. None of this worked. She was highly clever in her response. If I had not been so involved from the depths of my soul, I would have laughed.

As we drove to the doctor, I sat in the backseat with her. She rambled on about taking *me* to the doctor. She lowered her voice, saying, "Poor Mom, don't be sad."

We had to wait quite a while because our normal doctor was swamped. A time slot with Dr. Ziegler opened, so Joe, thinking of getting back to school, said, "We'll take him." I had not seen him before that day. Now I know Dr. Ziegler was the low man in his group as far as respect and following were concerned. We were about to learn why. He was affable but too eager to be a "hot dog" doctor!

With little data, he started to grill Claire using all the drug cult lingo the kids used, and we left knowing he could not give a prescription for sleeping pills, since they had no way of knowing, at this late date, what drug she'd taken. Mixing those drugs with prescriptions could kill her or fry her brain.

The following night, the sleep nightmare threatened to worsen. We called the exchange, but Ziegler was out of town. Another doctor wrote her a prescription, though, and she slept. I'm not sure what happened, but when Ziegler returned, he practically insisted on hospitalization. We followed his suggestion.

Packing Claire's things and leaving her at that hospital was the hardest thing I had ever done in my life up to that point. I picked up stuffed animals as I packed and cried into them, muttering, "What will she do there all alone?" In the hospital admitting office, she played a very comical charade in which I was the patient. I went with her to her room, which she would share with a well-adjusted patient who was fastidious to the max. This other woman had lipstick and complicated make-up on her dresser and in the bathroom. I went with Claire to the bathroom and could see that this was going to be very problematic as Claire immediately went into high gear, trying every tube and case and eyebrow pencil in there. She had not a trace of inhibition about touching what wasn't hers. I was finally as finished as I could be, and I left her in the room. I peeked back in and saw that she was reading her roommate's letter. Nurses encouraged me to leave, and I was glad they did.

When we went back in the evening, it seemed Claire was oblivious to us. I found her under her bed, kind of in a birthing pose again, and the roommate was after her. I think Claire had taken something of hers. This was the night Claire sat at the piano and played "Für Elise" so beautifully while all the troubled people in that family room area pushed up around the piano in a kind of group demonstration of reverence—a moment of grace.

I wept openly, thinking, *my sweet little girl may never snap out of this*. Joe kept saying, "Let's go now." I wanted so much to see her in bed for the night, but we had to get out for them to function. At first, I felt good about the doctor. He called after he had seen her there and said they had to keep her from eating the eggshells off boiled eggs. She had also been a wisenheimer with him several times, and Dr. Salvas and I mused, "What are we going to do with her?"

Within the first week of Claire's hospitalization, Joe went out to Claire's school to talk to the principal, who was almost too busy to give him any time. I guess Joe almost had to beg him to listen, but the principal finally acknowledged that Joe had a right to be riled as it was his daughter. I called Dan Culver (the principal at Claire's elementary school) and asked him about the kids Dan Jr. knew and what they knew about "druggies." We discussed all the kids we had ever heard anything about, and young Dan negated false rumors. He did not give me any reason to believe Mark might slip drugs to Claire.

I stayed out of school that week and went through every slip of paper in Claire's room for clues. I found much data about environmental concerns from her biology class. I saw notes from Valerie and other friends and to-do lists Claire had written. There were so many lists, with things on them like "don't forget the apple"—I began to think this apple business might be some vehicle for delivering drugs.

When the situation reached a fever pitch, we invited Mark and his dad over for the evening. They both entered, heads bowed, like people coming to offer condolences after a death. I called Dr. Salvas every day, and he reported that there was improvement. He also told me about another overdose victim who had finally come out of a coma. Claire may come out of the state she was in too, but then again, she might never come out of it. All during the time we didn't see her.

Anyway, Mark was contrite, and his father assured us that Mark was not on drugs. Mark, of course, denied drugging Claire. I couldn't tell whether he looked like he was lying or not. I begged him to tell us the kind of drug it was so that the doctors could give appropriate treatment. Dr. Ziegler had said it would help to know what we were dealing with. Mark's dad gave us his sympathy, and they left, heads still bowed. Mark's mom called and cried for Claire, but I wasn't sure what the truth was. It didn't seem we could reach real closure. Our trials with Claire were so great until Thanksgiving, and I just couldn't sympathize with the McCarthys.

Then Dr. Salvas and the in-house psychologist laid the Rorschach test on us. They said it would help them diagnose her, so we pinned some hope on that. It cost eighty dollars to administer, and insurance would not cover it. Still, we thought there would be a finding and that they would report to us about it. Dream on. Days passed. I thought it was still being analyzed, since no one mentioned it. Eventually I asked, and they said the findings showed her to be very mixed up, I guess. I thought they already knew that. Even if they didn't, we could have told them and saved the eighty dollars.

I felt so helpless and confused when I'd see Claire there, and I'd cry. I expressed my worry to a nurse, who said I should stay home. Finally, I asked another nurse, who said, "Why don't you stay away for five days or a week?" So, we placed our trust in the Lord and stayed away. Mothers of Claire's friends called often, as did so many other people from school, and Mrs. Benson said, "If Claire's on drugs, all the kids are."

Valerie's mother was a nurse, and I asked her to go see Claire and case it out. She readily complied and took Valerie with her. They came to our place the evening after and told us that Claire had looked clean and fed but had behaved highly inappropriately. She had tried to get Valerie in bed with her, and Val was so moved and sad that she'd lain down next to Claire and hugged her. These folks were the reason that Claire was eventually able to return to high school as easily as she did.

When Joe and I went back to the hospital after the days away, we saw Claire's geometry teacher coming toward us with his head bowed. He had just visited Claire. He was silent about the visit, but it meant a lot to us to see him.

The staff took us back into a different section of the wing than we had seen before. Claire was lying on a bed about one foot off the floor. There were no windows, only plain walls and a bathroom with a toilet and sink only. She and I went into the bathroom, and she said, "Mom, remember how I'd always say *turtle* when we went to the bathroom?" When I was potty training her, she had a little plastic turtle. She would stand on a stool, and I would put her hands under the water to help her go. Hearing Claire reference this was such music to my ears! Claire was back and rested, but I could not imagine at what cost, since I saw that there were loops on the side of the bed for binding patients to it. I still do not think too deeply about that, nor have I ever asked anyone who might know about the treatment of uncontrollably manic people what might have happened.

The next time we went to the hospital, she was situated in a room with a woman of around fifty years old whose bed was next to the door. I figured Claire would be safe at night. One time, shortly after Claire was integrated back in with the other patients following the solitary part of her treatment, this lovely lady stopped Joe when Claire was not there and said, "Young father, you do not need to be so frightened. Your little girl is going to get well. She'll go on with her life." She continued by telling him some of the history of her many hospitalizations. I know now she was an angel. The hope that her counsel gave us was the first that anyone, doctors, or nurses, had thought to impart to us. In fact, Dr. Ziegler had told us that she might never come back, and he would tell us stories about patients who did and shocking tales of those who didn't.

Eventually, the doctors allowed us to start bringing Claire home for parts of the evening, always with the warning "Don't forget the Trilafon!" lest she become manic again. Then, finally, the day arrived when she could come home. But first we needed to meet with the psychologist and Dr. Salvas. We know now that they were trying to set us up with all kinds of therapy. They took us into a small conference room. I think the rooms are designed for one patient and one doctor. Dr. Salvas explained that if Claire's condition worsened or if she had a relapse, she would have to be taken away to Chicago to a group home, where they would reform her behavior and old patterns. They would assist her in developing new ones and would teach her how to cope. I only remember this conversation very sketchily, but I do remember saying, "I don't see why she needs to change; she just needs to be free of these hallucinations." At this time, Joe and I were still trying to figure out how someone slipped drugs to her. The doctors evidently had come to certain realizations that they had never shared with Joe or me.

There was another day when we conferred quite extensively with the psychologist. While I do not remember the thrust of the meeting for sure, I think it may have involved me insisting on knowing the results of the Rorschach. Afterward, as the psychologist walked down the steps to go to lunch, he said something like "I don't want you folks to feel that you caused Claire's problem and carry a lot of guilt." I thought that seemed strange, since we still thought this had happened at school—that someone had put some drug in her drink. This had been Dr. Ziegler's theory. We kept asking him how it could have happened, and he kept telling us every drug horror story he had ever heard. Trusters of authority figures that we were, we worked hard to believe him. I kept saying that she was very sheltered, as far as carousing around at night went, and that for her to get into drugs was highly unlikely. He told of a teenage couple that got so wacky and hot that they shot water into their veins. He even said that drugs could be put into plastic cups as the cups were manufactured. A neighbor's sister had ruined her brain and was institutionalized somewhere.

So, we set it up for Claire to be in group therapy once or twice a week. The people in her groups were alcoholics, menopausal women, and probably teen drug addicts. Claire would come home stressed about all the problems with menopause. That therapy was short lived, and afterward we practically ignored Dr. Salvas except for medication checks.

In September, I had a great shock when we happened to see Phyllis, a church friend. She said she was so glad it hadn't been drugs with Claire but a nervous breakdown. I asked Phyllis how she knew, and she said her friend who was a nurse at another hospital told her. I felt like we had been duped.

While she was on Trilafon, Claire got fat, was totally uninspired, and had no pep whatsoever. She was very troublesome. I made monthly phone calls to Dr. Salvas declaring that the side effects of Trilafon were devastating, but he kept insisting, "No, the pills don't cause weight gain and lethargy." The talks with the psychiatrist were very confusing and not very helpful.

Chapter 8

Summer Depression and Back to High School

Trilafon

> Trilafon acts like a chemical lobotomy turning
> active human minds into bumps on a log.
> —Linda Mary Wagner,
> *Unearthing the Ghosts: A Mystery Memoir*

Having been assigned a psychologist, the day came for me to be released from the psychiatric ward to go home. The school year was over. I had missed most of the last three weeks but passed all my subjects despite my absence. My teachers were generous.

I was prescribed Trilafon, which is one of the first-generation antipsychotic medications that can be called *typical* or *conventional antipsychotics*. Trilafon was approved by the FDA for the treatment of schizophrenia, schizoaffective disorder, and drug-induced psychosis. At that point, I didn't have an official diagnosis. Trilafon had several possible adverse side effects. Weight gain, drowsiness, and drooling bothered me the most. When I started back to school in the fall as a junior, staying awake in class became a challenge. Trilafon was doing its job.

Trilafon (Perphenazine) offered me my first experience with the side effects caused by psychiatric drugs. I found In a couple of years, I would experience even more devastating consequences of medication. I looked online at WEBMD and found listed there 48 potential side effects for Trilafon. A psychiatrist told me that the medications then had not been tested on teenagers or children because no one wanted to have their children be subjects of an experiment. Even today, psychiatric patients are subject to uncertainty regarding what drugs may work for them. Because of the lack of formal testing, I was in fact a test subject for Trilafon, and later for a couple of antidepressants. I thought the FDA was supposed to protect us from unsafe medication.

Later, in 1974, this "testing" on real-life subjects nearly cost me my life. Perhaps mental institutions were going out of style, but for people struggling with bipolar disorder and other mental illnesses, there was still a great chasm between merely coping with the illness and living in freedom from the tormenting distortions of feeling and thinking. As early as 1951, research scientists Abram Hoffer and Humphrey Osmond were investigating the link between niacin and the reduction of hallucinations in schizophrenic patients. It would be another forty years before I could benefit from their findings.

The summer of 1971 was a difficult one for me. I was embarrassed by my recent hospitalization. As a result, I felt like hiding from my friends. Two of my closest friends did reach out and try to include me in activities, but for the most part, I was extremely depressed and assumed my life was over. The manic exhilaration had been replaced with hopelessness. I spent a lot of time in the dark living room of my home, depleted and lonely.

My visits to the psychologist were unproductive. I did not trust him. On a typical visit, he would invite me to take a seat and ask, "How are you?"

"Fine."

"What's new in your life?"

"Not much."

"Have you had any dreams lately?"

"Nope" was my reply every time. If I'd had dreams, I might have told him. For all I knew, the Trilafon chased my dreams away.

He made me mad. Why did I have to meet with him? The only thing left for me was to resolutely fail to cooperate. After a few fruitless visits, there didn't seem to be much point in continued appointments.

The truth was, I needed a lot of help. My family needed help also. We were isolated by superficial relationships. Church and Sunday school certainly were not places to talk about fears and embarrassing personal problems. In the Methodist Church, we did not even have a confessional where we could at least tell something to someone. The church I belong to now has a professional counselor on staff and classes so people can learn how to listen and pray for people. But it was a different time. Today, it seems that at least some people talk more freely and bond over a wide range of embarrassing problems.

At that time, the need to appear and be perfect was more intense. Most women stayed home as full-time mothers, measuring their success against the pages of *Better Homes and Gardens* and the advice of Dr. Benjamin Spock. Perhaps my parents had more perfectionism due to shame from their own childhoods. Loneliness and unhealed memories bothered them also. I doubt that seeing a psychologist or counselor of some kind ever occurred to them, but I was certain I wasn't the only one with a problem. A stubborn place in me refused to shoulder the burden for the whole family. That stubbornness hindered my willingness to open up to the psychologist.

A divine encounter that summer encouraged me and gave me a new quest. A friend named Patty invited me to spend the night with her, and she loaned me a book that fueled my search for a deeper, more meaningful relationship with God. The book, *Christy* by Catherine Marshall, told the story of a young missionary teaching school in the Appalachians. After finishing *Christy*, I searched for more books by the same author, each one making me hungry for the faith Catherine Marshall depicted in her writing. Her book led me on a path that eventually produced a source of life, healing, and happiness. I believe the spiritual awakening that eventually resulted has been the most important saving factor in my life.

Back to High School

Despite my uneven experience with prescription medications, my junior and senior years of high school were relatively enjoyable compared to the turbulent last few weeks of my sophomore year. In the fall, as a junior, I was taking Trilafon, and I gained weight. My grades dropped, and I was hungry all the time. Mom took me to buy new dresses, as I was becoming too chunky for my current wardrobe. At a school function, a neighbor lady from our old neighborhood, stopped me to say that she barely recognized me because I had gotten so heavy.

I was back in the orchestra with most of the same kids who had been on the orchestra trip to Texas with me the previous spring. I never really talked with Mark again. I don't even remember looking for him. I was in a psychiatric drug induced stupor. Rita and I still shared a music stand among the violins, but none of us talked about what had happened in Texas and in the days that followed.

I had experienced a major trauma that also affected my friends. Nothing was said. None of the trauma had been addressed by my psychologist. He did not seem to care about or even know about the people or events that had precipitated my hospital stay. I was desensitized by Trilafon, so I mostly existed in a fog.

School remained a great preoccupation. At the suggestion of my guidance counselor, in addition to my fifth-year French class, I added German to my curriculum. The teacher shared a last name with my mother. Mrs. Schluensen had long blond hair and a pleasant disposition. My friend, Michelle had decided to take German too, so we were able to sit next to each other on the fourth period every day. Being Jewish, she already had some exposure to Yiddish which descended from a German dialect. I loved that class nearly as much as I loved my French class. I am fascinated with language. Even now, I would love to take a refresher course in either French or German. Hebrew wasn't offered at my high school or I may have taken studied that.

It was during my junior year that Dad began taking me to a dermatologist who didn't use antibiotics. A nurse named Shirley hovered above me like an angel and asked about my life as she gently bathed my face in dry ice. Her kind words and gentle manner helped me maintain some level of softness and hope despite the notoriously superficial atmosphere of adolescence. Soon my face had cleared up without antibiotics. However, I didn't yet know the importance of eating yogurt and probiotics to replace the good gut flora that antibiotics wipe out.

I had trouble staying awake in my classes. More than once in study hall, friends awakened me so I could make it to the next class. I do not recall being terribly embarrassed, although the drooling was a bit humiliating. I was too dazed to really care. One day in French class, I caught myself as my head whipped backward while falling asleep. What did my classmates think? I did not allow myself to even consider it. It was a time of numbed emotions and living for the comfort of the moment.

My history teacher often sold good sized candy bars as a fundraiser. I made sure I always had the two dollars in my purse just in case it might be a candy day. At lunchtime, I sat in the sack-lunch room with a homemade sandwich and an apple, and I sometimes bought a piece of cherry pie. When I returned my plate to a tub of dirty dishes, I often grabbed partially eaten pie crusts off discarded plates. I tried to be discreet, but really didn't care much if someone saw me. Trilafon numbed me to the point that I didn't mind what other people thought. Besides, I was a loser, so what did it matter?

During that first part of my junior year, Trilafon kept me in a fog. I wondered about Mark. I think he was in orchestra that year, but I can't honestly remember. If he was, he avoided me. I wondered a lot about life as I worried about the future. In the fall of that year, for a creative writing class I took the time to write about Mark.

To Mark, December 1971

Once, I did not know you.
But you teased me with your knowingness—
Your good looks.
I noticed you and came to like you.
You flattered me with attention and jealousy.
Then I believed I loved you,
And just as I returned the attention,
I was taken away against my will.
Living in dreams that turned to nightmares,
I forgot you
And will never know if you missed me or even cared.
I cared.
When I returned from that nightmare, not easily forgotten,
I wanted you, asked for you, cried for you, and dreamed to no avail.
When I saw you again, you had traded the gift of attention for
Indifference.
Still, I longed and cried for you
Until that wicked indifference turned me cold and made me hate.
I hated to see your face. I hated to think of the lost you.
Finally, graciously, that hate mellowed, and I prayed for you.
The thought of you no longer hurt so much.
Even though all hope of ever loving you was gone …
Again, I do not know you.

At church on Sunday nights, I showed up for United Methodist Youth Fellowship, which preceded choir practice. We would have our youth meetings followed by a meal that included something like pizza, sloppy joes, or hot dogs. Most of the kids were from the east side of town and just being around them was painful. The daughter of our pastor was usually the center of attention. I did not feel like I fit in very well. If my friend Molly wasn't there, I would often go hang out in the bathroom to avoid the sense of isolation I felt as the other kids joked and messed around. I waited there until choir practice began.

I fared better on Sunday mornings in Sunday school, when we discussed ideas. Too often it seemed to me that the youth minister was having us participate in "love-in" type hippie events. They weren't sexual, of course, but It was the sixties. I found such events to be irritating. I needed personal understanding that people in church were not able to provide.

I mostly wanted to talk about the Bible and what it meant for our lives. There was a lot of religion at church, with little help in understanding what a true relationship with Jesus entailed. The youth pastor could have been helping shape us into disciples by teaching us how to pray and how to apply Christian principles to our lives. Instead, he spent a lot of time trying to keep us entertained.

However, he was helpful in other ways. He did provide opportunities for us engage with the community. At least once a month, we visited a county supported nursing home to participate with the residents in Bingo. The pastor also introduced us to other churches. For instance, Mormons came to visit and explain their beliefs. One Sunday, we visited a large Catholic Church downtown. As part of the service, the priest moved his way down the center aisle giving a hug to every person at the end of each row. Those people then extended the "love" by embracing the person next to them until the entire church had received a hug. I believe this practice sprang from the Jesus People Revival that began in the 1960's. That was when walls between Protestants and Catholics began to disintegrate.

In December, my mother took me shopping for a dressy dress to wear to a concert at the Masonic temple. The city's high school orchestras and choirs combined to play selections of Handel's Messiah. By the time of the concert, I had gained a lot of weight and was literally out of clothes that fit. Mom found the section for chubby girls, and we selected a dress with a black velvet skirt, a crinkly white top, and a red, plaid tie under a velvet collar. I didn't much mind the weight gain. Whatever dignity I had possessed became calloused by the medication I swallowed daily.

By Christmastime, I had gained at least thirty pounds due to the medications. Dad was alarmed and scolded me. He tried to help me exercise, and more than once he had a boiled egg or some other sort of protein waiting for me after school. Some days, he took me to the basement and encouraged me to do some exercises. If he stayed with me, I would follow his lead, but I had no inspiration to exercise on my own. After supper, I often got up to clear the table and would help myself to more food as I rinsed the plates.

Shortly after Christmas, in noncompliance with the psychiatrist, my parents decided to take me off the Trilafon. Their belief was that I was normally OK and unruffled. Mania was not a usual condition for me. When the Trilafon was removed from my routine, I rather rapidly lost the weight I had gained and began returning to a more alert state. I became myself again.

Dad studied what he could find on mental illness and discovered that B vitamins were important for mental health. He read that in the making of white bread, B vitamins and other nutrients are stripped from the flour along with the bran and germ. Somehow, he found a recipe for making stone-ground whole wheat bread. He made it regularly. We found it was easier to eat when toasted. It was a far cry from Wonder Bread in both taste and texture. The texture was closer to a shingle from the roof. I appreciated his gesture of caring and did my best to eat a toasted piece with peanut butter each morning.

As I began to detox from the Trilafon, I thought about Mark. He was still in orchestra, I think, but I'm not sure. The last thing

Mark knew regarding me was that he had been unfairly suspected of having caused my problems in the first place by slipping me LSD. It is no wonder he avoided me or did I avoid him? After I stopped taking the Trilafon, the rest of my junior year and my senior year I was mostly happy and without notable circumstances. I wondered a lot about life as I worried about the future.

I decided the time had come for me to stop dreaming about becoming a famous person, such as a missionary or someone found in history books. I finally came to realize that in my lifetime, I would take my place beside all the common, everyday nobodies. I concluded that the world is made up of a majority of unbrilliant people.

Those thoughts left me scared. I wondered why I was here on earth—or for that matter, why anyone ever breathes and lives. Living itself was such a mystery to me. It seemed to be an endless cycle, completely lacking any real purpose. It consisted of birth, growing up (as quickly as possible), working, struggling, raising a family, retiring, and dying.

Quite honestly, I would have liked to believe that there was a divine plan set by God with eternal life in heaven after death. Yet sometimes that seemed so phony. How could I believe? How could I find my reason for living?

Perhaps I was rebelling against independence. I was afraid of finding the truth about living, afraid of uncovering mysteries of the grown-up world and finding that everything is common and human and perhaps not as well-ordered or nicey-nice as I might have hoped. I was in that trying time between childhood and adulthood.

Another thing that really bothered me was that I felt that my life was becoming more complicated when I would have liked for it to be simple and easy to manage. For example, I had to think about my new clothes, new shoes, a car, college tuition, my contacts, and making money for all of this. There was a song by Peggy Lee called "Is That All There Is?" I hated it. I had not liked it when it was popular, and I still didn't. There had to be more than just going through the motions of life.

Maybe the reason I was often disappointed by things was that I expected to be entertained rather than putting some work and effort into my own projects to see the fruits of my labor. It was kind of like what Mrs. Benson told me: "You've got to take along your own fun. You only get out of something what you've put into it." Her words were so true and logical. But how could I follow that formula myself when I was such a dreamer? How could I fit into this fast-moving world when I felt like I belonged in an eighteenth-century rose garden writing poetry?

In the spring semester of my junior year, I took an expository writing class from Miss Sheldon. She was young, skinny, pretty and freckled with curly, dark, short hair. The class was open to both juniors and seniors, so I felt both intimidated and challenged by Miss Sheldon and the seniors in the class. However, I learned a lot as she taught us how to form five-paragraph essays on a variety of topics.

Usually, we had a day or two to finish a particular essay, but on test days, we had only the length of a forty-five-minute class period to pick from a list of topics and write a five paragraph piece as quickly as we could. The class was challenging and I loved it. I got a chance to prove myself in an area where I had some gifting.

On one assignment I had to write about a day in my life in the future depicting a profession I had chosen. Of two options, psychiatrist or mother, I chose to write a story about me as a mother with a little boy who was just learning to walk. The paper turned out to be prophetic, because seven years later, in 1978 I found myself caring for Nick, my first child.

Summer 1972 before my senior year

I had hope that our family could host a foreign exchange student for a year. My parents decided that wasn't the best idea but agreed that for about three weeks in the summer, we could be a host family for a student through an organization called People to People. We applied and were accepted to host one of the leaders of a group coming from Germany.

We met Dietrich Becker at the bus depot in Davenport. He was about twenty-five and blondish with a broad head. He encouraged me to practice my limited German on him. I don't remember the name of his hometown in Germany, but I do know he had aspirations to become a doctor. Almost immediately, I fell in love.

After his first night with us, my mom wanted to make Dietrich a nice big breakfast of bacon, eggs and toast. He deflated her plan by telling her that a hot breakfast could make him "womit."

Finding things for him to do with us, became a challenge for the whole family. We showed him sights around the Quad Cities like the Mississippi and the lock and dam near the Arsenal Bridge in Rock Island. We took him out to eat and one day gathered at a downtown restaurant with other students and host families. Reporters from the newspapers were there to take pictures and write a story. The article included a picture of me and another girl pouring water for the German students.

I introduced Dietrich to my Jewish friends Michelle, Kenneth and Franklin. Considering the not-too-distant past, I wondered about mixing a German with Jewish people. Together we travelled to a county park to share lunch and hike on a trail. Of course, none of us mentioned the Holocaust. Now, I wish I had asked Dietrich about his family during that horror filled time in Europe, but it was one of those "delicate" subjects.

For two days we took time out in order to visit the Mayo Clinic in Rochester, Minnesota so that Dietrich as a pre-med student, could see an American hospital. We packed overnight bags and all six of us piled into our '68 Bonneville Pontiac. Dad, Mom and Dietrich sat in front and the three of us girls filled the back seat. Dad had reserved two adjoining rooms in a motel. That evening after supper, Dad and Dietrich retired to one room, while Mom, Megan, Annie and I got ready for bed in another. The next day Dad and Dietrich visited the hospital while we waited. All in all, the trip bored me to tears. There had been precious little time for personal interaction.

On another day, our house served as a gathering place for the other students and hosts to come together for food and conversation. People brought food to share. There were card tables set up on our deck in the back yard, My crush on Dietrich suffered a blow that afternoon as I observed his relationship with Petra. He and she spoke quickly and easily with each other in German. She was pretty, lively, and like all the other German girls, had hairy legs.

Petra and Dietrich sat together on our living room couch with their arms about each other's shoulders. I felt jealous that she held his attention. They were so comfortable with each other. So much for my romantic notions.

We took Dietrich to the bus depot the day he left. I cried. He told my parents that if I ever wanted to visit Germany that I could stay with him and he would take care of me. The chance of that happening was remote. I doubted my ability to travel especially to a place as far away as Europe. The chance for a breakdown was too great.

Shortly after Dietrich and Petra had returned to Germany I received two letters in a single envelope one from Dietrich and one from Petra. In his letter, Dietrich specifically thanked me the Bible verses I had included in a good-bye note to him. He wrote that he didn't know if he were a pagan, atheist or and Christian, but who knew? The Bible verses could be just right for him. Folded and tucked into the envelope was a tourist guide to Berlin that included a map with check points and information on how to get to East Berlin which was on Friedrichstrasse on the corner of Ziimmerstrasse.

Chapter 9

Senior Year

I began my senior year, pessimist though I was, not entirely without hope. I was a hopeful skeptic. I had not really grieved my losses surrounding the time of my breakdown. Those losses remained untouched for a long time. However, I did enjoy orchestra, my French, German, English and Psychology classes.

I considered myself the kind of person who could not accept change very well. I could accept change if it were slow and gradual, but sudden surprises bothered me. I guessed I was the kind of creature who needed a feeling of security to function. I compared myself to a turtle in that I was very shy and passive. When confronted with danger, I pulled into my shell, wait for the danger to pass, and hope for the best. Wow! Talk about wasting your life! Where on earth can a turtle be happy? In the depths of its shell?

Friday Night Football

One Friday night at the football game, I sat with Valerie, and we talked about—what else? —boys!

"You know, I really have a weakness for blond guys with wire-rimmed glasses," I said, digging into our shared bag of popcorn.

"I prefer boys who look like Glen Campbell."

"No kidding. I know!"

"You like boys who resemble John Denver."

"Yeah," I admitted, "you know me too well."

"Who are you thinking of?" Valerie asked gently.

"I think Terry is nearly perfect. He fits the blond-with-wire-rimmed-glasses requirement."

"But he plays football, not the guitar," Val reminded me.

"Scratch the guitar; football is attractive too."

We both scanned the field. I could see Terry below sitting on the bench.

"He's perfect," I sighed. "He's intelligent, a Methodist, smooth voiced, and male. It makes me sick to even think about someone like him because I know I'll just get stuck with a loser."

"Claire, you have no idea yet! You do not have to have that all figured out. You're only seventeen."

"Yeah, I guess you are right."

The truth was, based on my recent history, I felt like a loser. How could I ever find anyone who loved me? I was disqualifying myself before I had a chance to be in the real world. Living in my fantasies of guys was much safer than communicating with them face to face. I was such a dreamer.

In the fall semester, I took a creative writing class. I wrote poetry that expressed my reserved, skittish, yet yearning nature:

Seventeen

Best time of life,
Or so some people say.
A time when you enjoy yourself,
A time of no dismay.
Well, I can tell them.
It's not so,
At least not so for me,
For in a vacuum

Now I stand,
Unable to get free.
I've had the easy childhood,
And now I have no choice
But to accept responsibility,
Leaving behind all childish joys.

Wild and Free

Wild and free
Against the sky,
Young boy runs to play.
His hopes, dreams, and spirit flies
Beyond the darkening day.
His eyes are those of a deer,
Penetrating but so shy.
A deer that knows it will be caught, tamed, and
civilized.

Later that fall, I wrote in my journal: "I feel as if I am being smothered alive. I want so much to write a good short story—I mean a really good one. Mother talked with me for at least an hour. She completely tore apart my current story. I'll have to admit it is rotten. But now what am I going to write about?" I ended up handing in the rotten story and got a B. I had to write another short story, but as I ruminated about the next one, I finished an epic poem about Mahatma Gandhi.

In January, a new semester began, and because I had enough credits, my guidance counselor recommended I take two English classes. I chose Contemporary American Literature and another course in world literature; both were taught by Mr. McKenzie. The American Lit class was filled mostly with kids who were just fulfilling their English requirements. Under the direction of Mr. McKenzie, we read John Steinbeck, Ernest Hemingway, Langston

Hughes, William Faulkner, F. Scott Fitzgerald, and a novel by Edith Wharton called *Ethan Frome*. I regularly spoke up in that class. I loved the subject matter and found Mr. McKenzie's responsiveness to be very encouraging. He made me feel comfortable enough to share any of my thoughts by answering sincerely. He responded as if I were on his level.

In my journal, I wondered about love and what it meant. I dreamed of inviting Steven Grady, a boy from my old neighborhood, to Gala, a dance sponsored by the Girl's Recreation Association. It was a reverse invitation dance—girls invited boys.

I was unsure—it was probably too late to ask him, and I worried that he wouldn't remember me very well. Sadly, I guessed that was the way old friendships broke off. Oh, well, I was glad I got to share the experiences I did with him. I just hoped that I could meet and marry someone as nice as he.

On Sunday afternoon, Michelle called and suggested that I ask someone to Gala. I told her I was thinking of asking Steven.

"You should invite him," she pressed.

"But I haven't talked to him for a long time."

"That doesn't matter. He will probably be happy that someone asks him."

"Do you really think so?"

"Sure! We can go on a double date. Franklin is going with me."

She promised that we would eat at a nice place. I worried that it would cost me a fortune and I would have to pay for it with money I didn't have. I knew my parents wouldn't mind. I figured it might be worth it.

And so, I did call. I was so nervous that I wrote out everything I wanted to say to him, ahead of time. I kept my notes in front of me to refer to as we talked.

His phone rang, and his mother answered. "It sounds like a girl," I could hear her whisper as she handed the phone to her son. I laughed to myself.

"Um, this is Claire Foltz. Do you remember me?"

"Oh, yes."

"Well, you know that Gala is coming up, and I was just wondering if you'd like to go with me."

He didn't hesitate. "Sure."

"Well, that's good. It will be a double date. Is that, okay? With my friend Michelle and her boyfriend."

"Yeah, that's fine."

"The girls buy a boutonniere for the boys, and the boys buy a corsage for the girls," I blurted out, anxious to make sure I had a corsage for my one and only dance of the year. I knew I was being pushy and controlling to bring that up, but I simply had to make sure he understood the rules.

Steven had said yes! I was so happy. After that call, I told my parents and of course I called Michelle. Later that day, I only had to think up a myth for Mr. McKenzie's class.

We made plans to go with Michelle and Franklin. Franklin was a friend of Michelle's family. Because Franklin had a car and was going to be the driver for the evening, he took his time and made me miserable in the process. He and Michelle were nearly an hour late picking me up. In addition, I had somehow managed to find the homeliest full-length, blue, plaid dress. I looked like I had stepped out of a scene from *Little House on the Prairie.* In contrast, Michelle had a cute, form fitting dress that was just above her knees.

In the school cafeteria, Steven and I danced, but he had grown tall, and we just did not seem to fit very well. We talked about old times in the neighborhood, but our conversation lacked the tension of the little neighborhood kids. In my journal, I wrote that the whole evening had turned into a disappointing flop. I thought of everything at that time as black or white. I had overlooked the meal at Earl's Gourmet House and the fact that Steven had kissed me on the forehead when he got out of the car. Looking back, I guessed it wasn't a total loss.

After the dance I decided that I didn't want to get married. I had built up Steven too much in my mind and then I was let down.

That seemed to be the story of my life—great expectations and SMACK, reality and big disappointments. I was still trying to lose weight, while still reaching for cake and peanuts. However, I had found someone new to have secret admiration for—Mr. McKenzie. I worried about my daydreams that I'd rather dream than get actively involved.

The afternoon world-lit class with Mr. McKenzie turned out to be a bit more challenging than the third period American lit class. However, a few days after Gala Mr. McKenzie chose the myth I had written, entitled "Timidius and Aphrodite," as one of two he read to the whole class! His approval was all it took for me to develop a crush on him. Ever looking for affirmation, I was smitten. My crush would carry me through the summer until I left home for college.

More than a teacher to daydream about, though, I needed a relationship with someone higher than any human. I needed to spend time with someone who deserved my worship and who really understood me. I had yet to be introduced to Jesus personally. At that point He wasn't even on my short list. Yes, there was talk of God and Jesus at church, but I hadn't yet been born again.

> There is a God-shaped vacuum in the heart of each
> man which cannot be filled by any created thing
> but only by God the Creator, made known
> through Jesus Christ. –Blaise Pascal

On the day of the talent show. I wasn't as excited about the upcoming program as I had been in past years, but Mr. McKenzie made me smile that day. I was in my usual seat near the door and Mr. McKenzie was in his usual position waiting at the door in order to close it at the ring of the bell so the class period could begin. I was feeling rather grouchy as he hovered near me talking to a feather-brained girl about *Who's Afraid of Virginia Wolf.*"

During the class we were talking about a poem with "Olympus" mentioned in it.

"What is Olympus?" Mr. McKenzie swiveled and turned to me. "Ah, Claire?"

I happily explained that Olympus was the mythical home of the Greek gods. That exchange made me smile. He knew I would know the answer because we had talked about it in world lit. I guessed that the thing I liked about him was that he gave special attention to everyone once in a while. I still greatly value leaders who listen and refuse to be the star of the show.

On the morning after the talent show Mom was super critical. She thought the dancing "fairies" during the string number spoiled it. I had to disagree. I thought the sophomore emcee who dressed as Groucho Marx, carrying a cigar, stole the show. He was good looking, creative and witty. Even though he was too young for me, I didn't think you could asked for anything more in a guy. But I figured that I would one day meet the perfect man.

In March, I recorded in my journal that I felt sick inside because of the feelings I had about Mr. McKenzie. I guessed I was experiencing a vague longing. I decided it was just one of my private agonies. I thought that maybe if I wrote some music or poetry about him, I could get thoughts of him out of my system. I was thankful that people couldn't read my mind. It would be embarrassing.

During the winter and spring, I often went to parties at Michelle's house. Her parents didn't mind that high school kids took over the living room. Franklin was usually there too. When he was there with Michelle, I got irritated by the way he would hang all over her.

I guess it bugged me because I was still hung up on the fear of being an old maid. I was afraid I would never get married and maybe I wasn't meant to be married, but I worried that life would be so lonely and purposeless. I guessed I just had to wait and trust God to do with my life as He willed.

After reading *Christy* by Catherine Marshall, I found another book of hers called *Beyond Ourselves*. She explained how to know if a decision was God's will. She said if a strong inner suggestion was from God it would strengthen over time. She didn't address what to do if a snap decision was required. Nevertheless, I was intrigued and wanted to enter into better dialogue with God.

After the basketball tournament in Des Moines the local news interviewed one of the winning coaches, who commented that they won with the help of God. Mom and Megan scoffed at his words, saying that God has nothing to do with our little affairs. I wrote in my journal that Catherine Marshall expressed a differing viewpoint. Christianity acknowledges material things and addresses the everyday issues we face moment by moment. She says, "As for whether God means for us to include material needs in our petitions, one answer would be that Christ was interested in the bodies of men as well as their souls…Christianity acknowledges material things." I agreed with Catherine. If God is everywhere, surely He is with us even in our seemingly unimportant moments also.

On the first day of spring, I began to get excited and decided I'd take our beagle, Pepsi, for a walk. It felt good to walk in a fairly warm spring wind. On my walk I hoped that I could come up with a creative short story—one with a good plot.

I was still trying to understand the meaning of my interrupted relationship with Mark. I figured I was currently in a winter season of my life as far a love goes. I did get to know Mark a little bit, but I wasn't ready for him. I decided I must know a sort of emptiness before I could not only fall in love, but also appreciate and sustain it.

At that point, I decided that the only sane way for me to do things was to center on following the will of God. I worried that I was a coward but resolved to set aside my worries because I would have enough troubles in life without contriving them.

On a weekend in March after talking it over with Mom, I decided I would travel by bus with the church choir in a three-day trip to Chicago. The choir planned to visit the First United Methodist Church of Chicago, located in the Temple building. Our director especially wanted us to see the Chapel in the Sky. We left early on a Saturday morning, planning to return Sunday afternoon, after attending church in the main sanctuary.

I learned a few things that weekend. First, I discovered that people, including me, were deeply concerned with themselves. It just so happened, perhaps because of poor planning, that four people would have to stand in the aisle. Molly and I were a few of the last ones to get on the bus. We had to split up. She sat near the front and I sat in back next to someone else. When another girl got on and started down the aisle, I reluctantly decided to offer her my seat.

At first, she said, "Oh, no you were here first." So I sat down, but eventually she began saying, "All I want to do is sit down." So, I ended up giving her my seat for the rest of the four-hour trip to the heart of Chicago. It was hard, but even harder was facing my own attitude. For the trip home I made sure to get on the bus early to ensure a seat of my own next to Molly. My "Christian" love wasn't very sacrificial.

One of the most generous of the whole outfit was Mr. Hartman. He acted as a lay minister and chaperone for the group. I think he was a Sunday school teacher too. His son Dan was my age and part of the church choir and youth group. Mr. Hartman spent most of the time up and back cheerfully in the aisle. I considered him a top-notch Christian. I liked him. He was largely responsible for a revival among the young people that year.

The temple itself was built in 1924 and its 24 floors were dedicated to church and office use. It was the tallest building in Chicago until 1930. The church had two sanctuaries. The first was four stories high, with seating for a thousand. The second was on the second floor. Although the entire Temple was beautiful, the 30-seat Chapel in the Sky had a charm all its own. Myrtle Walgreen, widow of the founder of Walgreens Pharmacies donated the chapel. With the lights out, the effect of the stained glass windows was glimmering beauty. It contained a wood carving panel called "Christ weeping over Chicago."

The trip was a whirl wind. I made it home in one piece and lived to tell about it. I didn't have time for a break down so all was well.

After State contest on the last day of March, I decided that my ego had been officially "slain." I was still reading Catherine Marshall's book, *Beyond Ourselves* where she talked about "ego slaying." On a scale of 1-5, 1 being the best, I had gotten a 3 on my piano solo and a 2 on my violin solo which wasn't unusual for me. However, I was really disappointed. The hardest part would be calling my piano teacher, Mrs. Michaels.

I wished I could go to sleep and wake up to find out it didn't happen. I remembered Emily Dickinson's poem: "Success is counted sweetest by those who ne'er succeed." I began to rethink my plans to become a music teacher. Maybe I could major in foreign languages in college.

A few days later, Mom surprised me. Discussing the 3 on my piano solo, she said, "Maybe you aren't meant to major in music."

I was listening.

"After all, how else does God talk to us?"

I looked at her stunned. I never thought of Mom as a spiritual person, but maybe the 3 *was* a directive from God. Although I loved music, a 3 was certainly an indication that I wasn't a genius as far as music was concerned. Perhaps Mom was right.

In April, I wrote a little poem about Mr. McKenzie.

I Wonder

I wonder if I told him how I felt if he'd shake his head and laugh
Or if he'd give a puzzled grin and show his quiet half.
If I told him how it was to sit near him and gaze
At his head bent so diligently if his eyebrows he would raise?
But I'll not risk the telling lest he know how I really feel
My precious secret I will keep and never will reveal.

And another poem about my mother:

To My Mother:

The Ones We Love

We seem to always quarrel
Wherever we chance to meet
Be it in the bathroom or on the stair
Just once I'd like to tell you the kind words I'd
hoped to share
But our moods fail to synchronize
It seems as though we're storing all our energy for those
With whom we must be civil.
So decked with pleasant smiles
We face the world of casual acquaintances using up
the love that was meant for each other.

My sister Megan who was in eighth grade and still at the junior high, came into my room one evening to read my latest poem. Naturally, she made fun of it. I would have wondered what was wrong with her if she didn't. Then she proceeded to entertain me with one of her poems. In her most sentimental gushy voice, she proceeded as follows:

How do I love thee darling?
Let me count the ways.
One, Two, Three, Four, Five
And Darling, how do I hate thee?
Let me count the ways
Five. Ten, Fifteen, Twenty.

It made me giggle just to think about it. I didn't plan on telling her I really thought she was precious. Or was "rare," "odd" or maybe "eccentric" a better choice to describe Megan?

I met for the first time; a senior girl named Debbie who was an artist. I was impressed and sorry I hadn't met her sooner. She was very easy to talk with. Somehow, as I was chatting with her, she made me feel as if I had known her for years. I decided that was quite a gift—to enable others to feel comfortable in your presence. I wanted to learn the art, but at that point, I didn't know the secret. I guessed it lie in forgetting yourself and emphasizing the other person.

On the second week of April, I defended my piano teacher, Mrs. Michaels when Megan and Annie were critical of her. I declared that she was a really nice person—genuine and sincere. Most of the time, I found her in a cheerful mood. I liked Mr. Michaels too. I thought they made a great couple.

On April 10th I recorded in my journal:

I seem to be so dissatisfied with everything. I'm craving or lacking something, but I can't pinpoint what it is. I think it might be love or attention. People need attention and I'm no exception. I wish I could solve it. I know God can.

I feel restless, like I want something to happen. Life suddenly seems so drab. Maybe it's just that I'm getting ready to fly from the nest and find my own way.

One day I was in my swimming class and felt humiliated and sub-human because of the cold treatment by a couple of girls. When I was at the pool, Mrs. Murphy, the gym teacher asked me to go and get her a towel. So, I went back into the gym office in my swimming suit because the room that held the towels was locked, I knew I had pimples on my shoulders and back but that didn't define me as a person.

There were two girls in the office and when I asked where I could get a towel, one girl—the kind who has every hair in place—a snow queen—just looked at me icily even though I smiled at her. Finally, I looked in desperation at the other girl who appeared to be running the show. I repeated my request and after looking me over carefully, she went into the back room to get a towel. I thanked her but there was no response. So, after I was out of sight, I made a face in order to make myself feel better.

Golly! I felt as though I had been trapped by a tribe of cannibals who were about to boil me alive. I actually think cannibals may have been kinder. Somehow I was glad that I had pimples so I could understand what people with deformities feel when around "normal" people. At least my abnormality would eventually dry up.

I began to feel sorry for the perfect doll, living in her own little world where everything fits in place. I imagined she might become bitter one day when she found that everything wasn't just right. People do function and have pimples. People are fat, or homely, or imperfect in one way or another. People **do** have problems they can't fix and they have to live with them, day in and day out.

I wished I had extra time to read. Even more, I wished that I could discuss my books with someone special. I thought that would be too heavenly to even be possible. I decided that just to read and have access to books was really enough.

I was feeling really thankful for Valerie after going to a school play with her one Friday evening. After the play, we returned to my car, only to discover that I had locked the keys inside. I felt so stupid. Megan chewed me out when I called her from a school phone, but she assured me she would ask Dad to come get me after he and Mom returned from "Man of La Mancha" at the high school where Mom taught. I felt so frustrated. I had done something stupid and I wasn't able to do anything about it but wait. Fortunately, Valerie was patient and didn't add to my anxiety by complaining.

When I walked back out to the car to see if I had left a window open, a guy pulled up and asked if I wanted to go drinking with him. I couldn't believe my ears, so I said, "What?" He repeated the question with a little less enthusiasm and I said, "No thanks." If I hadn't felt so miserable, I might have laughed. Me, going drinking? He didn't know that I was a Methodist and that Methodists don't drink. Besides I was underage. My eighteenth birthday wasn't for another month. My parents didn't keep alcohol in our home. Thomas Bramwell Welch was a Methodist pastor who discovered a way to pasteurize grape juice so it could be used instead of wine for communion. He called it Dr. Welch's Unfermented Wine.

One Sunday evening at church before choir practice I noticed the associate pastor's son Cory Lawrence sitting at the grand piano playing a popular piece from memory. Several girls were gathered around remarking how much they liked the song. For some reason, I piped up and said, "Yeah, it'd be nice if he could play it right."

One or two of the girls gasped and said, "Oh, Claire!"

Immediately I felt ashamed and sorry, not knowing what to say. I honestly don't know why I would say that about such a nice boy. I once had a crush on him. I guess I may have been trying to capture his attention by showing how unimpressed I was by his talent. Regrettably, I discovered, that my approach was a terrible way to make contact with someone.

Fortunately for me, Cory was a very forgiving person, and afterwards always treated me as if nothing had happened. But somehow it seemed even worse to do something nasty to a nice person, because they didn't fight back. It seemed to be a sin.

All that semester, I had been fretting about my feelings for Mr. McKenzie. He suspected nothing, but that did not lessen my one-sided love. I realized that one sided-love wasn't really love. I didn't want to hate him, but I wished that my "love" would mellow into a simple respect for a teacher. I definitely didn't want to go through that cycle as I did with Mark—blindly loving him, grieving over my loss, hating him and then mellowing into indifference. It was too painful. I took all of those things so seriously. I hoped that if I kept my mind busy, thought positively about life, and focused on my studies, my thoughts of him would pass.

There was so much to learn, so much to read and so much to do. I felt that it was a shame to waste time. I decided that for the most part, watching television was really an unnecessary frivolity. Actually, it was just a bad habit like drinking or smoking. A no-think way of relieving tension. Life was serious and I *had* to get it right.

From my journal while sitting on our back deck:

How calming a running creek can be. As I sit here at 7:00 PM watching the sky grow dark, everything seems so peaceful. Birds can be heard chirping their goodnight songs. Lights glow in the distance and faint sounds of traffic can be heard. The hour after supper is a nice one; after the dishes are done and everyone has settled down to his early evening activity. Peace and solitude are good for the soul.

Man can be killed off so easily. Yet, sometimes he dies slowly and pain lingers, as in the story short story, "A Visit of Charity," by Eudora Welty. It is a shame that some old people have to live their last years in waste with no purpose.

Does man have eternal life? Does his soul live on after his physical self is gone? We're thrust here blindly to this earth, with no choice but to trust those responsible for us. They too, were thrust here not long before. It's a slender chain that depends upon all its links. Although some links weaken and even break, the chain appears to be never ending.

What a unique and fantastic mystery life is. Life is a huge lesson to be learned. We must learn the lesson and be willing to grow and spring back from mistakes and hurts. It is quite a challenge to face, one that each person must accept knowing that someday he will lose all that he has known—friends, material possessions and all the things of earth. I believe our only hope is that Christ has promised we will have a home in heaven.

I worried about my friends, that Valerie seemed so touchy and different somehow. I found I had to be more careful about what I said to her or she would misunderstand. Molly at church also seemed extra touchy. I couldn't figure out if they had changed or if it was just me. Michelle seemed to be the same although her brother Ken was unusually quiet. Whenever I saw him, he said no more than three words which was very strange for him as he usually was quite talkative.

As I thought about Ken, I began to wonder if he weren't love stricken. There was a pretty girl in his class that he thought about all the time. He couldn't see straight when he thought about Julie

—poor boy. I wouldn't dare tell him or anybody that I didn't think she was worthy of him.

Mother and I watched the movie I had watched with Mark in Texas two years before. *Wuthering Heights* on tv. I thought it was quite a story—so dreamlike yet in a very real setting. On the moors of Scotland with the wind always blowing against a grey sky—Emily Bronte. I wished I could create a story like that. It is really a sad story and really rather violent. Heathcliff is such a lonely character and because he had been hurt so much, he was seeking revenge a good part of the time.

At one point when the maid, Nellie tells Heathcliff that it is for God to punish the wicked, he asks, "Why should God get all the satisfaction?" After overhearing Cathy say, "Heathcliff is an animal," he runs away. When Cathy discovers that she hurt him, she tells Nellie, "I don't just love Heathcliff, I am Heathcliff!" Having grown up together, they knew each other well. I loved the movie. I hoped no one would ever really have to suffer and live such a life as that.

On April 21st it rained all day, just as it had the day before. I wanted so badly to see the sun. The next day was Easter. I went to church that day and felt saddened and a bit superior to all the people who only came to church twice a year. There they were packing the pews, so ill at ease. I wondered why they didn't always come. I told myself that just because someone went to church didn't mean they were a Christian and just because someone didn't go to church didn't mean they weren't. I felt that the "Church" did provide a foundation for a person's faith. Church served as a place for inspiration and renewal of belief.

On Sunday afternoon I got sick with fever and a sore throat and recovered in less than twenty-four hours. Megan was not so fortunate. She got sick three days before and had a constant fever and sore throat since then. Mom took her to the doctor and he prescribed some medication. When I began to feel feverish Dad gave me one of Megan's pills and I went to bed. When I woke up the fever was gone. I felt lucky that my illness was stopped before it had a chance to get started.

Poor Megan! She could barely swallow a bite of food. She lost eight pounds in four days. I was beginning to worry about her.

I attempted to write about the orchestra trip to Texas—Mark, my initial breakdown, and the psychiatric ward. I wasn't sure it would work or if I could ever do it. I thought I would wait and see if the urge to write of my experience got stronger.

On Monday evening I watched "Man of La Mancha."

My journal records my reaction.

The movie is very strange, so strange I almost gave up on it halfway through. Now I'm glad I stuck with it because it expressed some good ideas. Through the entire story (except at the very end) Don Quixote is portrayed as being crazy in search of his dream.

* He says, "The truth of man is in his dreams."
* All the way through the story he keeps insisting "Nothing is impossible"
* After he begins to see some reality, his faithful companion tells him, "There is no greater monster than reason."
* Then as he gains his sanity, he says something that puzzles me. "There are no birds this year in last year's nests." –I'll have to think about that one.
* Something that he says, I have seen expressed in other literature. "Perhaps in this unhappy world of ours, wise madness is better than foolish sanity."
* When he was mad, he was also happy and wise living in ecstasy.

"The thing of it is, we must live with the living"
Michel de Montaigne

I felt that Montaigne's saying was perfect for me. I was stuck with the people around me. Of course, I realized that I was not the ideal person to live with either.

After staying up late, the night before to watch Don Quixote, I woke up still sick, It seemed that my brief period without a fever was only the eye of the storm. That next day it moved in full force. I drank 7-Up and grape juice until I felt ready to float away. What really bothered me is that I was that I wouldn't be able to go to school the next day. I hated staying home alone, but if Valerie was able to stay alone for so many days, when her parents were in Florida, I knew I could stand it for one day. Mostly I hated missing school because I didn't want to miss Mr. McKenzie's classes. I was already on a countdown until that awful day when I would no longer see him.

On Thursday, Annie's friend Sarah, from school and the neighborhood, stopped at our house with horrible news. Sarah's brother Jim had died the night before. He had been sick and when his father entered his bedroom in the morning, he was unable to wake Jim up. Sarah said her father screamed loudly. We were all so shocked and sorry for the family. We learned later that Jim had what they called Reye's syndrome, caused by taking aspirin for a viral infection.

It came back to me that my ninth grade Ancient History teacher had said that it's one thing for a son to bury his father but quite another when a father must bury his son. I had never thought of that. I began to understand just a little.

In my American Lit class Mr. McKenzie told me he'd break my neck if I missed the definition of "effluvium." I felt strangely flattered by his joke. I was glad he was thinking of me. In class I hung on his every word and felt jealous when he paid attention to other girls.

I was happy to note that Ken seemed to be back to his old self again. I talked on the phone with him for half an hour in the evening. He was just as gossipy as ever. I was relieved.

Poor little Sarah. She knocked at our door before supper to ask us to come to the funeral for her brother. When she saw Mom at the door, she broke into tears. She kept apologizing for crying and mom assured her that she needed to cry and told Sarah she should just sit down and cry.

She and Mom had a long talk. I didn't hear too much of it because the tv was loud. I didn't turn it down too because I didn't want to intrude. The important thing was that Sarah got to vent about her worries and sorrow. Off and on she sobbed. She said she hated to cry at home because then everyone else would cry and feel bad. Mom said Sarah could cry all she wanted at our house. Losing a family member like that must be a terrific strain.

We went to the funeral at the Unitarian Church in Davenport. The was a deep heaviness in the air. During the funeral, they played *Stairway to Heaven* by Led Zeppelin. I was saddened.

I thought about what I would want played at my own funeral someday. I decided I wanted Dvorak's New World Symphony. I loved that melodies were based on African American spirituals and native American melodies. The hymn *Going Home* was based on the Largo movement from the New World Symphony.

I talked with Mom about my fear of traveling with the orchestra to Texas again in June. I had been having sick feelings—a déjà vu sort of thing. When I saw something or thought of something that reminded me of a dream I've had, I felt like I'm going to throw up. I couldn't understand it. Could it have to do with travel? I used to throw up when we'd go to Grandma's and the summer we drove to Kansas a few years ago, I had some dizzy spells. Travel worried me. Whatever—I didn't want another experience like I had two years ago. If I didn't go, I'd feel like I was letting Mr. Michaels down. However, if that is the price I must pay for health, I'll pay it. I would go for sure if Mom would go too.

From my Journal:

> To prevent a pimple and perhaps ease an irritation, I must express this sickening observation. –Today in World Lit we were discussing a little boy' s dream as he talked in his sleep and said, "No fight. I'll give it to you." Jane, a really nice girl, said "Maybe he was talking to his friends." Mr. McKenzie about flipped. "Wow, I never thought of that," he said. "That's interesting. It intrigues me." Vomit. I was

feeling rotten anyway and I was just mad because I hadn't said it. I thought it was too insignificant to mention. But I always do that. Feel like I should say something and wind up kicking myself silently for not speaking up. I just ought to say it—who cares about my dignity?

By the way, I *am* going to Texas. I feel better about it after discussing it with Mom. I've decided simply not to sleep on the bus in order to avoid jangled nerves.

On May 18, my 18th birthday I felt ancient and sad that time flies by so fast.

I chewed on the idea that privacy was dear to me. When I was in the hospital and complained about having no privacy, they were horrified.—"Why, you must learn to live with other people!" the nurses said, and "not try to escape from them." Ok, I agreed. But wasn't it necessary also for a person to learn to live with herself? That is part of living with others. Each human being must collect her ideas and values in order to know who she is and what she believes. True- a person can become rather odd if constantly isolated. Yet, some solitude is necessary in order to know oneself.

That Friday evening, Dad took me to a fancy restaurant for my birthday. Eating at the Plantation was a big deal. I ordered lobster for the first time as a pianist played in the background. Dad handed me a poem:

Dear Claire,

You know I'm no poet.
It's obvious, you know it.
With profound thoughts and class,
You are such a smart lass.
You're way out in front,

And I hate to be blunt,
But I feel such a pride.
'Tis with you I reside.
Though I don't always show it,
My inner thoughts know it.
I will always revere.
Everything you hold dear,
For you're one of a kind,
Up on top in my mind.
I would like much to say,
Make this your great day.
Though not yet arrived,
Dvořák is still alive.
Love, Dad

In a time before the internet and online shopping, Dad had ordered Dvořák's *Slavonic Dances* on a record album for me! The poem meant a lot to me as did the gift. I had grown to love Dvorak while in orchestra. Dad's gift and sentiments were sweet, yet I wished they somehow could have erased the deep sense of inferiority that still festered in my heart. Something in me yet had trouble believing that Dad really, really loved me. I believe that he gave all he had. His own father was gone so much of the time and as far as I know never praised my dad.

Dad was a poor kid from a poor family. Nearly everyone experienced lack during the Great Depression, but my dad and his siblings were among the poorest of the poor. He also lived in an era where the common belief that praising children could feed their pride and spoil them. So, Dad gave the best that he could. I held on to that poem and read it again and again. Still, there *was* that God-shaped hole in my heart that only God Himself can fill. I was waiting for God.

Before bed that night, in a yellow, brand new, 200-page, spiral notebook, I began the story of my sophomore trip to Texas with the orchestra. I wrote an introduction saying that I finally knew that the breakdown I experienced at fifteen was **not** caused by LSD, because an LSD trip could not have lasted as long as my psychosis did. I had come to believe that I was a borderline schizophrenic. (Although, in later conversations with my psychiatrist we settled on the diagnosis of manic depression.)

I made a promise that I would share both the beautiful and very personal, embarrassing parts of my story through the eyes of a mentally ill individual. I ended my introduction with these sentences. "With some doubts, fears and hopes, I begin my story. As one who believes strongly in God, I know I shall complete it, if that be His will."

From my journal May 24:

> I've got to write some of my thoughts before my head bursts. First, I must write about the matter foremost in my mind. My "feeling" (pardon the expression) about Mr. McKenzie has not mellowed but rather has gotten stormier and more unbearable. He's such a nice man. I'll miss him but thank goodness I'm getting out of that class. I'll go crazy if I had to be in there much longer.
>
> It is so frustrating to love (I use the word loosely) someone who does not or cannot love back. Sometimes, I almost wish I had never met him. Yet, he is a very good teacher. In trying to analyze what makes him good, I've decided that it is his responsiveness. No matter what any student says, he replies in some way whether it be a nod, or a further comment or even disagreement, it shows that he listens. His way encourages kids to talk, which is important in literature classes. I know I've said more in his class than any other I've ever had. He has a kind of knack for making people feel comfortable. That is a gift.

My neck aches terribly. I swear I'm going to find myself a Mormon and move to Utah. Maybe out there my sinuses would dry out and my pimples too.

Finally, I'm losing weight. I've lost about ten pounds in two months. Now I'm down to 115 with the hope of leveling off at 110—Just so I don't lose any more than that.

Ethan Frome is a good story. We read it in Modern American Lit. Edith Wharton put it together very carefully. The book is so sad. It makes life seem to be not worth living. If life were as drab as it is in the book, no one would smile.

Tomorrow is the class picnic. Yech! I'm not even looking forward to it. Herds of people bother me. I much prefer a small group. Oh, well. It will be an experience.

My class picnic was even worse than I expected. It was almost unbearably cold. I had no desire to play baseball or volleyball. I felt like Valerie was snubbing me. She and Michelle went off to play miniature golf. I thought maybe I had outgrown her.

After the whole class had eaten, Michelle, Valerie and I went to Trey Hovorka's house. He got his motorcycle out of the garage. Valerie insisted on taking a ride. It didn't take much coaxing to get Michelle on the back of it either. I refused to get on. I wasn't going to put my life in the hands of an eighteen-year-old kid with only half his senses.

Something rather amused me while we were at the fairgrounds. A group of us girls decided to go look at the horses. We walked past a baseball game. I noticed Doug, a guy from my Modern American Lit class in the outfield. I already had the feeling he was insecure. Anyway, when I looked back, he had taken off his shirt. What a goof! The rest of us were shivering. It was no more than 55 degrees out there with a strong wind. It didn't take him long to put it back on again. Later, when we walked back from the horses, he took off his shirt again. I really almost felt sorry for him to have to go to such extreme measures to get attention. I hoped he would grow up.

From my Journal May 26

It seems the only time I am really comfortable and secure is when I'm writing in this stupid notebook. That is not normal. The only time I swear is in this blank thing. I'm sick of writing mournful poems about unrequited love as they say. But what am I to do? I feel trapped by what I am. Does that mean I hate myself? Not really. Part of me wants to be the center of attention, while the other part wants to sit in the corner thinking. I worry that my imagination is too wild and it frightens me. I must write, maybe in story form, some of these strange ideas, if nothing else to merely get them out of my mind. It's probably the only answer.

Devoted friend that she is, Valerie is the only one I really talk to about my personal feelings. She doesn't have much of a blabber mouth. She told me something tonight which I think is good as far as making me think more realistically about Mr. McKenzie. She found out what his wife's name is. At Val's job, they have a listing of everyone in Davenport. She looked because she knows I'm fond of Mr. McKenzie. His wife's name is Marie. That at least gives her an identity. I know she is a living, breathing human being out there—I give up. I will mind my own business and work hard at getting an education.

After watching an episode of "Mash" one evening and viewing all the blood from a particularly raw ugly scar on a man's chest, I decided that physical wounds, though more obvious, were no more ugly than spiritual wounds. In fact, I speculated that mental illness is uglier, harder to treat, more frightening and elusive. It presented a great challenge. A person who has cancer can still think and love and know that he has a mind—a mind which is such a beautiful gift given to human beings. Humans must take care of that gift and work to make it healthy. It is our duty to develop it and fill it with questions and ideas. A healthy mind would be constantly searching for wisdom. Without healthy minds, we are no better than animals and only a burden to others.

I was reading Norman Vincent Peale's book *The Power of Positive Thinking*. He said that a positive mind could generate power. Our minds were useful tools that should not be allowed to rot in front of a television, dwell on a pornographic magazine; spaced out on drugs or trapped in a mental hospital.

Mr. McKenzie made an observation in class one day that people *on* tv never sat around watching television. I journaled that it would be a shame to waste something that had the possibility of bringing so much good into the world. I felt it was a sin to fail to care for such a precious gift as the mind. I thought that children needed to be educated about mental illness so they could take precautionary steps against it or at least recognize warning signs so illness could be treated.

After my frightening, sometimes ugly experience in the psychiatric ward, I appreciated more than ever a healthy mind. So many did not possess such a treasure. I felt that those who were lucky enough to have a healthy properly working mind, should in gratitude, work hard at making their minds even better. I realized that I needed to live up to my ideals.

May 30, 1973, was my last day of high school and possibly the last time I would see Mr. McKenzie. That seemed harsh and even cruel. Philosophically, I knew life was like that. You meet people you like a lot, they become part of your day-to-day experience for a while and then one day you realize that life has pushed them out.

I did stay after my World Lit class left that afternoon to wait for Mr. McKenzie to correct my test. I think I got a B. In reference to the matching part, which he called a "give-away," he said, "That part saved you Toots." I wondered if I looked like a "Toots"? Honestly? I only nodded in agreement and then asked if I could have my "Aphrodite and Timidius" paper. He looked through his file cabinet and handed me the paper. I still have it.

In my journal I agonized over writing about graduation. I fretted that if I didn't write down my feelings, they would be lost forever. I knew it was a dumb thing to worry about.

I thought about Ethan Frome, the novel we had read in Modern American Lit. I decided that as a girl I wanted to be a "Mattie" but I was really, more of an "Ethan." I felt cloddish in social situations because I was not good at expressing myself. I would have liked to be the center of attention, but too often I found myself on the outside looking in. How typically Ethan!

I knew I never wanted to marry a man as cold as Zeena Frome was. I needed someone with a warm and outgoing personality to draw me out. That's what Ethan found in Mattie—someone expressive and uninhibited. She brought out the best in him.

On Thursday, May 31ˢᵗ, I graduated from high school. It was a beautiful sun shiny day, just as I hoped it would be. We were preparing for the ceremony which was scheduled to be held outside at the stadium.

From my journal:

> It's funny but I've got a feeling of hunger—like some characters in literature. It's not imaginary either. I really feel it. Even as I was eating lunch today, I felt hungry. I can't understand it.
>
> Grandma and Grandpa Schluensen are here, along with Sean and Aunt Rosie. They came for my graduation. Aunt Rosie is so nice. The more I'm around her, the easier she is to talk with. She's

young, yet mature. I'm young and immature—oh, maybe I have a few glimmers of maturity now and then.

Sean is such a cute little fellow and he is smart, too. I was going to take a shower this morning and wash my hair, so he asked if he could come in the bathroom. I said "no" and he said "yes." I said "no" and he said "yes." After about thirty-five of each, I somehow got to saying yes." When I had said, "yes" about three times, he said, "Okay..." –meaning "have it your way, I'll come in." I giggled and said to him, "Oh, Sean! You fooled me!" He laughed too. I told him he could stay in the outer bathroom with the sink and I would go into the inner bathroom where the shower was.

When he sees me, sometimes he says, "You look like a stinker." Of course, I wrinkle my nose and disagree. And to anybody, he'll look up innocently and say, "I like you." Of course, you tell him that you like him too. He knows he'll get a positive response to that.

The day after graduation I was thinking about Clifford Beers, a man who in 1900-1902 was confined to two private and one state run mental institution while suffering from hallucinations, delusions and manic and depression episodes. To top it off, he received horrific treatment in the institutions where he was hospitalized. Among other things, he was beaten and restrained by mechanical straps. He had this to say in his book, *A Mind that Found Itself:* "Certainly the one afflicted deserves no punishment. As well punish with a blow to the cheek that is disfigured by mumps."

Two days after high school ended, I must have been missing Mr. McKenzie. I wrote this:

That Empty Space

The place beside your picture in my yearbook
Is void of your signature.
Oh, not because I did not long to have you write
it there
But because of me
So many times, I nearly approached you---book in
hand
Something held me back.
shyness, maybe
fear of what impersonal, hurriedly scratched
note you might jot down?
In just a few moments I would have had some words
from you
written in that empty space.
Looking at it now,
A sigh catches in my throat
I feel an ache.
Away with the selfishness that held me back!

That night after going out to dinner with Aunt Rosie, Sean, Grandma, Grandpa, Megan, Annie, Mom and Dad I went to the tail end of Michelle's graduation party. Franklin was there putting ice down her back, kissing her, hugging her and so on. Ignoring them as best I could, Valerie and I did discuss the lovely note she wrote in my yearbook.

Phil Vernier was there. He was in my creative writing class in the fall semester and world lit in the spring semester. I had talked to him several times before. He was reserved, quiet and handsome.

I danced with Ken in a brotherly fashion. When Franklin smoothly placed his arms around me, I knew it was only to make Michelle jealous and told him so. He laughed and assured me it was all in fun. I was irritated because it seemed with him that everything was a joke.

Then, as Valerie and I were standing talking with Trey Hovorka, much to my surprise and delight I felt a pair of arms encircle my waist. Thinking it was Ken, I let out an "Oh," and turned around to discover Phil.

I said, "Oh, Phil, it's you!" I

I was surprised at how much taller he seemed up close. He chuckled. We talked about something, while he held me in that pleasant position for a while. Then, without saying goodbye, he climbed the stairs and left. I guess he had to work the next morning.

The following morning, I couldn't remember anything we had said. I mused over his actions. It seemed as if he *had* to hold me before he left. I wished he would ask me out, even though I was sure I'd probably be disappointed if we did go on a date. I decided that was usually the case with me.

The next day I wrote yet another poem about Mr. McKenzie. It was more of the same, sappy longing. I wasn't happy with my last two poems and felt that because they displayed more emotion they were harder to write. Awkwardness still described my deep poetry.

I was feeling pretty good about Mom at that time. She was more relaxed than usual because school was out for her too. I felt conflicted because I hadn't written much in my journal about her or those closest to me. In preparation for the orchestra trip to Dallas, she took me downtown to shop and helped me pick out a large purse, blouse and some pants. I really appreciated her help because I never would have done it myself.

She really was cheerful most of the time and fairly easy to live with when she *was* happy. But like all of us she had her spells when she was frankly, like a bear. I knew I could be that same way. Nature seemed so fickle.

Chapter 10

Summer Before College

On Wednesday, June 6th our orchestra left for Dallas. The trip was anti-climactic for me. I took my journal with me so I could write on the bus. As we sat on the bus in Arlington, just outside of Dallas, I complained in my journal. I was tired of bus trips—the constant jiggle, the roar of the motor, mile after weary mile. Then we'd arrive at a restaurant or motel and wait on the stupid bus for Mr. Michaels to check with the management to make sure they were ready for all of us.

The thing about group trips was that all the people couldn't be happy all the time. When leaving a place, we wasted a lot of time waiting for Mr. Michaels or other kids to get on the noisy vehicle. I don't remember much of our actual performance. But I did remember Six Flags Over Texas in Arlington. It was clean, friendly and well-organized.

The most harrowing part of that trip was all the advice I was getting from well-intentioned friends. They wanted to prove to me that scrubbing my face like they did and using Noxzema would ensure the end of the unwanted pimples that still popped up on my chin now and then. Did they really think I hadn't tried scrubbing my face and doing everything I knew to do? I had tried Noxzema. It just seemed to add more grease to my face.

I felt so sorry for lonely people. I had a younger girl in mind. Karen Welby. Another girl, Pat went out of her way to reject and insult Karen. I tried to stand up for Karen whenever I could. I found it strange that Karen felt no hatred for Pat, rather she seemed shocked by Pat's attitude. Karen didn't understand it and neither did I. Pat was fun but also loud, almost coarse. I didn't want to judge her but I did want to understand.

I liked Lynn Werner. She was in my room on this trip. I noted how you really get to know someone after living with them constantly for just a few days. I talked to Lynn about Pat and Karen. I wanted Lynn's wisdom. She said that Pat was insecure. I decided Lynn was right. She *must* have been insecure the way she picked on Karen.

Karen took so much and yet remained cheerful but she finally cracked on day three of our trip. That morning, we told her we were going to eat at the motel coffee shop. Karen told us she would meet us there later. Accidently forgetting about Karen, we ended up eating at a different restaurant after being told by other kids that it was a better place to eat. Woops! I shouldn't have left Karen. I felt guilty.

When Karen got on the bus I said, "Good morning," as cheerfully as I could.

"What's good about it?" she growled.

I didn't blame her. I would have felt horrible too. How could I possibly explain that I was only thinking of myself and didn't want to be left out of the group while waiting for her?

When we were traveling, I sat part of the time with Charlie, a junior and also my seatmate in orchestra. After challenging a couple of other people in order to move my way up in the first violin section I had decided to remain seated next to Charlie. I was tired of competition, and Charlie made me laugh with sly comments during orchestra practice every day. It helped that he worked at McDonald's and smelled familiar, like hamburgers and French fries. I felt safe— at home—with him.

When we pulled into the school parking lot at the conclusion of our trip I took my time in gathering my things. I was feeling a bit melancholy, because I knew I wouldn't see much more of Charlie. In fact, I never saw Charlie again. As we were packing up, Charlie stopped me more than once to tell me he loved me. I loved him in a way too. I guess I liked his personality. We got along quite well. But he had a little girlfriend and they were cute together and I was sure he was happy with her. I knew I would miss him—the familiarity and the laughs, but I did not really know how *much* I would miss him until I was away at college, where I yearned for anything comforting that I could rely on like a pair of worn, old shoes.

After the trip I thought about the idea of God's forgiveness. No matter what did we know that we shall be forgiven? What about murder. Did God forgive that? I didn't understand. From all that I had been reading, it seemed that all that we had to do was claim and accept the forgiveness of God. It was supposedly so simple. Then, why was I so confused? Aunt Rosie said that when she stopped trying so hard to make the Bible fit and understand it, her confusion ceased and the meaning became clear.

I marveled that I could see a change in Rosie. She seemed happier than when I last saw her. She seemed more content and oh, so eager for new ideas. That was wonderful and encouraging for me. It was beautiful that she had "discovered" God. As for me, I still felt as though I was in the darkness.

I thought about the book I had begun writing about my earlier experience in Texas and the following breakdown. I wondered if a writer feels an irresistible compulsion to write. If so, I decided I must not be a writer. For I seldom felt a need to write, though I did enjoy writing. I knew my writing would not be read by many but that I would always write.

I didn't have to write, but I liked to. I guessed it was an escape like drinking, tv, driving fast, smoking pot, golfing, growing flowers, sex, smoking pot or even prayer. Oooo—that one. I knew some would disagree but prayer too is a form of escape. I believed that it was a healthy form and I used it.

After I returned from Texas, I received a Campus Crusade for Christ booklet from Aunt Rosie. It contained instructions on what I needed to do to be saved. I read eagerly. I wanted everything God had to give. Church alone did not engage me to the extent that I longed for. In the eighth grade, I completed confirmation classes and was confirmed as a member of the church. That formality caused no obvious change in me or in my relationship with God.

So, one day in June, alone in my bedroom, following the instructions of Bill Bright, founder of Campus Crusade for Christ, I invited the God of the universe to come and take up permanent residence in my heart as Lord of my life. I did not know at the time that my commitment to Him would eventually affect every aspect of my life.

Love Now Dwells

Worry fell from my neck today.
In its place grew a flower of faith.
Shame burned in my soul.
I threw its ashes to the wind,
Feeling for the first time the glory of forgiveness.
Hatred hid in my heart, lurking behind burning passion.
Disgusted, I threw it to the ground.
It shall return, but I'll be ready.
Love now dwells in the vacuum left by shame, worry, and hatred.
Peace fills my soul, making life worth living.

In my journal, I wrote, "Lord Jesus, I am Yours totally and completely without reservation. Use me as You wish. Send me wherever You will, for I am dead and my life is hidden with Christ in God." My promise to the Lord was earnest even though I didn't completely understand my sinfulness and need for a savior.

Through his book *Ten Basic Steps toward Christian Maturity*, and in particular the chapter outlining step three, "The Christian and the Holy Spirit," Bill Bright became my mentor. "To abide is to keep God's commandments. To keep his commandments is to obey. The abiding life is an effortless life." "Christ will do His work through you. You do not work for Him." I aspired to abide in the vine (Jesus). If I had known the difficulties that lay ahead of me, my little-girl bubble would have burst. I still needed the Holy Spirit teach my heart to trust and let go enough to truly abide and rest in God and His leading day by day.

That same summer, I got to see the new movie *Godspell: A Musical Based on the Gospel According to St. Matthew*. It premiered at about the same time that the Jesus People Movement began winding down. The opening scene of young people ridding themselves of idols, material possessions, and relatively worthless pursuits intrigued me and resonated with the part of me that wanted to embrace Jesus with everything I had. I bought the Godspell album and got to know most of the songs. I loved them all.

Here and there, I heard testimonies of how young people were suddenly changed and life became *so* beautiful. Everything was brand new once they received Jesus. You could call those summer months after my life-altering experience my "honeymoon with God." Almighty God is a transformer. At my invitation, He took the old, immature, self-centered me and began the process of making me holy. At first, I thought it was about love and feeling good, and it was. But God is alive, vibrant, and very real—not an abstract, ethereal concept. He began His reign in me by becoming a part of every thought, every motive, and every deed.

Many will be purged, purified and refined,
but the wicked will act wickedly.
—Daniel 12:10 (NASB)

In my journal in the summer of 1973, I ruminated about the causes of my prior breakdown:

> I believe now that my experience of two years ago brought me back to God and eventually much closer to Him. My ninth-grade year was an unhappy one. I cried nearly every night and prayed also with no apparent response. Often, too often, I was buried in self-pity. Coinciding and seemingly in contradiction, superstition in the form of astrology became a fascination. I read bits and pieces of some astrology book nearly every night. That reading gave me a sense of security but didn't help with much else.
>
> During my tenth-grade year in high school, a new world unfolded before me. Life seemed beautiful again. Then, after the psychotic break, satan was expelled from my life, though for the next year I was still removing scraps and remnants left behind, like old astrology books and magazines.
>
> Why do I believe God would allow the breakdown? Paul gives the answer in 2 Corinthians 7:10 (TLB): "For God sometimes uses sorrows in our lives to help us turn away from sin and seek eternal life. We should never regret His sending them." I do not regret God's sending it. I am thankful because I know He cares.
>
> My manic flare-ups and bouts with depression were the result of several things coming together to create a perfect storm. The law of sowing and reaping is as impersonal as the law of gravity. When I called upon God to work in me, He heard my cry, and He has been working in me ever since to realign my thinking with wholesome principles, heal my hurts, and connect me with people and resources

that will not only bless me but also help me get to a place where I can increasingly be a blessing to others. I have come to know Him as patient beyond patient, gentle beyond gentle.

The stories of people like Moses, David, and Abraham encourage me. Despite many flaws and failings, they were friends of God, growing to be like Him through ongoing conversations and experiences of living in His presence. I can trust a God who knows that I make mistakes and that I will even fail miserably at times. Yet He loves me anyway. His love keeps me going and coming back to Him. He already knows all, so He is not surprised when I confess a sin. Rather than taking me out of the world, away from the nasty toils, snares, and fears, He strengthens and empowers me to choose more wisely during the next trial. The key has always been the relationship with Him. Difficult circumstances are an inevitable part of life. Testing comes to give us an idea of where we are in the school of God.

On those summer evenings, I sat outside in front of our garage to read, write, and watch the sun set. My thoughts often became wistful, as I would think about my classes with Mr. McKenzie. I wrote this in my journal at the time:

I don't miss him. No, I do not miss Mr. McKenzie. Why should I? He was only a lot of fun and a gateway to better enjoyment of literature. Why should I miss a man whose humor I enjoyed so much? Whose voice I savored. Whose face was a constant display of feeling? Why, there is no sound, down-to-earth reason for missing him. It's senseless. Don't miss him, Claire. You do not have to … then why do I? I want to. I want to capture what few memories I have that are not already faded. But then, could I do justice to such memories? Surely not. My awkwardness would only destroy the humorous, funny circumstances that are in the past.

Suddenly, I know why I must stop missing Mr. McKenzie: (1) He is a married man. (2) No use pining over that which is past and now impossible to gain. (3) I believe it is God's will that I forget him. God's will must now be my will.

I am thankful to God that I could know Mr. McKenzie for the brief time that I did. I am also glad that I now have some of what Mr. McKenzie had to offer. My love for literature was revitalized. I am now eager to read many great authors and some unknowns. Goodness was gained.

He was also the inspiration for more than one poem:

Clouds

The clouds have changed
Since I looked last
And so have thoughts of you.

They're grayer now,
Grown indistinct.
I fear to look again,

For if I do,
Will I find
Your image altered?

Your Voice

I'd like to hear your voice as I drift to sleep,
Like the voices of relatives long ago
From Grandma's fragrant lilac bed,
Softly, lilting voices soothing me to sleep.

Your voice is like a sea captain's words of assurance.
As he scans the horizon,
Steady at the wheel,
Guiding his vessel to port.
How like you is your voice.
Laughter, correction, guidance coming.
From a gracious, kindly heart.
I would like to hear your voice as I drift to sleep.

On June 13th, early in my new spiritual adventure, I applied for and got a job at the Lutheran Home. I was raised to be a good girl by a mother who had endless compassion for outcasts and the needy, and we attended a church where I was taught to love others. Thus, I earnestly began my new life with God while working as a nurse's aide.

I took my job seriously, setting out each day determined to show God's love to every patient and coworker. In a short time, I memorized the names of all eighty patients. I took coffee to the residents in the mornings and was soon recruited by the head nurse to be the bath girl. Each morning I received the names of five or six patients who were to receive baths that day. I wore out a pair of shoes spending the bulk of each morning in a damp room assisting people with their showers. Although I enjoyed talking with the residents, the work itself was exhausting and wore on my nerves.

A couple of the men were embarrassed by my help. I felt embarrassed too, and I hated to feel like I was troubling them when just giving a shower was hard enough. But I persisted because that was my job. Around ten o'clock each morning, I took a break, which consisted of coffee and a sweet roll or donut. I did not understand at the time that coffee and sugary treats were among the worst things I could eat if I really wanted to maintain calm nerves and steady energy.

One morning after I had individually distributed coffee to residents, I slowly walked into Linda's room, carefully laying a tray of hot breakfast on the chest of drawers by her bed

"Linda, how about some breakfast?" I asked.

I walked over to the window to pull the curtains open. Looking out I could see that the day was going to be a beautiful one: hot, but beautiful. Already, at 8:00 the sun burned brightly in a blue, cloudless sky. By 3:00 I knew the steering wheel in my mother's green Nova would be too hot to touch. But that didn't matter now.

Across the courtyard, through the glass doors I could see the dining room. People were moving slowly to their assigned tables. Some were in wheelchairs, pushed by a resident or an aide. Some walked with help of a walker or a cane, while others walked by themselves, slowly, carefully, upright with dignity. Another day was beginning at the Lutheran Home.

"It's a lovely day outside, Linda," I said, trying to be cheerful. I hoped she heard me.

"Huh?" Linda opened one eye.

"I say it's a beautiful day," my voice rose.

"Oh, it is?" she moaned.

"Yeah, but it's going to be hot."

I pulled a chair alongside Linda's bed, wrinkling my nose. How on earth could she stand to eat that hot, cream of wheat cereal day after day? And without sugar? I knew the dietician didn't put sugar on it. I had watched her. Surely, they had some saccharine around this place. Linda may have been diabetic but cream of wheat without sugar was awful.

"Linda," I gulped. "We've got some nice hot cereal, and apple sauce, prunes and orange juice." Yum, I thought.

Linda said nothing. She lay still on the bed with her left arm pulled tightly across her stomach. It was paralyzed, probably from a stroke, I guessed. Gray frizzy hair sprouted from her head. Her eyebrows drew together causing several wrinkles between pinched eyes. She appeared to be in pain.

I took an extra pillow and placed it under her pillow so she could eat. I sat on the chair by the bed and opened the paper straw on Linda's tray.

"Well, how about trying some of this cereal?"

"What?"

"There's nice hot cereal for you Linda."

"Uhh, ohhh."

Frowning, I dipped the spoon into the "nice, hot cereal." "Yech" was my only thought. While lifting the spoon from the bowl to her mouth a glob of cereal fell onto her gown. Linda didn't seem to care or even notice for her eyes were closed. And so, my day went.

At noon, in a separate dining room from the main one, I fed people no longer able to feed themselves. In the afternoons, I gathered laundry, clipped chin hairs on the ladies, and checked with residents as to the date of their last bowel movements. Of course, that topic cleared the way for some laughs. I had a few minutes to chat and get to know people.

By the time I got home at three thirty each day, the only thing that interested me was sleep, and I regularly slept for two hours every afternoon. The head nurse knew I would be leaving for school in the fall and she worked me hard. Sometimes I worked eight days in a row without a day off. I remember wondering about the women who did not have school to look forward to. How could they stand the thought of working in that place day after day, month after month, year after year? The thought was more than depressing.

One day after lunch, I walked down the hall to help residents return to their rooms. As usual, I smiled at everyone as I went and greeted those who looked my way. Mr. Bauer saw me and said to another lady, loudly enough that I could hear, "With that smile, I'll bet she has a thousand boyfriends." I thought, *Dear Mr. Bauer, if only you knew!*

He had a nice smile himself. He was tall and broad. I think he may have been blond. Once when I was in his room, making his bed, he told me his philosophy about the Watergate scandal. He thought that the whole ordeal was awful, that leaders, whom we are supposed to be able to trust, are so conniving and crooked. Frank Bauer seemed to be a man of God. I liked that.

Nellie was one of my favorites. She had a habit of making noises by pulling her tongue down from the roof of her mouth. Strangely, her smacking noises did not bother me but were rather soothing. However, if I ever had to listen to some saucy girl in a classroom clicking her gum and swinging her leg, I would be greatly annoyed. Yech.

I guess Nellie's noises were tolerable because she was so sweet. I liked to go to her room and make her bed. In that pleasant atmosphere, she looked quite a bit like the witch in *The Wizard of Oz*, but beyond her appearance, no comparison was possible. Sometimes, I watched as she sat in her wheelchair, bent over a newspaper, her mouth moving constantly as her long finger ran under a line of print. As she read, her head moved back and forth slightly while her brow wrinkled according to the content of an article. A table full of crackers, cookies, candy, tissues, a telephone, and a clock stood beside her bed. On the floor sat a stack of well-used newspaper, ready for the trash. She studied them diligently to remain well informed.

Then there were Mr. and Mrs. Pratt. Poor Ernest suffered a stroke on a Saturday night. Mrs. Pratt had been on the verge of tears ever since. Her husband, whom she called Ernie, could not talk but mumbled and groaned. He could not eat but shook and coughed. Today, as I wheeled Mrs. Pratt into her room after dinner, I asked if Mr. Pratt was feeling any better. She shook her head sadly and said she thought he was worse. I told her I had been praying for him. She said, "Oh, thank you," ready to cry. I left quickly so I would not break down in front of her.

Another aide saw me in the hall and said, "Smile, Claire!"

I smiled.

While working among the elderly, an unfulfilled, still yearning part of me found solace. My closest grandparents lived four hundred miles away. I loved them and missed them terribly in the months between visits. Whenever we left, I felt as if a part of my heart were being torn from my body. I never got to know them well enough that I felt safe being anything but polite and reserved in their presence. Yet, when we visited, I often sat at Grandma's kitchen table listening to the adult conversation—Uncle Herbert's yarns, Grandpa's occasional corrections, and Grandma's gentle murmuring about the neighbors.

In July, my parents and I visited the University of Eastern Iowa and tied up loose ends regarding my enrollment for classes in September. I had earned a work-study scholarship and would work in the cafeteria. I found another girl from my high school, Susan Elsner, who, like me, needed a roommate. We arranged to share a room in an older dormitory for girl's in the Chablis wing. During the summer, we got together and planned a blue room with curtains made from red, white, and blue striped sheets. She agreed to sew the curtains, and I found royal blue bedspreads to match. Susan was a dark-haired, rather sad-looking little girl. Her dad was older than mine and quite ill with heart problems.

Bill Bright wrote in *You Shall Receive Power,* "I assure you that Jesus is far more eager to give His love and forgiveness, His power for service, and a life of victory over sin than we are to receive them. Jesus is far more eager to fill us with the Holy Spirit than you and I are to be filled." I hoped that the Lord would help me remember Him in my day-to-day life. I needed His love.

I finished *For Whom the Bell Tolls* and began wondering about literature and life. Life is beautiful, but *must* we always suffer before we can realize just how beautiful? I thought about Hemingway's writing. His story depicted nothing of beauty. The people and their actions were ugly; their conversations and living situations coarse and vulgar. Granted, life is not always beautiful. Hemingway certainly did a good job of showing ugliness. But must writing always be ugly to be good? I hadn't read *The Old Man and the Sea*. It was unfair to judge Hemingway's writing from just one book. But not all creations have to be ugly, do they? If I could create some beautiful fiction, I would be thrilled. But was that possible?

As the time to leave for college drew near, I began to get excited, thinking of the new adventure that awaited me. I looked forward to each day without dread. Oh, how wonderful! God was truly a part of my life.

I wrote in my journal, "If all my life I can see pink clouds against a soft-blue background at sunset, I will be content. If I can always see flocks of birds and be filled with amazement and a wish that I too could fly, I will be content. If I also can feel the ever-present breeze upon my face and in my hair, I will be content to know that my God lives."

One patient at the home, Florence, presented me with a conundrum. I did not like going into her room because she would unfurl foul, bitter language to greet me. At that time, I had very little understanding of prayer or how I could offer Florence some reason to hope. She really needed people to listen, but there was not time for that in all the caregiving I had to do. Besides, I didn't have the confidence, experience, or wisdom to even know how to begin to approach her.

To Florence

I have seen your long, stoic nose.
Your brow wrinkle with harshness,
Mouth curled toward your chin.
Florence—where you have been,
What you have seen, I don't know.
I do know a dignity in your smile—
Rare and full of teeth.

I know the elegance of your angular face,
Your long fingers clasped together on your lap
Are beautiful,
Your head held high.
With steel-gray hair pulled back straight.
Florence, if that beauty is yours,
Why does ugliness always form on your lips?

I had learned a lot at the home. Interaction with the residents distressed and disillusioned me, challenging my idealized notions of life and death and everything in between. In old age, it seemed, so many people still had long-unresolved issues. Life continued to be such a challenge for so many of the residents.

Mom called from the hospital in Omaha where Grandpa was undergoing tests. She mentioned that it hurt his pride to have to be held down by a restraining belt. I could understand. It must have been degrading.

At first on hearing that, I was angry and felt mad at God. But once I stopped to think of the degradation Jesus suffered on the cross, my rebellious feelings passed. As it says in the song "What Wondrous Love Is This," "He laid aside his crown for my soul. He bore the dreadful curse for my soul." I winced as I thought of the Son of God dying on an old cross between two criminals with a "crown" of thorns upon his head, blood dripping from his side, nails through hands and feet. I thought of the unbearable ache in His heart as He watched with weary eyes an ungrateful mob jeering and cursing Him even as he was dying for their sins so they might have eternal life.

In my journal I wrote,

Oh be glad, my soul. Sing to Him, praise His name, and weep with joy, for He is good. For us—you and me—He came. He came with love so bountiful and unending that we as relatives of Adam cannot hope to understand. Generously, He has provided the chance for us to abide in Him, as well, by accepting the Holy Spirit, as it says in 1 John 4:13. Our understanding of His love can grow more each day if we can accept His forgiveness and rejoice that condemnation has no part in His relationship with us.

Never ever did I wish to become like some poets, like Edna St. Vincent Millay, so drunk with poetry in my soul that I could not reason and enjoy the beautiful, logical realities of life. That would have been a pure disaster. Life for me had to have meaning. I did not want to rush off on wild tangents in my mind, leaving the solid base of reality in the dust. That could have led to madness like I had experienced when I was a sophomore. God could and would help me with this. For what good were moaning poets to God, if all they could do was sit around and write the overgrown imaginings of their minds.

Still, I wondered if I were not forgetting things like the genius which some poets possess. I did not wish to condemn Edna St. Vincent Millay or any of them. I didn't know how they lived or felt. I did want to always keep my mind open.

I ended my work at the home after the third week in August, which gave me time to buy notebooks and some clothes and prepare to leave home for the first time. The Lutheran Home was a good learning place for me. The work was exhausting. I wondered how the women could stand to work there day after day, year after year without something better on the horizon.

Before I left, most of the aides had insisted that I meet with them downtown to hear from a man who wanted to help them begin a union for nurses' aides. I wanted to stay out of it, protesting that I wasn't going to be around, but they stopped just short of threatening me. They practically demanded that I go with them. I did. In retrospect, I better understood their plight. People who are called to care for the loved ones of others should be paid well. The work they did was both physically and emotionally demanding.

The head nurse found out about the whole thing. I felt as though I had betrayed her. She said nothing. What could I say? I had given the job everything I had and earned $1.75 an hour, which was minimum wage at the time.

I now had school to look forward to, but I was still undecided about a major. I considered German but dismissed that idea for fear that I might have another breakdown in Germany during the mandatory year there. I had looked for a school where I might major in music therapy, but the closest was in Kansas. Once again, my past mental health difficulties were a deciding factor when considering a school farther away than my grandparents in Nebraska. So, the time drew near to leave for my new school, I decided I could major in social work and minor in German.

I ended my time at home by studying Bill Bright's *How to Pray* booklet and made plans to live simply—just jeans and T-shirt for clothing. The opening scenes of "Godspell"—young people throwing the trappings of wealth and ambition into the garbage had affected me. I looked to the future optimistically. I was sure that God would see me through to a fulfilling, productive life.

I said my goodbyes to the residents of the nursing home. They touched me. I wished I had more time to spend talking with them. I still did not know the history of most of the people.

Earl and Edith

With age, she grew rounded like a pumpkin.
He shriveled like a partially eaten apple in the sun.
When he pushed her wheelchair, he didn't need his cane.
A peculiar pair.
Edith, understated like a queen,
Accepting with the dignity her lessened ability,
Eyes bright, soft, bleating voice …
Earl was abrupt, grudging existence day to day,

His pride wounded by every humiliating bath I
gave—
Every ache, every hindrance, a reminder of all that
remained unfinished in his life.
One day, he knocked her on the forehead with his
cane.
A purple bruise appeared beneath her fleece-white
hair.
Four nurses could not pry the cane from his fist.
It took a fifth to remove the staff that made possible
his daily walks.
He may have lost that fight, but he still had Edith's
wheelchair.

Underneath their pain, borne alone, their stories remained
unknown to me. Goodbye, my friends.

Chapter 11

Maple Crest, University of Eastern Iowa

After Labor Day, my parents and I drove with my new roommate, Susan Elsner, to Maple Crest. We pulled up to an older girls' dorm, where we were assigned to the second floor. At the time, I was very devout in my faith, but I confused a spartan lifestyle with Christianity. I didn't pack stuffed animals or sentimental items. Only children needed such things. Grownups certainly did not need teddy bears or reminders of home. As an eighteen-year-old adult, surely, I could get by without pleasurable belongings. After all, I was in college to get an education and be a witness for Jesus.

The windows were high. The walls were composed of an interior stucco-like plaster. I put up a calendar and a picture of a girl with long auburn tresses and a straw hat. Unsure of my own looks, I thought she was pretty and wanted to look like her.

On move-in day, Mom and Dad bought Susan and me Big Macs. What more could we possibly need? After they left, the reality of my separation from my family began to really sink in. Could I really deal with the melancholy that began to seep into my heart?

Adjusting

I was enthusiastic about my classes; hopeful about the new friends I would meet; and pleased with the new clothes I had purchased with a portion of my summer earnings. Looking forward to my classes, I got up early in the mornings to prepare for the day. As I washed my face, got dressed and combed my hair, I tried to be as quiet as possible so I didn't bother Susan.

After my preparations, I walked downstairs and outside to the nearby cafeteria, where I ate breakfast and drank coffee. Then, I went back to the room to gather my books and notebooks. I'd get back to the room humming and eager. By way of greeting, Susan sometimes growled at me. She had scheduled her classes for later in the day and found my bustling around annoying.

In the evenings, she seemed particularly perturbed when she'd notice me standing in front of the mirror over the sink, pin curling my hair and dabbing a bit of perfume on the end of each strand. I get it. How prissy was that?

I had a work-study scholarship. On several days in the late afternoon, I checked into the dish room in the cafeteria to work at removing silverware, cups, glasses, and napkins from the trays as they entered the room on a conveyor belt. Sometimes the trays came down the line so quickly that I could barely keep up. Always eager for something to read, I'd help myself to the pithy little sayings attached to the used tea bags.

Finding Other Believers

Susan's father had heart problems, so she usually went home on the weekends. I was left to find things to do on my own. I found a group that gave rides to church on Sunday mornings. On those days, I boarded a bus with other students, and we were taken to a church that televised its service. A well-dressed, enthusiastic lady met a line of us college kids at the door.

"Babes in Christ," she warbled as she hugged each one of us. "Babes in Christ." She seemed genuine in her delight over us, and I welcomed the hug. But I felt somewhat suspicious at the whole atmosphere of the production. We returned to a dorm that offered no lunch on Sundays at one o'clock.

Eager to find fellow believers on campus, I met Mary Atkinson, a junior who simply called herself a Christian. I was intrigued that she identified herself as a Christian rather than by her denomination. I found it refreshing to think that followers of Jesus need not be divided by various peculiarities of their denominations.

Mary drew me under her wing, took me to Bible studies and special events and often shared with me a special verse or idea. She was always neatly dressed and quietly confident in the way she presented herself. She had a patch of a one-way arrow sewn onto the upper right sleeve of her jean jacket. I wanted to be like her. On Sunday evenings, I found the Wesley student house to be a welcoming place. I attended meetings there as I could.

The dining hall was typical. Part of my eventual undoing, however, was the coffee in the morning and the free-flowing caffeine-filled soft drinks available at any time. I did not have any awareness of my super sensitivity to caffeine. Apparently, some people can release toxic substances from their bodies more easily than others. Although it seems obvious now, despite my previous trouble with sleeplessness and excitement, neither I nor my parents recognized the possible contributions caffeine made to accelerate mania.

One Friday evening, I walked with a group of girls and two guys who were grad students to the college hill. Iowa's legal drinking age had changed on July 1, 1973, to 18. I was legal! We ate at a restaurant, ordering dessert first because we could. Our parents were nowhere in sight!

After supper, we walked to a bar where I planned to order beer. I wanted to know what it felt like to be drunk. I ordered a beer and stopped at four or five. Before we all left, I went to the restroom. As we began walking back, it seemed like the sidewalk was rising up to meet me. About a block away from the bar, I stopped.

"Wait, I've got to go back for my mittens. I think I left them in the restroom."

One of the grad students offered to walk back with me to retrieve them. I returned to the restroom and looked around. No mittens. Then I stuck my hands in my pockets. Ooops. There they were! I didn't tell my thoughtful escort that I found them in my pockets. I decided he didn't need to know. Like a gentleman he walked me back to the dorm and took me safely to the door. I survived my first experience of getting drunk and wasn't overly impressed.

Lonely for People who Knew Me

Even though I was busy, I did miss my family terribly. The university was about 160 miles from home and given that all but 50 miles were two-lane highways, driving home took nearly four hours one way. I did not have a car, so I tried to wait patiently for the reunion with my family when I would be able to really let go and talk about things. In those days, when I had to share a phone with others on my floor, having a private conversation with my parents was nearly impossible. I believe now that one factor in my eventual second breakdown was my lack of connection with the familiar and the resulting feeling of having lost love and support.

Given my history of having had a serious breakdown in high school, I wondered later about my parent's seeming lack of concern about how I was adapting to a completely new environment. Dad did write me letters, but an occasional letter wasn't enough. Perhaps Mom and Dad thought that because I had finished well academically in high school and had worked a full-time job in the summer, I would be fine. They themselves had overcome great hardships to even get to college. Dad had spent four years in the navy near the end of World War II and after.

Because of the GI bill, he was able to go to college. Mom had taught in one-room country schools to earn her way. Surely, I should be able to overcome any difficulties that were minor in comparison to theirs.

One day, Susan told me that she and I would get along better if we could just have an argument to clear the air. The thought of arguing with her was terrifying. I was too insecure to risk an argument. I felt I needed to hold close the few friends I did have.

It really was not surprising that amid the excitement of starting at a new school, meeting new friends, and being presented with a smorgasbord of activities, that my thoughts began to race. During the night, I often thought about my parents and how mismatched they were. My dad was athletic to an extreme, and my mother couldn't walk fast due to her deformed hip. Mom tended to think things to death, while Dad was more eager to get up and move on. Looking back, I can see how perfect they were for each other—not that they were a perfect match but that their souls were designed to grind against each other. "As iron sharpens iron," scripture says in Proverbs 27:17 (NASB), so Mom and Dad sharpened each other.

I found myself lying awake all-night thinking about things like the relationship between Rhett Butler and Scarlett O'Hara from *Gone with the Wind*. At five o'clock one morning, I called a friend to share my profound insights about Scarlett and Rhett. I was certain that she would be delighted to hear from me. Her sleepy voice failed to dampen my enthusiasm as I explained my revelation.

One day, Susan received personalized checks in the mail. Her last name had been misspelled.

"Say hello to Susan Elsneroni," she urged.

"What? Since when are you Italian?

"Since I got these checks. Guess I'll have to reorder."

"No, wait. I know! I want to be Italian too."

"OK? How do you propose doing such a thing?"

"I could change my name to Claire Foltzio."

Susan joined arms with me. "Elsneroni and Foltzio. I like it."

We laughed at our solution.

Delusions Begin

There were signs that I was losing it. From the beginning of the school year, I was moving in fast motion. In my search for belonging, I attended the group meeting of the campus Methodist ministry and other Bible studies with Mary Atkinson. One evening, one of the boys in the Wesley house group was talking very slowly explaining something. In my accelerated state, his slowness became nearly unbearable. I spoke for him and finished his sentences without consideration of how my rudeness might make him feel. Oh, well! I was on top of the world. I had a chance to break out of my previously mediocre place in the social order and really be somebody. My confidence soared at his expense.

I noticed almost immediately that my Argument and Persuasion professor looked a lot like my high school orchestra boyfriend Mark. Considering how that relationship had ended abruptly, I harbored a strong sense of unfinished business. There was something about this young professor that tapped into my primitive brain. I can only guess that because he was long and lanky like the men on my mother's side of the family, I was drawn to him—cigarettes, Buddha, and all. I thought I might be able to "win" him to Jesus.

One day I ran breathlessly into his class.

"I can see without my glasses!" I blurted. "Jesus healed me!"

He looked at me quizzically and said, "Well, you can check it out. There is an optometrist right over on Twenty-First Street. You can go right now."

"OK, I will." I hurried from the room, ran through the campus quickly, and crossed Twenty-First to find the eye doctor. I burst into the waiting room and said, "I think my eyes have been healed! I can see perfectly without my glasses or contacts."

A man looked across the counter at me and said, "Your contacts can shape the lens of your eye, giving you better vision. But it will not last."

My bubble of wishful thinking had been burst, and I walked back to my class a little more slowly to soberly explain the truth I had run up against. At that point, reality still held some sway over my increasingly convoluted thinking.

One weekend when Susan stayed at school, we attended a horror movie called *The Other*. It involved twins—one innocent, the other purely evil. The movie left a lasting impression on me. Apart from the murders and the horror of it all, I found the connection between the twins to be utterly fascinating. One of the twins died, and the other maintained contact with his brother as though he were alive. This concept of communicating with someone who was not physically present raised its head days later as I was being drawn more deeply into psychotic thinking and behavior.

As my psychosis deepened, the normal rules faded, and I began believing that anything was possible. I had a mission, and miracles were an everyday occurrence. I recall finding coins falling into my shoe, which proved that Jesus was with me, favoring me with little miracles. As in my 1971 breakdown, I was fairly certain I could fly if I could just get off the ground. Retaining walls made of brick, lined the paths on campus. They were of various heights and rose at an angle from the sidewalk, so I could run a little on the path and then on up one of the walls. I became certain that with just a little more faith, I could take off flying. For the most part, my mania was happy and hopeful.

My nights were filled not with sleep but with thinking. I would lie in bed analyzing and reanalyzing movies, books, things I had seen, and words I had read. When I was out and about on campus, I was basically sleepwalking. Interactions and dialogue with others all fit into my life as if in a dream. If I had been checking in each evening with my mom and dad for supper, they would have noticed my peculiarities sooner than my friends did.

One afternoon, well into my unraveling, I showed up at my folk-dance class feeling utterly drained. I loved the class, where I had learned many dances including the waltz and minuet. I also became quite good at performing an Irish jig. The only drawback to the class was the lack of boys. That afternoon, I had worn a dress, and I sat on the floor along the wall, legs spread wide.

The professor came over. "Please keep your legs crossed." she said sternly.

"OK." I sat up straight and pulled my dress down as far as I could.

She did not address the fact that I appeared able bodied but was opting to sit out. I watched as the rest of the class danced. I was very tired due to little sleep. By that point, I had conjured up a scenario that involved me helping to start the world over. I believed I would soon be joined by several young men and women to be new Adams and Eves. I had yet to meet my Adam, although there *was* that cute boy in my biology class. My "theology" was not yet fully developed at the time, nor do I remember it well, so I cannot tell just why I believed it was necessary for humanity to start again or how all the ruined humans would pass away. I guessed that was God's problem, and I was just his handmaiden.

One day, during my morning sociology class, the professor was waxing eloquent, talking about families and sharing illustrations from his own life. In my psychotic mind, the professor became my father and I, his daughter. He had dark hair like my dad and was similar enough in looks to satisfy the requirements for a manic delusion. Mania, as I have experienced it, is like a dream state lived in real time. One person can morph into another, and during an episode the transition seems perfectly natural, only seeming odd upon awakening or returning to sanity.

This happened with my professor/father. As class ended and students were leaving, I began weeping while remaining in my seat. I truly was sad and missing my family. The professor approached me and questioned me in a concerned manner. I am now uncertain what sort of inappropriate remarks I made, but apparently, he was satisfied with my answers, or they were not psychotic enough to cause him to take action on my behalf.

I had been at school for about six weeks before I came completely undone. At times, I would sit in the closet for privacy, talking to myself, keeping Susan awake because of my insomnia. One Friday night, after some increasingly bizarre behavior, Susan and some other girls found me around midnight in a lounge just across from my room. I was sitting on the floor against the wall, tucked into a fetal position, talking to my unseen "twin" through the wall. Susan called my parents.

Leaving Megan and Annie at home alone, Mom and Dad arrived around 4:00 AM. It was the first time I had seen them since school began. Without much convincing, I went with them, sitting in the back of the car. They talked quietly to each other.

"I've really missed you. I thought you'd never come. Did you miss me? Did you know I have a twin? Why didn't you tell me?" I filled the air with nonsense. "Are you going to use the wings?" I was telling myself that the car had wings enfolded in the doors that could emerge and fly us home.

"This isn't an airplane," Dad replied.

"But isn't this a new car plane?"

"No, it's just our same old car."

Once at home, my parents arranged a meeting with Dr. Gould, who was aware of my history. She immediately prescribed Trilafon along with Elavil, an antidepressant. The mania wore off quickly, and I began to sleep again. By week's end, Dad and Mom faced a decision regarding my possible return to Maple Crest.

A Difficult Decision

I remember pleading with my dad to allow me to return to my life at UEI. I thought my life would be over if I could not make it. Reluctantly, he agreed, and we packed my pills—one package for each day. If I stuck with the Trilafon, mania would not surface, while the Elavil would keep me from depression—or at least that was the hope. It was the best psychiatry had to offer at the time, and in our limited experience it seemed possible that it could work.

Two Sundays later, a little over a week after I had left, Mom and I began our trek back to school. Along with my books, clothes, and sundry items were the Trilafon and Elavil, tucked neatly into small packets. Each packet was marked with the date and time I was to swallow them. This strategy seemed to be a worthy, reasonable risk. If only this were the 1940s when dorm mothers closely monitored the comings and goings of young people. Mom and Dad thought that I could ask the dorm mother to help me keep track of the medication. I did not dare ask her. I thought she might laugh at such a notion. She lived in an apartment just down the hall from my room, but I barely had any interaction with her other than a nod in the hallway.

I felt embarrassed by the behavior that had sent me home. In my journal I recorded my heartbreak and frustration. But I resolved to swallow my pride and decided that though I felt like a fool, my ego had been slain. I wanted to go back. I hoped to finish school successfully, just as I had planned.

In returning to school, I attempted to pick up where I left off. In contrast to the previous manic weeks, my confidence was at an all-time low, and when my biology professor failed to show up to administer a test I had missed, I gave up and did not try to reschedule. I eventually ended up getting a D in that class. So, I returned to reality with a thud, hoping I could make it and fill the emptiness in my heart.

I kept going to Bible studies, and dear Mary continued to reach out to me. Sadly for me, I learned that she was moving out of my dorm into an apartment with some other Christian girls in January. One evening, she invited me to have supper with her new friends. I became concerned, as I could see how possessive one of the girls was of Mary, hovering over her, full of warnings, and questioning Mary's decisions.

Life was filled with uncertainty and fear. I forced myself to make an appointment with a college counselor. He seemed like a nice enough person.

For a while, the relationship between Susan and me seemed to flourish. At the time, there was a popular game show for married couples on television. The activity committee of the second-floor Chablis wing of our dormitory hosted a game night. Susan and I wound up winning a roommate version of the *Newlywed Game.* We knew each other quite well.

In November, a theater major asked me to play Dorothy in her adapted stage play of *The Wizard of Oz.* Under the influence of Trilafon and Elavil, I declined her sweet offer as I could not imagine having the energy to play the lead. Gone was the playful girl who had pretended to be Dorothy in the hospital in 1971. This sinking girl did settle into the role of a munchkin alongside Susan, who was more suitably short. I scrunched down as much as I could and adopted a squeaky voice. In practice, Susan and I welcomed Dorothy to Munchkin City in the Land of Oz. I invited my parents to come and watch our production, but a Sunday evening show, four hours away, did not work for people who had to get up and teach the next day.

I visited the campus psychologist a few times. Just as I began to feel that I could open up and really talk to him, I apparently said too much, because he suggested that I find a doctor in downtown Maple Crest. I think he even gave me a name. What? Did I hear him correctly? Surely, he wasn't passing me on to someone else. He was turning me over to a phantom, as far as I was concerned. Maybe he felt inadequate to meet the needs of someone who had suffered from mania.

I was stunned. He led me to the door and wished me well. That may have been a good suggestion, but it was too much for a girl short on courage and confidence. I still did not have a car and lacked the energy to find a bus schedule or hire a cab, so I let it go. He let me go, and I let go of potential help and hope. What could I do?

The counselor failed to follow through or check up on me, and thus I found myself facing a cold, dreary winter without an adult confidant. I honestly believe that a sympathetic adult to talk with could have helped me tremendously and may have prevented the inevitable slide into desolation. Really listening with compassion is possibly the greatest gift one can give to another human being. Lacking that, the nearly tragic decision I would make in March had become inevitable.

Christmas at home came and went. Because the semester didn't finish until mid-January, I had homework during my Christmas break. Worst of all, I had to write a paper for my Argument and Persuasion class.

My maternal grandfather died in January, and I made a quick trip to Nebraska with my family to attend the funeral. I became increasingly distressed at my lack of feeling. I wanted to cry and knew I needed the release that tears could bring, but all I felt was the brittleness of disconnection. I don't know if it was the Trilafon or the Elavil, but something was making me numb.

Unbearable Reality

By March 1974, the darkness had deepened. The high hopes that had carried me to UEI in September had flown away. The gray sky loomed once again. Wind howled through the leafless trees as desolation descended more deeply into my spirit. My second-semester classes were uninspiring. My literature class felt like having a meal of leftovers, as most of the short stories we studied I had previously read in high school. The algebra class had so many students that we watched the professor on closed-circuit television. My German teacher had the warmth of a statue, and the Old Testament class was so lifeless and uninspired that if I had not previously been exposed to the sacred texts, I may have chosen never to bother reading from the Bible again.

Unkindnesses

Adding to these rather grim circumstances, the fact that I had few real friends only opened the gash in my reserve of hope even wider. One weekend when Susan was gone, the sorority girls next door had a party that spilled over into the hallway. Boys and girls talked and laughed while tipping drinks. I was not invited. I stayed in my room that night, only leaving to go to the bathroom. The music was loud. I couldn't sleep. I learned later that someone had called campus security to complain about the noise from their party. My neighbor girls were sure I was the one who had called. Talk about adding insult to injury! Yes, they were loud, and I was hurt by the exclusion, but I had not called anyone about it. I was faced with yet another painful incident to deal with on my own.

I felt as though the link between my brain and mouth had been severed. I could not express myself. My feelings were dampened to the point of being unreachable. Sadness is one thing; the absence of feeling is another. I felt terrifyingly dead. I was going through the motions of living, entirely detached from anything but physical pleasure, which consisted mostly of eating.

> Scorn has broken my heart and has left me helpless.
> I looked for sympathy, but there was none,
> And for comforters, but I found none.
> —Psalm 69:20 (NIV)

I was certainly no longer manic, yet I was still suffering greatly at the opposite pole of bipolar disorder. The medications (an antipsychotic and an antidepressant) had failed to bring me into a place of balance. The depressive side was a place of mere existence. I had lost my humanity—my ability to feel, to laugh, or to cry. I was rapidly losing even my ability to think. Shame, a sense of rejection, loneliness, and more than a little anger and disappointment toward

God worked on me to bring me to a place of hopelessness. I was a loser. I decided that it was no wonder I had trouble making friends.

Early in March, I made a trip home on a Greyhound bus. I left Maple Crest early on Friday afternoon and arrived in the Quad Cities a little after supper time. Dad came to pick me up at the bus station and explained that Mom was gone for the evening with Annie to a see a play at her school. After going to so much trouble to get home I was deeply disappointed that Mom wasn't there to greet me. I could tell that Dad had hoped to be enough for me.

On Saturday morning, Mom and I went to visit my psychiatrist. In her office, Mom and Dr. Gould discussed my situation. As I look back, I wonder why Mom went with me to *my* psychiatric appointment. Mom just happened to have one of Dr. Gould's children as a student in English.

As she often did, Mom spoke for me. "Claire didn't make any effort to contact her local friends."

"Really? Why do you suppose that is?" Dr. Gould asked.

"Well, if I had limited time at home, I'd probably do the same thing. We all need time to ourselves," Mom said.

"Is that it Claire? Do you just need time to yourself?"

"Well, yeah, I guess." I didn't have the energy or motivation to explain and figured my friends were all busy with their own lives anyway. I had neither the will nor the courage to really talk about what was bothering me with my mother and the expert in psychiatry. In her office that day, I felt lonelier than ever.

When I returned to Maple Crest after the weekend at home, I decided to kill myself. Life had become unbearable. The only thing I looked forward to was eating. A week or two prior, in an attempt to help myself, I had rented a bicycle, thinking that exercise might do me some good. As I pedaled the standard old bike up and down the hills and into the cold March wind, my attempt to lift my flagging spirits fell flat. The wind and the effort only discouraged me more. When I finished, there was nothing to anticipate as I looked forward to another lonely Saturday night away from family and the people who knew me.

The high hopes that had accompanied me to school had been dashed. The high had become low. I was depleted and exhausted. Nothing inspired me. I am sure there were layers of hurt and disappointment deep inside my heart, but I was without a skilled counselor to help perform the necessary spiritual surgery. God did have plans for me, and his hand was upon me. There was help on my horizon, but I did not know it.

The path to healing and wholeness would take years and input from many sources. It was a divine plan in the midst of a broken world. At that point in time, I had no such hope. Because of my introverted nature, I rarely gave voice to my misery. I did share at times with Mom. When it came to sympathy for an illness, Mom was top notch. However, the pain that I suffered from was invisible and not something that her comforting Jell-O or milk toast could help.

The medications I was taking served only to dampen me more. The balance between the poles of mania and depression had not been achieved, and I was suffering the consequences of a complicated situation—me. My heart was broken. My strength was gone. I could not think clearly to see my way out. Being young, I had yet to gain enough life experience to know that things could get better.

Trilafon may have prevented mania in me but it contributed to something far more sinister than overexcitement. I recently googled Trilafon (Perphenazine) and found a long list of side effects and warnings. My horrible feelings and follow-up actions were not entirely my fault.

I had been incapable of making genuine attachments to people, and I believe that was the main source of my desperation. My manic state in September had been a frantic attempt to make attachment happen. I had been performing and striving but was unable to find safe places to be authentic—to be myself. By March, I was dealing with abandonment depression, feeling bereft and alone without the skills I needed to make it. Ineptly, I had abandoned my very self to try to fit in and belong with others. Later, I came to realize that I had many symptoms of rejection. My feelings were easily hurt, and I would see hurt where none was intended. I withdrew and found it difficult to share with others. I spent too much time and attention on my appearance. I did not feel I really belonged with anyone in particular.

Bottom line, I was basically unattached to anyone. I believe if I had been able to connect with and regularly confide in just one other person, like the counselor who turned me away, I would not have reached such a point of desperation. Yes, Mary Atkinson had reached out to me and checked in regularly, but I was more her project than her friend. I knew she cared as much as she was able. It just was not enough. I needed a wise adult to advise me and tell me that things would be better—a kind adult and a funny friend would have worked miracles. I had neither.

So, the day after the weekend at home, I decided to research suicide to find a painless method to end my misery and loneliness. I went to the library Monday afternoon but could not find much on the subject. I decided that aspirin would be my drug of choice. I walked the three few blocks to a little drug store.

One Last Chance

The next morning, I had a little Bible study with Mary, who had picked out several verses in the New Testament to show me.

"I found something amazing to share with you today," she began.

"That's good."

Mary did not know how much was riding on our interaction.

"Let's look at Galatians 3."

We flipped the pages in our New American Standard Bibles. "Would you like to read the first five verses?" she asked.

"You foolish Galatians, who has bewitched you, before whose eyes Jesus Christ was publicly portrayed as crucified?" I started and read a little more.

Mary followed with more verses, ending with verse 24: "that you might be justified by faith."

"Isn't that awesome?" she asked. "We *cannot* earn our place with God. We *already* have a place with Him as His children because we believe."

"Yeah, I guess so."

"We belong to God no matter what. We can't earn it!" she exclaimed.

I wished desperately that I could share her enthusiasm. As usual, she was practically squealing over the amazing truth wrapped in the Word, while I was unable to muster equivalent delight. The medications that were keeping me "sane," had deadened my spirit. The words were just words. They seemed as dead and lifeless as I felt.

In the past, I had seen life in the Bible. I remember being very amazed that after I had committed my life to Jesus for the first time, the Bible had begun to make sense. But now it seemed as though God himself had abandoned me. In my mind, meeting with Mary was giving God one last chance to impart some hope. Failing that, I decided to swallow the bottle of aspirin I had purchased the day before. I figured that if I swallowed enough of them, I could just sleep my life away. I mentioned this idea to no one, although I had fantasized that if I explained to Mom the futility of life, she might want to die with me. That gives a clue as to how delusional my thinking had become, as well as how enmeshed I was with her. I knew enough to refrain from talking with anyone about suicide.

My Last Lunch

I went to lunch that day with Susan and some other girls for my last meal. I did not feel nervous about my impending death, I guess because I did not feel much of anything. After lunch, Susan left for class, while I got a large, pink plastic glass of water. I began my grim task, swallowing aspirin one after another, refilling my glass several times as I ran out of water. I believe there were 250 tablets in the bottle, and I swallowed over two-thirds of them. Later, Susan counted the remaining tablets, and it was determined that I had swallowed 170 in all. The choice of aspirin over sleeping pills may have been what saved my life. I had thought that I would take the aspirin and nap, as I often did in the afternoons. If I had swallowed a large number of sleeping pills instead, I may have slept my life away.

The aspirin did not bring sleep. Instead, I found myself with time to think. I thought of how Catholics believed that people who commit suicide were destined for hell, and I began to worry, because I did not want to go to hell. The longer I thought, the more I worried. What had I done? How was I going to get out of this mess? I began to get frantic. Finally, I went to the bathroom, hoping to throw up. I bent over the toilet and tried to vomit. Nothing happened.

In the bathroom stall, I shriek-whispered to God, "I don't really want to die. I just can't continue like this."

I knew I could not, absolutely could *not* continue living in my current painful, removed existence. I was trapped and couldn't find a way of escape. The thought came to me (prompted by the Holy Spirit) that I needed to tell my roommate about the aspirin. Oh dear! That would be rough!

After Susan returned from her afternoon class, I ashamedly confessed what I had done. She knew what to do. She called the infirmary immediately. She left briefly, and a girl from next door came in our room to sit with me. She looked at me with soft eyes and told me that she was here for me. Where had she been? Why had I never connected with this gentle person? When Susan returned, she walked with me to the infirmary, where upon learning what I had done, they yelled at me and gave me something to induce vomiting.

They put me in a car with a campus security officer and a female student in the front seat. I sat in the back alone, my stomach in knots, gagging and spitting into a bag. The driver carried on lively chit-chat, seemingly oblivious to my plight, as he drove slowly to a hospital. I wondered at his apparent lack of empathy and urgency, not to mention his indifference. Did he realize I could very well be dying in the back seat? Did he care? I guess it was just another day at work for him.

Once at the hospital, I was placed on a table in a room with nurses and a young, concerned, focused doctor. At last, someone seemed to care. I listened as they talked about what to do. I slipped in and out of consciousness, oblivious to the chaos I had caused, and awoke in a dreamy twilight state.

I vaguely remember later, after being placed in a regular room, looking at a doctor through a haze. "We'd like to move you to the psychiatric ward of the hospital, young lady. What do you think of that idea?" The orange-pinkish glow of the setting sun filtered through the window as he spoke. I agreed with him and sensed that maybe I might be able to make it.

Chapter 12

Freezing in Minnesota

I did not wake up again for a day or two after my conversation with the doctor. When I did, I learned that during my unconsciousness, my folks arrived and Dad had cried. Dad crying was not unusual. I had one of those dads who cries easily. What I needed to know in that moment was that Dad still loved me, even though I had let him down. I was the one who had convinced him that I would be fine if they sent me back to school. Against his better, masculine, more mature judgment, he chose to trust my naive, little-girl decision. He chose to trust little old me, all the while knowing I could blow the whole thing—big time. I nearly did.

On that Monday back in October when Dad had decided to let me go back to UEI, I was ready and armed with the best medications that were available. I clutched the Trilafon and Elavil, packaged neatly, and walked back into an environment that was not equipped to help me with belonging and social skills. It was the seventies, and everybody was being set free from the old rules. Boys and girls then were living in the same dorms; eighteen-year-olds could drink and be drafted. Freedom was the name of the game.

I had obtained a prescription for the best that science had to offer: those pills. I came to hate them. As sure as I know anything,

I do know that God hates poison or anything else that damages his children.

In 1974, when I swallowed all that aspirin, I was thinking *only* of *my* pain. But all it took was a hint of Dad's concern for me to focus on his pain rather than my own. That is why his tears meant so much. Underneath it all, I loved my daddy, and I truly did not want to hurt him.

The doctor determined that they needed to move me to a medical center in Minnesota for dialysis. Mom travelled with me by ambulance.

Hospital in Minnesota

A day or two later, I woke up in a hospital room with Archie Bunker and Meathead having one of their familiar arguments in the background. As I opened my eyes, I became aware of a presence in the room. I glanced over to see my mother sitting about two feet from my bed with tears in her eyes. Mom. The sight of my mother encouraged me. The familiar sitcom was a taste of *one* of the best things in life: laughter. I was still here! I had hope. Maybe life could get better.

"Hi, Claire," she said quietly.

"Hi, Mom."

My stay at the hospital was short lived and plans to place me in the psychiatric wing of another hospital came next. I was moved to a bed in a single room. Nearly all my possessions were locked up in a ward that was locked down. I was still severely depressed, and I spent a lot of time in bed. I met with a psychiatrist named Dr. Chavda, who was from India. She wore a sari and a colorful dot on her forehead. The color of the dot changed from day to day to match her clothing. Unfortunately, I experienced no great relief or insightful conversations with Dr. Chavda. I was too pent up, too sad to express myself. Often, the good doctor and I would just sit and stare at each other.

One day, I sat down across from her. Her dot was red that day. I said, "I wish I knew why I am so messed up."

Dr. Chavda thought for a minute and said, "You're not so messed up." That was the most encouraging thing she ever said to me.

"How can I ever be anything useful? I've already messed up so bad."

"It takes time. You will be fine."

I wasn't so sure. She had yet to give me anything solid to hang on to.

On my own, I tried to understand what had happened at school to make me such an outcast. When I would find that people were not what I wanted them to be, I'd withdraw from the situation, rather than actively speaking my part. I would become sour and bitter because everyone wasn't the way I wanted them to be. Then again, I wouldn't be the way they would want me to be either. So, neither silence *nor* passivity were ever, ever enough when faced with misconceptions about me or someone else. I did need to grow and learn in order to avoid drying up.

Did life have meaning for other people? A real purpose? Maybe that is where I had gone wrong. I had been searching for a meaning in life when there was none to be had. I wanted to find out everything right away. Here and now! Like all teenagers, I was impatient, but I was also sluggish and sad. Just months before when I was manic, I had been sure that *I* was a gift to the world! But now I was hanging on to hope by a thread.

I truly wanted to start anew. That was my only possibility. I guessed one had to be bull headed and one sided, because when you tried to be just and see both sides of a situation, you could only become confused and split. Humans could never reach perfection. For one thing, if they did, they would have nothing left to work for.

One day, I ran into a girl in the hallway. She told me of her situation. She was not adjusting well to a recent conversation with her husband. I felt bad for her.

"My husband doesn't *luff* me anymore," she said in her sad, little-girl voice. I didn't know what to say. I listened and tried to comfort her, without a clue as to what I could say or do.

How could Dr. Chavda help me? How could any doctor help me? Would going over my past be of help? I did not know. I did want to get out of my mess-- but how? I had been telling everyone that I saw no meaning to life. I did not see the reason for living. Reverend Willard from a nearby Methodist Church stopped by one day. I told him that life had no meaning. He said that perhaps love could be my goal.

Nothing made much sense. Because I did not want to live in a sick world, that meant I was sick. How ironic. I wanted to scream. This couldn't be the way God meant us for us to live. All I did here was stagger to get dressed in the morning and shuffle between meals and the activity room—what an existence.

People would say, "But Claire, that's the way people are."

Why? To me that meant that people were no better than animals. I felt deeply frustrated and angry.

I was so extremely bitter, and I could not put my finger on what it was that made me so. I guessed I had to be willing to get up and out and start fighting in this venom-spitting world.

One evening in the community room, Father Jeff, a fellow patient, made a comment to an orderly and a couple of people nearby. I probably deserved it.

"You know? After being in here so long, even ugly girls start to look good." He paused and then added, "Claire's looking good." He, the attendant, and another guy laughed. I hurried from the room and went back to my bed.

Dr. Chavda said I ought to consider teaching music as a profession—perhaps she was right. My life couldn't be over now. I had a whole life ahead of me. I had to be willing to get back into the game and start fighting. They say God helps those who help themselves. That is probably true.

Sunshine

Sunshine spilled pale upon my bed
With it came a new day
But like the sunshine
I was weak.
Lacking depth
Lacking vigor
Like the pale sunshine
I too spilled upon my bed.

How could there not be a God? I wondered. *Where did we come from if there is no God?* My faith was barely hanging on. I felt utterly desolate. Depression was thick, and the grief over the loss of college hopes and dreams seemed to be getting deeper.

Part of my problem in being a Christian was that I questioned rather than accepted blindly. Wouldn't it have been easier if I just blindly believed? But after I'd read the Bible and learned of Jesus Christ, my doubts arose. Whatever. I had to decide on one or the other—atheist or Christian. I leaned at that point more heavily toward Christianity. I wanted to have Jesus be a part of my life so badly. One of the reasons I leaned toward Christianity was that what Jesus taught was realistic and human. He taught how to live without being barbaric.

My experiences with other patients in the ward were no better than my relationship with Dr. Chavda. There was Father Jeff, the mean priest who seemed bent on letting me know how awful I was. And indeed, there was not much that was attractive about a sad girl with long, straight hair and no access to a curling iron or make up. Somehow, I still managed to care about my weight. I thought that maybe if I were thinner, I would be more acceptable, and people would like me. I weighed about 112 pounds and decided to ask my doctor if she would put me on a calorie-restricted diet. She declined my request. This hospitalization was as grim as my first hospital experience had been fun and liberating.

On the weekends, my parents took turns coming to see me. Megan told me later that she and Annie had accompanied Mom and Dad on those overnight trips to southern Minnesota. I felt bad for my dad who sat nervously near me, quietly and tenuously trying to think of things to talk about. He brought me a book called *I Ain't Much Baby, But I'm All I've Got.* Dad's presence alone was reassuring, and yet I felt the pain of his awkwardness at not knowing what to say or do. Still, I was incapable of performing and putting on a happy face.

I never really had a breakthrough moment while in that psychiatric ward. I attended occupational therapy and made moccasins and other meaningless items. If they wanted to reach me, making me attend an adult version of art class really was not the way to do it. Even though I failed to make a breakthrough, I did have a humiliating encounter that I could say was educational in a reverse way.

One morning, some young, bright-faced professionals—I assume they were interns—trooped into my room and stood around my bed. There were five or six of them. I cannot recall what they asked me, but I do remember what I felt. I felt like a frog about to be dissected. The air about them was cold and clinical. I was an object, and they were practicing their skills on me. The fact that there were several of them made it even worse.

I also remember their stern charge that I needed to cooperate with my doctor. I felt shocked and betrayed by the accusation. At the time, I was honestly unaware of any lack of cooperation with my doctor. I felt completely misunderstood and hopeless. It may have been then that I resolved to find a better way to kill myself when I got out of there.

At some point, my mother suggested to Dr. Chavda that she take me off the medication, which had consisted of Trilafon and

Elavil. Dr. Chavda reduced the doses of each medication. When she did, the heaviness began to lift, and after a few days, she decided that I could be released from the hospital. Mom arrived to take me home. On the way out, she asked an orderly if this was where Ernest Hemingway had been hospitalized. Yes, Hemingway had been released from this very place in 1961, a couple of weeks before he fatally shot himself.

The trip home was grim. We stopped at school to gather the belongings that were still in my dorm room. I was nervous and embarrassed at the prospect of running into people I knew. Mercifully, my roommate, Susan, was not there. I worried about how my actions may have affected her the day she took me to the infirmary. All I know is that she did the right thing and I am grateful to her for that.

We gathered the rest of my possessions, making several trips up and down the stairs, so that we could finish the trip home and begin the rest of my fragile life. I could feel my mother's depression and disappointment. She generally was not one to suffer in silence, so understandably her feelings came out in waves of complaint. There was no one there to comfort us or offer hope. We were desolate and facing an uncertain future with little support. I knew some of my mother's difficult history, and here I was making life even harder. My parents had been told not to expect much from me—that I would probably have to live with them the rest of my life and that I could not be expected to ever get married, have children, or obtain more than a low-stress job.

Years later, I contacted the hospital in search of records from that time. I was curious about the diagnosis. The first notes indicated that I had poisoned myself with the 170 five-grain tablets. The salicylates in the aspirin are toxic to the central nervous system. Tinnitus, which I still suffer from today, is known to be a result of high salicylate levels. They gave me mannitol through an intravenous infusion to force urine production.

Dr. Chavda had administered the Minnesota Multiphasic Personality Inventory (MMPI), which showed me to be "very sensitive and touchy, very aware of the opinions of others, an excessive worrier, and mildly depressed." Yes, the MMPI and Dr. Chavda did well in assessing what was wrong with me. Yes, I was highly sensitive and indeed an advanced worrier.

But, wow— I was only mildly depressed? The MMPI sure missed the mark on that one.

Dr. Chavda went on to say that I showed no signs of "psychotic behavior or difficulty in thought processing." Lately I have heard more about bipolar depression as a unique form of depression. I guess I never heard of psychotic depression. Apparently, it is possible to be psychotically depressed? I wonder what that looks like.

The Rorschach Ink Blot Test caught the severity of my depression better than the MMPI. Dr. Chavda had this to say about the Rorschach: "The patient took a very long time responding to the blots. She showed no bizarre responses or looseness in association. The Rorschach is most indicative of a *significantly* depressed person who is having a difficult time dealing with some of her environmental stresses. The manner in which she handled the blots would make one wonder whether she has the tendency to sit back and let time solve some of her problems. The most consistent finding was a *significant degree of depression.* She expressed some thought of suicide."

Yes, indeed I had a tendency to sit back and let time solve my problems. You could call me lazy, but that label didn't begin to describe the complexity of what had caused me to shut down. Years later, I discovered that I had developed a habit of "learned helplessness." Learned helplessness can be described as a condition in which a person suffers from a sense of powerlessness, arising from a traumatic event or a persistent failure to succeed. It is thought to be one of the underlying causes of depression.

Also, I was on Trilafon which blocks the neurotransmitter Dopamine. Dopamine is what enables us to feel motivated, focused and have psychological drive, to accomplish goals. It's not normal to be psychotically manic but it's not normal to want to stay in bed all day either.

Dr. Chavda summed up my stay with these words: "Depressive reaction with suicidal attempt by overdose of aspirin in a rather passive, dependent, idealistic girl. No evidence of present thought disorder. However, in view of history, could either fit in the picture of schizophrenic reaction, schizoaffective type, or manic-depressive illness." In other words, even though I was showing no signs of psychosis, they were still considering whether I might be schizophrenic or have schizoaffective disorder. In truth, I was stone-cold sober and deeply depressed. At the time, there was no physiological test that could lock in a diagnosis.

According to my understanding, schizoaffective disorder can include manic and depressive symptoms but has psychotic symptoms at its core. While manic, I had experienced symptoms of psychosis—disorganized behavior, speech and delusions. Yet, these manifestations were not a chronic part of my experience.

In reading through the notes, several times, I was amazed by several things. Before I go into that, I want to emphasize that I hold no grudges or ill will toward any psychiatrists, doctors, or nurses. I believe that those who serve people in hospitals and clinics have noble desires to help people. I understand how wearying, frustrating, and thankless their jobs may be. In 1974, much less was known about human behavior and the brain. I hope that my children and others that I have hurt forgive me for my ignorance, my neglect, or the downright harm I have caused. Likewise, I have purposefully forgiven and asked God to cleanse me from any bitterness I may have harbored toward any caregivers for being so inept in their attempts to help me. I am aware that if I'd been in their shoes, I most likely would have done the same things. However, I was astonished by how little understanding the doctors and staff seemed to possess concerning depression.

They knew that *some* medications seemed to help *some* people in *some* way. Dr. Chavda, my primary psychiatrist, voiced the complaint that I was not "trying" hard enough. She said I was passive and lacked "ego strength." She was good at analyzing and prescribing medication. The summary at the end of my stay at the psychiatric hospital stated, "There was no significant improvement, though subjectively the patient felt her mood to be less depressed. Her involvement in the ward activities was minimal. It was difficult to draw her out, though she was encouraged to socialize and verbalize her thoughts."

On my behalf, let me say that I had no energy to express myself. I had nothing to say. I needed encouragement. Had any of them ever been depressed? People suffering from deep depression are unable to pull themselves up by the bootstraps. I had been taking crippling medication. At that point in time, my thoughts were dark and pessimistic. Verbalizing them again and again was pointless. My spirit needed to be fed. I needed to hear stories of others who had overcome similar situations. I needed to laugh and view beautiful scenery. I needed confident people to tell me that I could make it.

Instead, I was stuck in a colorless hospital at the coldest, darkest time of the year. I found that they were surprised that I was reluctant to spend time in the day room with a television blaring and a priest making fun of me. And by the way, where was a nurse or attendant to protect me from his derision?

The doctor, nurses and therapists were surprised that occupational therapy, which consisted of making moccasins and hammering on pieces of copper, failed to wake me up. If they had taken the time to get to know me, maybe they would have found that I had never cared much for crafts. I hated coloring pictures and had merely endured art class in school. Perhaps as alternatives, they could have given me short stories to read and discuss or a piano to play. I would have listened to stories of people who had suffered severe depression and lived to talk about it.

Most of all I needed to talk. While at UIE, I had gathered multiple experiences that I never shared with my family or anyone. I needed help in getting to the roots of my fears, frustrations, and anger. My mind needed to be cleansed from the residue of past disappointments with people. I needed help to grieve and work through my loss, hurt and sorrow.

> In the world you will have trouble but take
> heart for I have overcome the world.
> —John 16:33 (NIV)

It has been forty-plus years since April 1974. Since that time, many advances have been made in understanding human motivation and behavior. In my lifetime, there has been a surge of awareness and comprehension of the human brain, emotions, and relationships. Yet we still have a long way to go.

An entire lesson in a course I took through Elijah House Ministries was devoted to understanding depression—both how to and how not to minister to one who is depressed. Not only were the doctors and staff at the medical center enormously ineffective in reaching the depressed in 1974, but many in the mental health field still fail to comprehend effective ways to help those who are mired in depression.

It is interesting that Dr. Chavda mentioned "ego strength." Sometime prior to moving to UEI, I had read a chapter from a Catherine Marshall book that advocated "ego slaying." I had prayed the prayer the chapter suggested. Were the experiences I had at school a perfect storm to deliver me from a self-centered existence? Or did they merely expose the fact that I first needed to acquire a self before I could trustingly bring it into submission to God. I think *ego* as used in Marshall's book was a reference to self-exaltation, while the ego strength mentioned in the hospital report referred to a lack of healthy self-knowledge and resilience.

In an attempt to understand their analysis of me, I googled *ego strength*. The word *ego*, of course, comes from Freud's theory of personality. In Freudian psychology, the human id consists of primal urges and desires, the superego consists of internalized rules and standards, and the ego is the part of us that deals with reality and attempts to find balance between the conscience of the superego and the basic urges of the id. The analysis from the psychiatric ward seemed to be correct. I was definitely lacking in resilience and the resources needed to obtain it. Resilience does not happen overnight. I could set resilience as a long-term goal.

People who are depressed need counselors or guides who are confident that God can restore such a one to hope, strength, and joy. The helpers need to respect the space of a person whose spirit is tender from discouragement, disillusionment and disappointment. John and Paula Sandford explain in their book *God's Power to Change: Healing the Wounded Spirit* that, in much the same way that a burn victim must be touched carefully, the spirit of one suffering from depression needs careful handling. Things that work for a normal person who is feeling a little down, like parties, joking, and fun, will not work for someone suffering from despondency. They do not have the strength for vigorous activities or prayer from groups of people. A gentle person who can affirm and speak confidently of a better day will go a long way toward reaching the core issues that may need to be carefully uprooted in a precise manner under the direction of the Holy Spirit.

Family members who are caring for the depressed need to be aware that good progress can be thwarted by clueless staff, unkind fellow patients, or family members with their own problems. In order for the "broken" member to recover, the whole family needs counseling. Patients must be heard by people who believe what they say and can stand as advocates. True healing takes time, and a person needs to be in safe hands in order to risk the sharing that is necessary to get to the roots of depression. Guilt, shame, fear, judgment, trauma, and unresolved grief in many forms contribute to the bitter roots that cause us to fall short of the grace of God, as we are told in Hebrews 12:15. If the patient's diet is poor, help is needed in selecting healthy foods and meal preparation.

The idea that mental illness is caused by a chemical imbalance has been debunked. Studies have shown that there is not a strict dichotomy between mental illness and mental health. There is rather a continuum between the two. You cannot really point to a person and say—now SHE is mentally healthy! Having many friends and being popular could be considered signs of mental health. However, if the so called "healthy" person gossips and tears other people down to feel better about herself, is she anymore helpful to society than a mentally ill person? Because we are comprised of a body, mind, will, emotions and spirit; good counseling, forgiveness, regular confession of sin and support groups also need to be part of the prescription for healing and wholeness.

Ego strength and resilience are things you can build. At the time I was in the hospital, I was obviously lacking in each of these essential "bricks" that together make a wall of inner strength. Little by little over time, however, the Lord began working in me to build that inner vitality and stability. I was to meet and marry a man who loved me. Through pursuing affirming books, finding a welcoming church, listening to sermons, and learning how to read and be nourished by the Bible, my outlook became more positive. By God's grace and with increasing maturity, I stopped resorting to sarcasm or gossip as regularly as I once did. The Holy Spirit revealed better ways to let off steam and feel at peace with myself. With increasing experience, my sense of worth, confidence, and ability to communicate grew, but my upward climb to a good outcome could only happened gradually.

Chapter 13

Joy in the Mourning

Re-entry into the Quad Cities, Spring 1974

With my defeat and return, another battle had just begun. My new challenge involved living the truth in the real world with real people. Laying aside fantasies and unrealistic hopes and dreams, I faced the glaring harshness of the noonday sun, not entirely without hope. I had been given parents who truly did love me and had the means to support me through a prolonged and unexpectedly difficult adolescence. Likewise, I did have a handful of friends who loved me as best they could, as they too were navigating the rough waters that even "normal" kids face just trying to grow up.

I fretted about humankind's selfish nature and confessed my sin of overeating and laziness. Speaking of laziness, it never occurred to me to blame the numbing properties of medicine I was taking. The medicine wasn't even close to what I really needed. I certainly wasn't going to have another manic episode any time soon, but neither was I going to feel capable, confident and motivated to keep going. Only my mother's prodding kept me on track.

I watched the tv miniseries *QB VII* based on the novel by Leon Uris. It concerned the trial of an author who brought to light the sadistic atrocities committed at concentration camps during World

War II. As I recall, Mom watched it with me. The movie portrayed the inhumane treatment that Jewish men and women experienced at the hands of doctors who had vowed to do no harm. My thoughts most naturally turned to dark things, and I focused on sin more than I did on goodness. I wrote this in my journal at the time:

> People are basically selfish. It hurts to find that out. It is difficult to find people who are not sourpusses, generally unhappy with the world. I often wish I could wake up to find it not so—to find that people love more than themselves, that they love everyone.
>
> My overeating is a sin. In fact, I think that almost anything done in excess can be sinful. And I believe that every time someone sins, he is giving in to satan and denying God. It is so easy but so wrong to pass off our sins as human nature. If we keep telling ourselves *I am only human*, that is all we will ever be—only plain old run-of-the-mill humans. We must look to God for strength to overcome our weaknesses. He forgives, but it is our duty to try to do better.

I slept a lot and worried that I was nothing more than a vegetable. I was living strictly on a sensual level, no better than an animal. Mom didn't know how to motivate me. She came into my room one morning and, in her abrupt fashion, asked, "Are you going to lie there and stink all day?" Her question only made me want to burrow deeper.

Mom didn't realize that the medicine I was taking had put a damper on my motivation. She failed to take into consideration that Trilafon was a hard hitting anti-psychotic medication. It blocks dopamine receptors in the brain. My drive and hope for life was being depleted by medication. In addition, I was still taking Elavil, an antidepressant. Elavil now comes with a black box label warning that studies showed antidepressants increased the risk of suicidal thinking and behavior in children, adolescents and young adults. At the time I was taking Elavil, there was no black box warning. This girl (me) who wanted to die wasn't entirely at fault for swallowing all those aspirin.

When I returned home, two of my best friends from high school, Michelle and Valerie were super busy studying at college to become nurses. I landed first at one Catholic college that had originally been established for boys. Within a year I transferred to a gentler Catholic College that was once primarily for girls. Both had recently become co-ed.

In May of 1974, I applied for a job at the boys' school. I joined a lot of other kids to serve at a large catered event. After the flurry of the two-day event, I was given no further assignment. So, at Mom's insistence I went back and asked about a schedule for more work. I was offered a position serving in the priests' kitchen.

It was in the priests' kitchen that I was challenged by Father George. One day while pouring coffee, I spilled some on the table. "It's sure hard to find good help," he harumphed to the priest sitting next to him. I retreated to the kitchen to cry. Rather than writing him off, I internalized his comment as proof that I was defective. I wiped my tears and returned to the table to wipe up the spill.

For a while, I was still taking low doses of medication and I remained depressed. I still wanted to end it all. Having learned that aspirin was not the most effective choice for such a final solution, I bought a bottle of sleeping pills. With sleeping pills, I would fall asleep and be unable to change my mind. I stuffed the pills in a drawer of the desk in my room.

One morning while I was still in bed, Dad, ready to leave for school, walked in and glanced hurriedly about my room. He appeared to be looking for something. He didn't say anything, but I thought that he may have sensed the sleeping pills. He was worried and knew I was depressed. He left, and I decided that the sleeping pill idea would be devastating to him. I was sorry that I had already caused him so much trouble and anguish. I took the pills to school with me and tossed them into a trash can.

In June, I took a class in sociology at school as well as a class in music history from Palmer Junior College. I also continued serving meals in the priests' kitchen. That fall, I began taking piano lessons as well as classes in German, psychology, sociology, music history and philosophy.

In addition to Valerie and Michelle, I was also friends with Michelle's brother Kenneth, who was now also taking college classes. Ken had dreams of going to Hollywood and making it big as a movie star. Ken was tall, dark, handsome, and goofy. One day I picked him up after school.

"How do I look?" he asked.

"Good, Ken. You always look good."

"Do you like my shirt?"

"Hey, yeah. Blue's a good color on you."

"I know." As we drove around town, he scanned our surroundings. "Slow down, slow down," he directed.

I started to brake.

"Pull over," he said.

I pulled to the side of the street.

He rolled down his window and shouted "Hello, Bessie!" to an elderly woman in her yard. We were far enough away that the lady only knew that someone had yelled and waved. Bessie waved back as Ken contorted into fits of laughter. In a few blocks we repeated the routine, only this time Ken shouted at Henry. "Hello, Henry!" This scenario unfolded nearly every time we were together in a car. Ken was a tonic, the silly brother I never had.

We stopped at McDonald's. Ken ordered a fish sandwich. He was Jewish, and his family kept kosher. He and his sister, Michelle, allowed themselves fish sandwiches at McDonald's and onion pizzas at Pizza Hut.

"What are you doing next year?" I asked.

"I guess I'll go to college in town for a while before I head for Hollywood."

"Oh, Ken. Yeah right!"

"No, I'm serious."

"OK. I believe you."

"You just wait and see."

I met a super nice guy named Philip on campus, and we began dating. He lived just down the hall from a kindly priest. Philip took care of me. He was big and like a teddy bear. I felt very safe with him. As a gift, he bought me some basketball shoes. We regularly ate lunch together.

In the spring, we rode in a van with a group to enjoy Six Flags over St. Louis. One day he asked if he could kiss me. It was nothing monumental. I wasn't knocked off my feet with boundless passion for Phil, but he was truly kind. Eventually, I tried to ease out of the relationship. I wrote in my journal around this time:

> Philip's world is far different from mine. His is made up of things you can see, feel, smell, and eat. I want my life to be more than that. If I cannot get new ideas daily, I'll grow stagnant. I will be smothered.

After about six months, feeling just slightly bored, Philip and I broke up. I recorded my feelings in the time leading up to this in my journal:

> Right now, I am trying to let go of Philip (gently), and it is not easy. As Mom says, he is a kind person, and I do not want to hurt him—ever. But he doesn't take hints very well.
>
> One day when he came to see me, I purposely left curlers in my hair. He told me I looked cute. I am attempting to be unattractive and as cold as possible yet be civil. Then I see the hurt in his eyes,

and I hurt for him and seem to go in the opposite direction.

I am truly at a loss. I will have to trust God to work things out as they are meant to be. I guess that just as it takes time to begin a relationship, it also takes time to end one.

That year, we spent part of Christmas week in Nebraska with my dad's mother Clara, Grandpa, aunts, uncles and several of my cousins. That particular day, my Grandma Myrtle and Mom came for dinner at Grandma Clara's also. Two days later when we were back at Grandma Myrtle's farm, Dad got a call that his mother had a heart attack. He left immediately and was able to be with her when she died a few hours later at only 74 years of age.

We attended the funeral and drove in a procession several miles from the funeral home to the graveyard in Dad's hometown. I was touched by the kindness and respect coming from Nebraska people. As we drove the twenty miles, there were occasional men or women stopped and standing beside their cars, hands over their hearts alongside the road despite the December weather. They were paying their respects. My family and I spent time with Dad's siblings and most of my many cousins that I wished I could know better.

Back at school sometime in early 1975, I had my last manic episode. I started to "see" my cousins in other kids on campus. In my loneliness, I began once again to fabricate a fantasy world. Fortunately, my delusions never became full blown. This time they were held in check, by my familiar surroundings, my light schedule, and the fact that I was living with my parents. I found this recorded in my journal from that time:

This morning, Mom said to Dad, "Claire's eyes are back with us." And that's just the way I feel, like I've been away. Not really alive—just existing but not really living and feeling. God, I hope I can stay!

My journal also indicates that Dr. Gould, my psychiatrist, was adjusting my medication according to what I reported at each visit. I remember feeling disappointed that we never really talked about things above a superficial level.

I stewed about love and my life. I thought back to Mark and my original breakdown. What had I done to mess up my life? What could I do differently? In another passage from my journal, I reflected that my problem began when my imagination began to run beyond a mere boy-girl, high school relationship and into marriage and the great things we would do for each other and the world. Reason gave way to fantasy, and I began living in my dreams, which explained the delusions, euphoria, sleeplessness, loss of appetite, and so on. I lost control of my imagination. In my delusional fantasies, every hope and desire were fulfilled, and all parts of my life turned out with the happy endings that I wanted.

That is why I had to learn to accept things as they are at face value. I didn't want to allow my mind to wander beyond the here and now. That is not saying that I should expect the worst from any given relationship or situation. Rather, I wanted to accept reality and not project possibilities (good or bad) into my future.

By fall, I had found a new job at a smorgasbord in the salad department. Mr. Becher hired me and directed me to Phyllis, who ran the salad bar during the day. Phyllis introduced me to my assorted responsibilities. I got a tour of the dark walk-in refrigerator which housed large tubs of a variety of salads. I would learn how to run the potato peeler. A considerable part of my time would be spent standing at a sink, washing, and peeling various vegetables. Phyllis showed me the stash of recipes for salads like coleslaw, potato salad, bean salad and fruit fluff salad. She lastly showed me what my final task would be each day—breaking up the ice that surrounded the salads on the salad bar. That job required a huge butcher knife, muscle, and some chiseling expertise. At first, I worked alongside Phyllis, but soon I was moved to the second shift. I came to dread the last task of every work day.

While cleaning vegetables, some of the young guys came and told me their troubles. One fifteen-year-old especially confided in me. Paul was adorable. He was so cute but was miserable about his home life. He lived with his mom and stepfather, but I could tell that he missed his dad and felt the loss deeply. I commiserated with him and worried. Scott, one of the cooks, would stand and sing ballads to me. He sang like a crooner. He was a bit of a mystery. At first, I thought he didn't like me, but as I got to know him, I realized he was just moody. Philip had been so predictable that I got bored. Scott, though, said things that surprised me and helped me look at life from a different angle. Yet, I was cautious. I wrote a poem about my feelings:

Don't Ask Me Why

Don't ask me why I shy away; I'm not sure myself.
It's not that I don't long to know you better.
It's that I can't.
Not again can I face the fallen hopes, untamed fears, and childish doubts.
Not again can I stand the brief, joyful ecstasy of someone real.
Not again can I endure the bitter, tearful, unbelievable emptiness—
Left by one I loved.
So come no closer unless you wish to stay.
It's my own illogical solemnity that blocks entrance.
But this fence need not be torn away.
Fire isn't necessary.
The little gate of love will let you in,
And I will meet you there if you come with a cloak of candor.
But if your garment be only of frivolity and fun,
Pass by my gate and find another.

At the staff Christmas party, Scott and I sat at the piano together. I played, and he sang. I really liked Scott, but he had a girlfriend. A couple of weeks after Christmas, Scott found a different job. I was disappointed. I had enjoyed the friendly banter we exchanged at work. I wanted to find and marry someone that I could tease, joke, and laugh with. That is what I missed when Scott left. I got some give and take with some of the other guys, but it was not the same. Scott looked at situations quite differently than I did, and I liked getting his perspective. He created a balance for some of my ideas.

I continued to meet with Dr. Gould, who had me back to taking Elavil, an antidepressant, and Trilafon, an antipsychotic. The doses I was taking were lower than what I had been taking while at EIU. Although Trilafon was often prescribed for schizophrenia, Dr. Gould had not labeled me as schizophrenic. She admitted to Mom and me that she did not understand schizophrenia. Rather, she suggested that I was manic-depressive or merely a person who will need help during trying periods of life. In other words, she seemed to feel that a label was not necessary.

In later spring 1975, I wrote this to Dr. Gould and took it to an appointment with her and Mom. Both Mom and I wrote a note to Dr. Gould:

> Me: At this point, I'm feeling angry and upset. I am tired and sick of this whole ordeal, and I absolutely do not want to go through a fall of '73 or a March of '74 again. What can be done? We keep talking about noticing the danger signals. How come noticing them does not seem to work?
>
> I am OK now, but I feel ever at the exploding point. In other words, I want some help. Trilafon, as far as I am concerned, is a pain in the neck. (I want to be honest.) Is there another type of drug that would be better? Also, what exactly are the differences between Elavil and Trilafon?"

Mom:

> With Elavil, frustration seems to come up. She also
> has more of an alive feeling when awake and is
> sleepier at night. She feels like she is withdrawing
> from people to some extent while on Trilafon. She'd
> rather sleep than engage with others. Would night
> and morning Elavil and 8 mgs of Trilafon keep this
> balanced? Or is that too much drug?

I did not record what the decision was concerning the medication,
but I know that with the backing of Mom and Dad, I did eventually
stop taking Elavil and Trilafon. I do not remember whether Dr.
Gould was part of that decision. For most of my early adult life I
did not take any kind of psychotropic medication

I wrote in my journal, "At this point I would like some answers
from Dr. Gould. If I must endure another mania or depression, I
know that I can say 'Who cares?' and 'Delusions live on!'"

At work, I met and eventually began dating a younger dishwasher
named Vincent. He was a cute kid with a curly lip and a squeaky
voice. He took me out to eat and to movies. He was still in high
school, and I demanded too much from him. After we had known
each other for a while, we would go on a date and end up making
out in the front seat of his car. My folks did not think he was good
for me and did nothing to encourage our connection. Early in our
relationship, I wrote this about him:

> Let me just say that I like Vincent quite well. I
> cannot really say I love him because I'm not sure
> what love is. I know that what I feel for him is not
> overwhelming and that I do love his mind—so our
> relationship is not at all only physical. I like the way
> he talks, thinks, acts, and laughs, and yet I cannot
> pinpoint the reason I am unsure about the love

aspect. I guess it might be because he thinks as I do quite a bit. I do not know. I cannot analyze it all.

One day I told Vince about my past experiences with mania and depression. He wrote me a sweet letter expressing his care for me and what a tragic loss it would have been had I been successful in killing myself. His response was better than I might have hoped for. He thanked me for telling him and said it made him cry.

> Claire,
>
> I am glad you told me about your disaster and hospitalization. I just thank God you were saved … When I think of how you are now, I am filled with joy. Ever since I met you, I have thought you were an extraordinary person. You have always demonstrated feelings of compassion and love and great interest in other people. Now, to know what personal pain and anguish you have gone through and to see the beautiful person you are, my admiration and love for you abounds. When I think of how lucky I am to know you, I feel so happy I could bust. When I found out you wrote a poem for me, I really felt like someone. Although not poetic, this is my way of telling you that you are someone to me.

It became a practice of mine to get to know someone, size them up, and decide whether or not to share my previous mental problems. It served me in getting to know a person—to determine whether they were safe to tell other personal matters. I found people to be kinder and safer in my young life than later on.

One evening, Vince showed up at my front door, guitar in hand. He had been working on songs he could play for me. He loved Jim

Croce and learned some of his songs so he could sing them. We sat on the deck in the backyard.

"This is how I feel about you," he began and with some faltering, he began to sing. "If I could save time in a bottle, the first thing that I'd like to do is to save everyday till eternity passes away, just to spend them with you ..."

I tried to sing along. Vince strummed through as best he could.

"That's really nice," I said weakly. Vince may have been thinking in terms of forever, but I wasn't really sold on the eternity idea. I was rolling my eyes in my mind. It seemed so confining, and I felt a bit squeamish at the thought.

"What else are you working on?"

"Oh," his shoulders sagged. "Do you like John Denver?"

"Yes, very much!"

"I'm working on 'Take Me Home, Country Roads,' but I'm not ready to play it yet."

"That's OK. I can wait."

After Christmas, Mr. Becher fired me. On one of the few times, I went into his office, I noticed he was wearing a bra beneath his long-sleeved white shirt. Some of my coworkers had also noticed that he was starting to wear mascara and lipstick. Mr. Becher had a wife and daughters. I thought maybe he was envious from watching them apply make-up and do other girly things. There was an intercom system between the break room and his office, and I later wondered if he hadn't heard my voice among the other kids discussing his unusual behavior. Maybe that was why he fired me. Losing that job was not overly distressing. I certainly did not miss breaking up the iceberg in the salad bar each night. After I left, Vince continued working there but also found another job at the mall so he could afford to keep taking me out to eat and to the movies.

Vince took everything we did so seriously. The fact that my parents did not like our affiliation probably only prolonged it. I just wanted them to be kind to him. They kept acting like they could not wait for me to be done with him. The reality was that Vince was too young for me and too young for what he was attempting to do. Worse, I was using him up. I didn't stop to consider how much pressure he felt in trying to measure up to my expectations. At that point I couldn't really analyze our interactions. I could have used a trusted older advisor, but neither of my parents seemed to have the time to invest in the intricacies of my life.

So, I used him. At first it was mildly amusing. It was nice to have someone always taking my picture and taking me out to eat and to movies. We went to so many movies that summer that Vince really needed that second job. Because his mother sometimes needed the car, she drove us places for our dates. She was patient, but I did catch the absurdity of it all, not to mention the embarrassment.

Vince and I were both rather moody and thin skinned. He had taken up photography, but after the initial novelty, I didn't really enjoy being constantly photographed. One day at my house, I beat him at Scrabble, and he left in a huff. By September, I had written him a letter:

Dear Vince,

My heart is truly broken, and I hurt and ache inside. For the past few months, I have felt mostly misery. It just seems that we can't be happy together. When for some reason we cannot be together, you curse and swear. It truly hurts my feelings, and I feel rotten for the rest of the evening. I can't even concentrate on my schoolwork, which is the thing that keeps us apart.

Isn't love supposed to be happy and forgiving and understanding? If it is, we have missed the boat. We used to be so happy together. What has happened?

Vince, I have never asked this of you before, but would you pray about it? I know Jesus loves you and me, and He will help us if only we ask Him. Please do, Vince. I still love you, and I want things to get better. We can be happy. I know it.

With love,
Claire

The end was near after Vince accompanied me to a high school dance that my sister Megan was legitimately attending as an actual high school student. Revisiting high school did not work. It failed to make up for the little bit of dating I had done in my senior year. I felt ashamed to show up at high school two years too late. I became increasingly disillusioned and began to agree with my folks that Vince wasn't "the one" I was looking for. I began to tell him that it just wasn't working. If anything, he was too young, and we were at different stages of development.

One day I found a single rose and a note of apology on my car parked near school. He appeared just as I was plucking the rose from the door. We had a dramatic scene right there on the sidewalk near Sister Janet's residence.

"Vincent!" I cried, dropping my books. "This is it! It's over."

"I didn't say it's over," he wailed, as he scrambled to pick up my books.

I felt for him. I really did. I knew I too, would have been really upset if I had been in his position. I stacked my books, thanked him for the rose, and headed for my Introduction to Social Work class. I took the rose with me. As sweet as his gesture may have been, it was over. I knew it had to be.

I felt sad for him and wrote several fretful letters expressing my concern. Poor Vince! He did not handle the breakup well. One day he came over when I was the only one at home and nearly broke down the door from the garage to the house with his loud banging. Another day, he slammed his hand on the brick wall right behind my head. He scared me. I certainly did not care for that reaction.

And so, we were on our own, letting go of the hopes that love would materialize. I hoped and prayed that I wouldn't forget the sunny feeling. I knew how likely it was that I could forget because life is so terribly hard. Just when you think the prize is nearly yours, it fades from view, and a black, dark cloud that obliterates the sun moves in again to stay—day after never ending day. And you give into its oppression, its gloom, its promise of nothing, because giving up is safer than hope and easier than trying to maintain a happy face. Sleeping for hours on end may be wasting daylight and violating several Proverbs that warn against sloth. It may also disappoint God, who expects you to be more productive to prove that your love for Him and others is real. And so, you sleep and wait and sigh, hoping that He'll find you, wake you up, and care enough to send His very best—a heavenly prince charming.

In looking back through the years, I realized I was being unfair to Vince. I had viewed our relationship as an experiment and deep down had not felt the connection and attraction that I had wished to feel with someone I planned to marry. The age difference was one thing, but the temperament clash was another. Somehow, I knew I needed someone who was older, more stable, and more easygoing than Vince.

Although I felt the lack of any kind of mentor and wondered how I could survive spiritually, I did return to my childhood Methodist church. While in Maple Crest, Mary Atkinson had given me two books, *Abide in Christ* by Andrew Murray, and a devotional called, *Hinds' Feet on High Places* by Hannah Hurnard. I faithfully read a chapter from Murray's classic each night before shutting out the light to go to sleep. Although the words were rather dull and repetitive, I found them comforting and calming.

I continued in classes and soon was settled into a place of security at church. I loved the large Sunday school rooms, which brought back memories of classes and vacation Bible school. I also loved the sanctuary—especially the sanctuary! The way the pews were set in a semicircle, how the dark, polished wood smelled, the deep red carpet in the aisles, and the velvety curtains in the chancel area. I loved sitting in a pew about five rows back from the front where I had sat with my parents as a kid. From there, I looked up at the ceiling, the two-story curve around the choir area, and the magnificent stained-glass windows.

When I was in third grade, I began to enjoy the sermons, listening and watching as my mother scratched notes on her bulletin. Dad often served as an usher and would slip into the pew beside us during the sermon. We sang "O For a Thousand Tongues" and "A Mighty Fortress" and repeated prayers printed in our bulletins.

When I had returned to church after my fall from a "normal" life, I was invited and encouraged to attend a young people's Sunday school class called Pairs and Spares led by a lady who knew my parents. I was one of the only "spares" in the class, but I joined in with the reading and discussion. On Sundays, after that class dismissed, I had enough time to find my way to the choir room to warm up with the chancel choir before the second service. My former favorite teacher, Mr. McKenzie, was a tenor in the choir. I didn't mind being near him on Thursday evenings either when we'd practice the inspiring four-part harmony music in preparation for the upcoming Sunday.

To replace the smorgasbord job, I got a job at Pizza Hut. It was the easiest job I'd had so far. The hardest part was staying up until 2:00 AM on Saturday nights to vacuum the red shag, carpet. I learned how to run a cash register and count back change. I took orders, served up salad, soft drinks and beer. I carried piping hot pizza and pasta dishes to waiting customers. Best of all I received tips!

I went to classes in the mornings, still on track to major in social work. For one class I wrote a paper entitled "Social Welfare and the Great Depression." I got an A on the paper and the professor asked if she could have a copy. For my U.S. history class, I wrote an A- paper on Herbert Hoover. As a result of the research for those papers, I began to experience empathy for scapegoats and unsung heroes. The more I read about Herbert Hoover the more saddened I became that such a brilliant and charitable man was forced into the position of scapegoat for the Great Depression.

Every day, I drove home for lunch. I'd make myself a sandwich, sit in the family room and watch a rerun of Brian Keith and Sebastian Cabot in "Family Affair." Sometimes I'd go back to school for an afternoon class. If I wasn't in class, I used those afternoons to cook.

Mom had taught me basic things like how to make meatloaf, scalloped potatoes and various forms of jello. I came to believe that anyone who could read could cook. I soon learned how to make lasagna. In high school we had a yearly potluck attended by the kids who were learning foreign languages. Through that period, I learned how to make crème puffs. Somewhere along the way I had obtained both a German and French cookbook. I learned to make German stew, French salads, and apple strudel. I experimented with new dishes and my family didn't seem to mind being the taste testers for my concoctions. I didn't know yet that my motivation to create new dishes would accelerate and be helpful to me in the coming summer.

On April 30th I went out with Ken, Michelle and Michelle's boyfriend of the hour—not Franklin. Ken was so nice and responsive—not too moody. I half-way wished that Ken weren't Jewish. But I decided that if he were available, we wouldn't be such good friends.

He was sensitive just like me—too easily hurt. So, we seemed to understand each other. He was protective of me, like I thought a brother might be. I guessed that's just what I wanted with him – a brother-sister relationship. I was happy with it that way.

Chapter 14

Bill Lieber

At the end of that spring semester, I met my future husband. One evening while I visited a local discotheque with Michelle and Valerie, Michelle met a guy named Larry who wanted to take her on a date. Wisely, she said she didn't want go out alone with Larry, but she would go on a double date with him. He said he'd bring the extra guy if she would bring me. Larry chose his friend, Bill Lieber for the big event.

A few days later, Larry, Michelle, and Bill pulled up in front of our house. I met Bill for the first time at the front door of my parent's house. He had light, reddish-brown, wavy hair and smelled good. I liked what stood before me. After introductions, we went out to Larry's car. Bill and I decided to sit in the back. When faced with a malfunctioning seat belt, I insisted we share the working one.

That night the four of us ate at the Gay Nineties, located near the Arsenal Bridge. I learned that Bill had a good job as an engineering analyst at John Deere Plow Planter in Moline. Larry, who was about six inches taller than Bill, told us that once when he was drunk, Bill had the audacity to kick Larry out of his own apartment! Despite that story, I liked Bill right away. After we ate, we all went to see *The Duchess and the Dirtwater Fox* starring Goldie Hawn and George Segal. After I arrived safely at home, Bill, who was working third shift, reported to work.

I savored the good time I had that night. I hoped that Bill would soon call asking for a date. I fretted when it took him four days to call me back. I wasn't tuned into the limits that third shift places on one's social life. I don't remember the second date, but we began getting to know each other.

By May 24th, I had this to say about Bill.
From my journal:

I am going out with the nicest person and I can't believe it. Bill is a sensitive, good-looking guy with a neat sense of humor. I'm just lucky enough to share the pleasure of his company on occasion.

When I first met you, the earth didn't move,
Stars didn't fall from the sky,
Nor did birds sing
Yet, I was captivated and knew you were special
And now as I know you I love you so much I ache
A pleasant ache, but an ache just the same.

Darn it! I love you. Wouldn't life be less complex if I didn't?
No 5:31 am phone calls…
But I do and I'm willingly stuck,
Tangled by your charms
And somehow how as the bits of our love unfold,
I'm held fascinated by each new crease, new line.
And for all the world I'd not change the complexity of this
Thing called love. I'm willingly trapped.

Part of the process of getting to know each other, included going to church together. I went with Bill to visit his Independent Baptist church. The pastor was from the south and spoke with an accent. Bill was in a young people's group, and I had hoped I would love it and fit in right away. That didn't happen. It wasn't the music; I liked some of the words and lilting melodies of the Baptist hymns. It was not a lack of devotion on the part of the congregation either. Nor was it Bill's family, who seemed nice enough. It was the pastor and his associate. One summer Sunday evening, I was sitting next to Bill in a section of young people. I had just slipped off my shoes when the associate pastor stood in the pulpit.

"Sit up straight! Put on your shoes," he barked. He then proceeded to lecture us on the proper behavior of Christian young people. By that time, I was already beginning to mentally check out of the church. Bill's grandma Elsie later confirmed my discomfort by expressing her own displeasure at attending that church when she was in town. She said she did not like to be yelled at. Well, neither did I!

I attended on Wednesday nights, when we would sit on the same pew with his parents. They all seemed to be waiting for me to walk down the aisle so that I could be properly saved and baptized right up there in front of everyone—dripping wet like all good Christians, who had to be baptized just the way Jesus was. I just could not do it. I had already asked Jesus into my heart to be my Savior. I was never given the opportunity to express my feelings, and I had great fear that if I did, a deafening silence or gasps might follow my words. It just was not done in those days; honesty was not very popular. No one dared express genuine feelings when the truth was already so well known. Jesus was the way. You could not argue with truth and God-given authority. It simply wasn't done.

At that time, governmental authority reigned supreme. This was more than my imagination. There were nationwide protests made by young men old enough to be drafted into the Vietnam War. Young men unlucky enough to have their birthdates drawn in the national draft lottery were headed to war. Many young women reluctantly said goodbye to boyfriends and husbands who were soon gobbled up by the war machine. Bill had turned eighteen in 1972 and was given a number that all men born on his birthday shared. By the time we met in 1975, the threat was over. Bill's number had not been picked, and he was safe.

But the times had not changed much. Rejecting authority, no matter how rotten, was simply not acceptable. Helplessly hating war and hating the cruelty inflicted by the one in charge was just the way it was. Sadly, those of us who hated war and the governmental authority were in danger of becoming the very thing we judged. Change was in the air, but societal change seems to move at glacial speed, too slowly to be felt by those who are suffering the most from the current way of life.

Despite my less-than-ideal experiences at Bill's church, I liked Bill a lot. He was adorable, good natured, and able to make me laugh with his corny humor. Of the few times I had "fallen in love," this time with Bill was the least giddy, the most peaceful. On nights when we couldn't get together, we spent at least an hour on the phone. I talked a lot and found acceptance and a willing listener. Bill had a calming effect on me. For perhaps the first time in my life, I felt that someone really heard me.

When we rode around in his brown AMC hornet, we listened to a rock music station on the radio. I was more of a WOC "Pure Gold Music" kind of girl. But I listened to his music and developed a taste for it.

Bill was in a Bible study group of young adults. One time Bill and I went out to eat with another couple from his church. As we waited for our food, I asked Bill for some money to stick into the juke box. He gave me a dirty look. I didn't understand, but later realized he didn't want his church friends to know that he listened to anything besides gospel music.

In spite of my ongoing contributions to supper, my life at home with my parents was rather tense. Maybe they were sad that I was still at home. At times, I felt guilty for taking up space. I got tired of trying to be a referee of their arguments.

I knew from past experience what loud, accusatory bickering could do to the kids. For one thing, it made me feel sick to my stomach. I was twenty-one and still their arguing had that effect on me. I felt that if they wanted to fight they should go off by themselves. It wasn't common in those days for couples to seek marriage counseling. Fortunately, now, counseling of all kinds is available.

It seemed especially that Mom and I could not get along, so I avoided her as much as possible. Mom could be extremely critical, and in the stress of raising two other daughters and teaching full time, she often unloaded critical remarks onto me in passing. While in my creative writing class at college, I wrote a poem that described my unspoken response to her unwanted observations:

Your Little Men Are in There

You see you can't convince me
With your boneless logic.
Another tactic is required, so
You've sent out your legions,
And your little men are in there,
Digging at my heart.
Relentlessly picking and scraping,
Tiny buckets of red at their feet,
I hear them snickering as they toil.
Please—whatever you say!
Just tell them to leave and
Take their shovels with them.

Bill worked while I studied and engaged with others at school. I loved the nuns and various classes. It was in my Introduction to Social Work class that I began to question my decision to major in that subject. A visiting professional talked about the burnout she had experienced while serving as a caseworker on child abuse cases. A visit to a social welfare office downtown confirmed my doubts; it was loud, overcrowded, and filled with sad, overwhelmed people. So, I began reviewing my options. English was my strongest subject, and I had observed my parents' careers in teaching every day while growing up. Without regret, I shifted to a degree in English secondary education.

For the English aspect of the degree, I took a Shakespeare class, several literature classes and creative writing. I got to know two nuns in the English department- a younger nun, Sister Francisca, who had short, reddish-brown hair and the older Sister Janet. I don't remember Sister Janet's hair. I never caught even a glimpse of it because she still wore a habit. Because she was younger, I asked Sister Francisca to be my advisor. However, Sister Janet also played a significant role in my young life. At a time when I was extremely needy, unsure and wobbly, Sister Janet was a steady, comforting presence. With her warbly voice and her kind, reassuring comments, I was slightly bemused but mostly reassured.

In the Shakespeare class, on Mondays, Sister Janet introduced a play. Our job was to read one of the plays like *Othello, Hamlet, Twelfth Night* or *Romeo and Juliet* and come back to class on Wednesday ready to discuss it. On Tuesdays I always went to the library to checkout an LP record so I could listen to actors speaking the lines. As I listened to words of antiquated English, the inflections of the players voices helped me tremendously in understanding the dialogue. Fridays were test days. The test was made of essay questions. It was easy to memorize a few lines from the play and receive extra credit on my exam by incorporating the lines into one of my answers on the test. I was thrilled to receive an A in that class.

Sister Francesca taught several subjects including an American Literature class. The one I most remember was a World Religions Class, where we studied not only Christianity and Judaism, but also Hinduism, Buddhism, and Taoism among others. I came to learn that belief in reincarnation is central to both Taoism and Buddhism. I personally unequivocally hated the idea of reincarnation. The idea of coming back into this world with all its problems and difficulties carried no appeal for me. In the ninth chapter of book of Hebrews we are told "it is appointed for men to die once and after this comes judgment."

In a secondary education class, I enjoyed the class where we learned how to make lesson plans. I loved picking out a poem, or short story, creating discussion questions and finding music and pictures to enhance the lesson. As I recall, one of the poems I chose was by Lawrence Ferlinghetti. I had first learned about Ferlinghetti from a book my mother owned called *Reflections on a Gift of Watermelon Pickle*. I don't remember the name of the poem but from that point on Ferlinghetti was a preferred poet of mine.

My favorite English class was Creative Writing. In my writing class at IUE I had learned to read my works out loud in order to catch mistakes. In this class I learned to love criticism. For the first half of the semester, we were instructed to bring enough copies of a poem so the whole class could critique our work. The very first poem I shared was a poem about the demise of my relationship with Vincent. The professor mocked my overly dramatic line about our love being "smashed and smattered." He was right. I took note and I learned.

He taught us to be precise and sparing. Words didn't have to rhyme. In the class as we shared our works, we were allowed to critique our fellow poets. We shared what we liked and what didn't work for us and why. I learned to dish it out and accept what others said. I didn't always agree, but I listened and my poetry got better as a result. The instructor asked us to grade ourselves at the end of the semester. I gave myself an A-. I knew I had written some good stuff. Words didn't have to rhyme. Yet, one of my favorite poets is Walt Whitman who wrote two poems about his sorrow after Abraham Lincoln died.

On Thanksgiving day that year, I knew I had a lot to be thankful for. Bill and I were each having Thanksgiving with our separate families. I had trouble sleeping and I was feeling the need to talk with someone so badly. All I had was the paper from my journal so I ended up talking to a piece of paper. I acknowledged to my paper that I had a lot to be thankful for.

That year I was happy about almost everything in my life except for a few minor irritations like zits and petty girlfriends. I enjoyed the choir at church immensely but I really missed Bill. Talking to him on the phone just wasn't the same as being with him. When I was away from him for long periods of time, it was like being with a stranger when I finally did get to see him.

I had so much energy, that I didn't know what to do with it. I drank a lot of water and noted that it interfered with my ability to sleep peacefully at night. I missed my Grandma Myrtle and Uncle Herbert. I also worried that I used the word "I" too much.

Before Christmas it bothered me, that it seemed like a sin to have children. There was so much emphasis placed on finding yourself— finding a career and finding what you were meant to do. Couldn't having children be part of what one was meant to do? I knew the world could be cruel…maybe so cruel that it was unkind to have children.

All that I knew was that it was essential for me to be around people who also knew Jesus as their Savior. I was weak and a sinner. My strength was not in myself but in my God and Redeemer. In the troubled times He was my only true Rock. He was the only constant part of my life. He was the only existing being that is constant in love, wisdom, strength and virtue.

Around that time, I wrote this in my journal from the winter of 1976:

> Bill is a comfort to me. I'm a serious person, and
> he is rather lighthearted. I tend to take myself and
> everyone else too seriously. When I'm around Bill,
> he makes me realize with a joke or a mocking tone
> of voice that something I take earnestly is nowhere
> near a life-and-death matter. That's all good.

I love life, and yet it scares me sometimes. I guess what worries me most is my lack of self-confidence. I need to be bolder, more ready to say, "Who cares?" and move on without regarding what people think.

Sunday—a good day, though cold. It was below zero all day. We had church in the fellowship hall today because it was only fifty degrees in the sanctuary. That was fun. I spent the rest of the day with Bill. He cut my hair and did an amazingly good job. I was pleasantly surprised.

A few weeks ago, he asked me never to leave him. It was tender to me because he admitted his vulnerability and need. Those few words meant a lot. I never want to hurt Bill or ever leave him. I pray that we can be together and know each other for a long time. I hope that is not too much to ask.

In May, on my twenty-second birthday, Bill took me to the park where Dad had managed the pool just a few years before. On a hillside, under a tree Bill asked me to marry him. He produced a black-and-silver ring so modest that people would remark on how small it was. I didn't care. I told myself that I wanted a frugal man. My father was cautious about money. That trait seemed to serve him well. I would have preferred a gold ring, but I didn't say anything because I was so struck by the fact that he pulled the ring out and got on one knee just like in fairy tales. We began to plan for a December wedding right after Christmas. It would be easier for my Nebraska relatives to come at that time since there were fewer chores to attend to on a farm in the winter.

Only my mother wasn't pleased with the date. It was hard for her to squeeze a wedding into the brief time she had off between semesters at school. She usually counted on that time to rest and get ready for the second semester. I, on the other hand, wanted to get married as quickly as possible because it was difficult to wait so long to legitimately have sex. I felt guilty because we were already violating my moral code. I felt caught in a double bind.

One Saturday when we had gotten back to my house after a date, Mom brought up a touchy subject. She came into the living room and wanted to know if Bill knew what he was getting into by marrying me.

"Do you know about the breakdowns Claire had?" she asked.

My heart caught in my throat.

"It took her a long time to recover from the depression she went through when she was at EIU. It was hard on all of us. At the hospital, they told us that she probably should never get married or have kids. She would need to find a low stress job and most likely live at home with us."

I groaned inwardly. Is that what she wanted? She wanted me to stay home and make meals for her?

Bill sat down not saying much.

"Mom, I'm going to be fine. The past is past, and I've already told Bill most of this." I felt shredded—depleted of whatever joyous thoughts I had been harboring.

Mom seemed a little frantic, like she was just doing her duty in warning him of how I might be. "Well, I just want to make sure Bill knows. Life can be awfully hard. You have been doing well enough, but you never know what might set you off."

"Oh, Mom."

Bill said, "I'm sure we'll be fine."

Mom's sudden sharing of her concerns made me nervous. What if Bill backed off? Where would I go? What would I do? I needed him. Bill was not perfect, but then neither was I. I was damaged goods, and I could not allow myself to think about things concerning him that did not quite line up with my ideals. To spend the rest of my life with my parents was unthinkable. I was still in a fairy tale stage, and therefore Bill simply had to be my prince charming. Getting married was like magic. It was the step that preceded living happily ever after. Wasn't it?

In late August, we took a quick trip to Nebraska so that Bill could meet my still living grandparents. On the first day, we spent nine hours on the road to make it to Grandpa's by early evening. There we found my dad's dad, Grandpa Samuel, who lived alone in an old, two-story house. When we pulled up, Dad's little sister Jeanie walked from her house down the street to greet us. I introduced Bill to my aunt just as Grandpa emerged from the house.

"Hi, Grandpa!" I called out and ran up to him for a hug.

"Hello, Claire," Aunt Jeanie said, giving me a squeeze. "This must be Bill," she reached out to shake Bill's hand. "How was your trip?"

"Too long," I moaned.

"Well, let me give you a tour. Do you want to bring your bags?" Aunt Jeanie asked, heading for the front door.

Grandpa's living room wasn't remarkable. As we passed through Jeanie said, "Follow me. I'll show you the bedrooms."

We passed through a narrow doorway and climbed a winding staircase. At the top Jeanie said, "There's this bedroom" We looked into a small bedroom with one small bed. "or there's this room."

She pointed toward another small room and a bed. "It's up to you where you sleep." No mention was made of an unspoken moral code or a suggestion that, of course, we would sleep in separate rooms.

'Wow! It's hot up here," I said. "Do you have a fan we could use?"

"It will be fine," Bill said.

"I'm afraid we don't, dear. The windows are open, and as Dad used to say, if you lie really still, you can get to sleep." She chuckled, and we laughed nervously with her. "There are clean towels in the bathroom if you need to take a shower."

And so that night, after going to bed in the second bedroom, I sneaked into Bill's room, and we did what good Christian young people are not supposed to do: we slept together and used a condom.

I knew it was wrong, but in defiance of God's law and our parents, we had sex anyway. At the time, I was not sure what to do with the desires that conflicted with my faith.

The next morning, we stopped at Auntie Evelyn's ranch. Evelyn was Dad's oldest sister. We visited her lake and took a ride in her paddle boat. For lunch she made both of us a large cheeseburger. Although she didn't offer a salad, the burger was delicious and no doubt directly from their herd of cattle.

Our next stop would be Grandma Myrtle's farm in northeast Nebraska. Grandpa had died a couple of years before. So, Grandma lived in a six-bedroom farmhouse with my mother's oldest brother, Herbert. Herbert cultivated the 160-acre farm and presided over cattle, hogs, kittens, and dogs. When we pulled in, Smokey, a collie rushed out to inspect our unfamiliar car. Smokey's barking had alerted Grandma of our arrival. She walked out to greet us. It was comforting to see her familiar face and give her a big hug.

Carrying our bags, we entered her house through the kitchen door. The aroma of fried chicken, and the familiar kitchen comforted me. In addition to chicken, Grandma had prepared green beans, mashed potatoes and her Watergate salad—a fluff made from green Jello and pineapple. It was all delicious. For dessert, Uncle Herbert got a gallon bucket of ice milk out of the pantry freezer. It was all delicious and I took it for granted. Grandma was simply doing what grandmothers do. After supper, I helped clear the table as Grandma poured Palmolive dish soap to create warm sudsy water in the sink. I grabbed a dish towel and happily dried dishes as Grandma and I chatted.

Before sundown, Grandma and Uncle Herbert accompanied us to the yard. Above us was a line of very tall Cottonwood trees. Near the trees sat Uncle Herbert's Bobcat Skid Loader and 1955 Farmall Cub tractor. Bill admired and talked with Herbert about his equipment. My uncle and grandma heartily approved of Bill who knew about farm implements because he worked at John Deere.

We meandered down to the barn to check out the cows and the nearby pig barn. Then Bill and I walked to the side of the house so I could show him what Grandma called the grove. We walked into the woods, that consisted mostly of box elder trees—an enchanting place that reminded me of childhood days where Megan, Annie and I could play and pretend.

As it got dark, we moved inside to the dining room that also served as a tv room. There we talked of our trip across Iowa and half of Nebraska to Grandpa's house. Grandma asked about our wedding plans for the big day, just three months away. We watched the local news at 10:00 and then settled in to watch The Tonight Show with Johnny Carson. Johnny was a favorite in those parts as he had grown up in nearby Norfolk.

At bedtime, there was no ambiguity as to where either of us would sleep. Bill was shown to an upstairs bedroom near Herbert. Grandma made it clear that I was to sleep with her—no monkey business. I felt a mixture of conviction concerning my rebellious actions at Grandpa's house and comfort knowing that Grandma was holding the line on morality. It took me a while to get to sleep, but once I got into the rhythm of Grandma's breathing, I slept well.

We left the next morning, as I had to get back for my fall classes and work at the uniform shop at the mall. After breakfast, we drove for about six hours, found our way to Decatur and crossed the Missouri River there. Our journey across Iowa was pleasant because of the frequent rest stops along Interstate 80.

Shortly after we returned home, I began a new semester and a new job at a uniform shop at the mall. In late September, my period was late. I began to worry that I might be pregnant. Throwing my scruples to the wind and having no security in myself apart from the approval of my parents, I began to investigate the possibility of driving to Iowa City to get an abortion. I knew my parents would be terribly disappointed if they found out I was pregnant.

Chapter 15

Wedding

I worried for a week, and then my period started. I was relieved, but from that point forward, Bill and I reformed our weekends. We no longer had sex on Saturday nights. From then on, I was going to do my best to be the image I wished to project—a virginal bride. At that time in my life, I needed a lot of inner healing. I was more concerned with appearing to be good on the outside than I was with being worthy of God's approval on the inside.

To think I might have aborted a baby two months before our wedding makes me shudder. I was so thankful I wasn't pressured into that based on faulty reasoning. I certainly did not judge anyone who ever had an abortion, because according to Jesus' strict law of love, I'm just as guilty for having even considered it. Plus, mercy and understanding needed to replace all tendencies I had toward self-righteousness.

In November I felt so irritated with another of Mom and Dad's accusatory arguments. Just as their habit did to me as a kid, the latest argument made me feel sick. I looked forward to moving out of the house.

In November, Bill and I also met several times with my pastor who would be conducting our wedding. He gave us a small book that we read and discussed with him. I remember feeling dismayed when he implied that it didn't really matter who you married just so God was at the center of your marriage. He said he could be married to any number of women and still flourish and accomplish God's will for his life. I disagreed. I was sure that Bill was my one and only—the very best person, handpicked by God for me.

In early December, my advisor at school, Sister Francisca, stopped by our house to drop off a wedding gift. She sat in the kitchen and chatted with my parents. Unfortunately, I wasn't home but was pleased to discover she had left a gift for Bill and me. Even though I had invited her to the wedding, she told Mom and Dad that she couldn't attend, but wanted to give us something. Later, I thanked her for the red Oxford English dictionary.

Brenda, my boss at the uniform shop proved to be an ally. I was able to do homework when nobody was in the store. One day Brenda heard that I had failed to approach a lady who had entered the store. She understandably corrected me. I was thinking about how I liked to be treated when I was shopping. I preferred to be left alone unless I needed help. My boss wanted me to at least make my presence known while people were there.

So I changed. I began welcoming people and informing them that I was available to help. I was often at the shop alone in the evenings. I took a lunch and heated it in a toaster oven in the back room. Brenda amazed me. One afternoon a pre-med student looking for a uniform, stopped by and took out some pent up anger on me. I was alarmed and felt very undeserving of his wrath. Brenda heard of my unfortunate experience. She found his number and called the man to let him know that his behavior was uncalled for. Relieved, I felt supported and understood.

When Brenda heard that I was getting married and that no one was having a shower for me, she took it upon herself to host one. Although, I needed practical things like small appliances and towels, she decided I needed a lingerie shower. So she gathered the few employees that she had and on a December afternoon, I opened boxes of red and black underwear.

I did not share much about Bill with people at school, though he had attended *The Taming of the Shrew* with me and my Shakespeare class at a downtown theater. Some of my classmates thought that I was marrying my English class buddy, Bill Lang. Bill and I usually sat together in classes to commiserate and share observations, but I had a different Bill in the wings. My dad called ours a match made in heaven.

On Christmas Eve, Bill and I had two services to attend. In the late afternoon we drove to Bill's parent's house where they were waiting with Bill's sister Hannah, two brothers, Joe, Tim and Grandma Elsie. After a light supper, the whole family went to a service at their Baptist Church except for Bill, Grandma Elsie and me. Instead, we cuddled together under a blanket. Bill's parents liked to keep the thermostat low by tossing tree branches into a wood burning stove in the living room.

After his family returned, Bill and I left to join my family at my Methodist Church for a candlelight Christmas Eve service. The chancel choir sang, the bell choir rang their bells and Bill kept muttering under his breath that all those candles were a good way to burn down the church.

The day after Christmas, Valerie and I ate at a pizza restaurant and worried we'd both die of food poisoning because the sausage was a bit pink in the middle. THE Wedding was only 48 hours away. We didn't get sick.

When Aunt Sophie and Uncle Mitch called the next day from a small town in Oklahoma reporting car trouble, Mom cried. That same day, my dad's dad, Grandpa Samuel Foltz pulled into our driveway. Grandma Myrtle, Uncle Herbert, Aunt Rosie, Uncle Joseph and my cousin Sean also arrived safely from Nebraska. Grandma Myrtle had a calming effect on Mom. It was comforting to hear her homespun wisdom and to have her bustling around the kitchen.

That afternoon Aunt Rosie, accompanied by Megan practiced her songs for the wedding. Grandma went into the hallway, embarrassed because it made her cry. I nearly dropped my teeth when I discovered $100.00 in a card from Uncle Herbert.

On Tuesday night, rehearsal at church went well. Bill and I practiced our lines. Megan advised me not to bob my head up and down when I talked. We laughed politely at the pastor's obviously stale wedding jokes probably pulled from *A Preacher's Guide to Humor.*

The rehearsal dinner at Bill's parent's was delicious. I recall that in addition to other food, Bill's mom served something called "Dolly Parton's Cheese Loaf." Their house was located on the banks of the Mississippi River on the Iowa side. Although it was dark and cold, our rehearsal guests could step out onto the wooden deck that Bill's dad had constructed. From there we could see the light from a small city across the river and hear the gentle lapping of the river's waves against the shoreline. Bill's friend Larry dominated the conversation, deservedly proud that he, with the help of Michelle, had brought Bill and me together. He also informed the gathering that "bitchin'" was the latest word in California for something nice or good. I highly doubt that Larry's information impressed Bill's mother. I thought that Larry had probably caught trouble more than once for his candid comments.

I felt warmed by the nice evening. Bill took me home. Needless to say, I got very little sleep that night.

On December 28th, the day of the wedding, the weather was much warmer than it had been. The morning went by quickly. I took a shower and a bath. Grandma provided me with a pair of pearl earrings so I would have something borrowed. Anna Schneckloth, a lady from the Lutheran Home had given me a little gold cross necklace that I wore around my neck as something old. The garter from the Bridal Boutique was blue and of course my wedding dress was new. I tried to ignore the ache that began to form in my head.

Grandma, Megan, Annie, Mom, Dad and I got to the church before 12:00. Megan had taken Aunt Rosie early so she could practice with the organist. Bill's sister Hannah came a short time later and we all got dressed. Someone informed me that Bill had arrived at church. I was told that Bill wasn't nervous at all. I was extremely nervous. Everything was going according to plan. I cried when I noticed, Aunt Sophie, Uncle Mitch, and my cousin Lily, come in the church through the back door with less than an hour to spare. Dad's teacher friend, Brian came early to begin snapping photos.

Aunt Rosie had stitched a peony-colored wedding banner which was displayed in the front of the church. Poinsettias lined the altar and were displayed by the communion kneeling rails. Christmas trees still stood next to each pulpit. The bridesmaids wore long sleeved burgundy dresses which fit in well with the poinsettias and the carpet.

At about 12:50 the organist sat down to begin playing my favorite hymns. He didn't begin to exhaust my list. As time for the service drew near, I watched as Bill, his brothers Joe, Tim, and Friend Jess filed in following the pastor. His parents and Grandma Elsie were sitting up front. Dad and Megan gave me advice on how to keep from crying.

On cue, Dad walked me down the aisle. I learned later that Dad had to fight his own tears. As our sisters slowly made their way to the altar, Dad told me a "knock-knock" joke.

"Knock-knock."

"Who's there?"

"Elsie"

"Elsie who?"

"Elsie if we can get through this."

We did.

Bill Lieber and I were married on a Wednesday December 28th at one o'clock in the afternoon. Molly, my friend from church attended to the guest book. Aunt Rosie sang "The Lord's Prayer" and "The Wedding Song" written by Noel Paul Stookey of Peter, Paul and Mary. The pastor pronounced us man and wife.

The picture taking afterwards was a drag, although the pictures were lovely. Perfect was the only word for the reception. On the reception table In addition to the small, elegant cake, trimmed with little red frosting flowers, the reception table held homemade pink, cream cheese mints and mixed nuts. The parlor of the church was full of people, including Miss Vitale, my junior high orchestra director and violin instructor. Larry was there and spilled his punch twice. Michelle's sister caught the bouquet.

My friends Valerie and Michelle served punch and coffee. Before the afternoon ended, at Mom's suggestion, Megan and Annie drove to our new apartment and made our bed with brand-new sheets and blankets, wedding gifts.

Our relatives gathered at our house. When my sisters returned we had a cafeteria style meal. Aunt Rosie sang the Lord's prayer and I played the piano. Michelle, her little sister, and Valerie joined our family. I didn't really want to leave while everyone was still around. However, after an hour or two of talk about the wedding, Bill and I left. Aunt Rosie had constructed a "Just Married" sign to put in the back window of our car.

We spent our first night together in our apartment. Bill put a frozen pizza in the oven, and we drank the champagne that Bill's friend Larry had given us. We did what married couples do without guilt and then we held each other, content, secure, and tired.

I began feeling homesick and cried. I guess it wasn't really homesickness so much as it was the feeling that I had lost something. When you marry you gain so much—a partner, a new home, a new life, and more family. But some things are lost. You lose a way of life that can never be recovered and the security of your parents' concern for your life. You lose minor things such as access to a piano, a color TV, advice you trust, meals often fully prepared, free groceries, the ability to do laundry without having to leave home, and your dear, old dog. For some reason, the loss I felt the most right then was that of Chip, the half Dalmatian, half mutt -- my friend.

As I was thinking, I began to cry.

"What's wrong? Why are crying?" Bill asked, gently.

"Oh, this is going to sound dumb, but I miss Chip," I sniffled.

I feared that Bill would think I was hopeless to miss a creature he considered to be totally worthless. Wisely, he didn't voice that opinion. Instead, he said, "Even though it won't be easy, I will try my best to take his place."

I laughed.

Except for my brief seven month stay in Maple Crest when I was attending EIU, I had never really been on my own. Ideally, I could have lived alone and grown up a little bit before marrying Bill. Sadly, I learned that "Ideal" on this earth is only a fantasy. We are plunked down here amid worldly, ungodly influences and the best we can do is find others who seek the ideal God and shun the other guy. After my suicide attempt and time in the psych ward in that Minnesota Hospital, I had little boldness or energy to put myself out there. By God's merciful kindness I was revived and able to reattach to church, friends, a Christian (Catholic) college and obtain a bachelor's degree in English.

My heavenly Father knew in advance that there would be a man for me to marry—a kind man, well-intentioned and seeking God. We weren't a match as far as calling and gifting. However, we were a great match for parenting children and for healing each other.

I wasn't the only one who came into the marriage damaged by life. We both needed lots of understanding and kindness. I needed his calm nature and he needed my inquisitive one. His mechanical gifts required my linguistic ones. My romantic approach to life would eventually be able to meld with his more practical and pragmatic ways. Proverbs 27: 17 says "As iron sharpens iron, so one person sharpens another." God intended for marriage to be a means of refining for each other as He makes us fit for His kingdom.

Neither of us had any idea what lay ahead. Along the way, God hovered over us as we encountered many dangers, toils and snares. Interwoven with countless blessings and quiet streams, He frequently refreshed us, guided us to best paths and corrected us. None of it was easy, but He was always with us.

In the middle of that night, we were awakened by loud, vibrating music from the stereo in the apartment below ours. I began to wonder what kind of a nut I had married when Bill got up, went into the living room, and began stomping on the floor. The music immediately grew softer. Who was I to question something that worked?

On another night in the first days of our marriage, I had a nightmare in which a large spider dangled from a web over the bed. It seemed so real that I woke Bill, pointing at the "spider." A few years later, after reading M. Scott Peck's *People of the Lie: The Hope for Healing Human Evil*, I came to understand the meaning of the spider dream. The spider represented the emotional grip that my mother had on me but also my own tendency to be like a spider by wanting to own and control people I liked. Resolving that issue would take future counseling and inner healing.

After a three-day honeymoon in Chicago where we visited the Museum of Science and Industry, we settled into our apartment on Tenth Street. Each weekday morning, I walked just up the hill to school and Bill drove his brown, stick-shift Hornet to John Deere in Moline.

Epilogue

And He shall turn the hearts of the fathers
to the children, and the hearts
of the children to their fathers, lest I come
and strike the land with a curse.
Malachi4:6 ASV

My father wasn't perfect. Once he broke my heart, but mostly he healed my heart. I feel sad when I think about people who were not as blessed as I was with the father I had. Likewise, I am thankful for my mother. Most of the wounds I received through her were based on good intentions. She taught me discipline, the value of hard work and gave me a love for good books. I am so grateful for both of my parents.

At this writing, the enemy is raging against families, fathers, mothers and children. My prayer and belief is that God is raising up godly fathers and grandfathers to come alongside brokenhearted mothers, grandmothers, children and teenagers. In order to: come alongside children who have been exposed to drugs whether on the street or in the hospital, children who have been damaged by violence or abuse whether physical or sexual, children who have been exposed to theft, lying, cheating and abandonment caused by poverty, death or divorce and to children confused about their identities. God save the children worldwide, we pray. Protect them and station Your holy angels around them. May they all come to know The Truth for He will set them free, show them the way and grant them abundant life.

Recommended Media

Memoirs about Bipolar Disorder, Suicide and
misuse of Psychiatric Medication:

Coleman, Monica A. *Bipolar Faith: A Black Woman's Journey with Depression and Faith.* Fortress Press: Minneapolis. 2016.

Deere, Jack. *Even in Our Darkness: A Story of Beauty in a Broken Life.* Zondervan: Grand Rapids: Michigan. 2018.

Fisher, Carrie. *Wishful Drinking.* Simon &Schuster: New York. 2008.

Hines, Kevin. *Cracked Not Broken: Surviving and Thriving after a Suicide Attempt.* Rowman and Littlefield Publishers: Lanham Maryland. 2013

Lukach, Mark. *My Lovely Wife in the Psych Ward.* HarperCollins Publishers: New York. 2017.

Moezzi, Melody. *Haldol and Hyacinths: A Bipolar Life.* Avery a Member of Penguin Group: New York. 2013

Samet, Matt. *Death Grip: A Climber's Escape from Benzo Madness.* St. Martin's Press: New York. 2013.

Vonnegut, Mark. *Just Like Someone Without Mental Illness Only More So*. Bantam Books an imprint of Random House: New York. 2010

Vonnegut, Mark. The Eden Express: A Personal Account of Schizophrenia. Praeger Publishers: New York. 1975.

Wagner, Linda Mary. *Unearthing the Ghosts: A Mystery Memoir*. The Troy Book Makers: Troy New York. 2013.

Books Related to my Life

Frank, *Anne. Anne Frank: The Diary of a Young Girl.*

Sands, Bill. *My Shadow Ran Fast*. Prentice-Hall: Englewood Cliffs, New Jersey, 1964.

Wharton, Edith. *Ethan Frome*. Scribner: New York, 1911

Movies

Forbes, Maya (writer and director). *Infinitely Polar Bear:* Starring Zoe Saldana and Mark Ruffalo. 2014.

Greene, David and John-Michael Treblak (screenplay), Schwartz, Stephen (music and lyrics), Bayes, Sammy(choreography), Green, David (Director) and Lansbury, Edgar. *Godspell.* Starring: Victor Garber, David Haskell, Katie Hanley and Lynne Thigpen and more. Columbia Pictures: 1973.

Bronte Emily, Tilley, Patrick. *Wuthering Heights.* Starring Timothy Dalton and Anna Calder Marshall. American International Pictures. 1970.

Therapeutic Reading:

Amen, Daniel. *The End of Mental Illness: How Neuroscience is Transforming Psychiatry and Helping Prevent or Reverse Mood and Anxiety Disorders, ADHD, Addictions, PTSD, Psychosis, Personality Disorders and More.* Tyndale House Publishers: Carol Stream, Illinois.2020

Baker, John. *Celebrate Recovery: Getting Yourself Right with God, Yourself and Others,* Zondervan: Grand Rapids, MI. 1998

Breggin, M.D., Peter R. *Reclaiming our Children: A Healing Plan for a Nation in Crisis.* Perseus Books: New York. 2000.

Breggin, M.D., Peter R. *Medication Madness The Role of Psychiatric Drugs in Cases of Violence, Suicide and Crime.* St. Martin's Press: New York, 2008

Clark, Randy. *Ministry Team Training Manual.* Global Awakening: Mechanicsburg, Pennsylvania. 2004

Cloud, Dr. Henry and Townsend, Dr. John. *Boundaries: When to Say Yes and How to Say No to Take Control of Your Life.* Zondervan: Grand Rapids, Michigan. 1992

Diamond, Harvey and Marilyn. *Fit for Life.* Warner Books: New York. 1985.

Guyol, Gracelyn. *Healing Depression and Bipolar Disorder Without Drugs.* Walker & Company: New York. 2006.

Guyol, Gracelyn. *Who's Crazy Here? Steps to Recovery Without Drugs for: ADD/ADHD, Addiction and Eating Disorders, Anxiety and PTSD, Depression, Bi-Polar Disorder, Schizophrenia, Autism.* Ajoite Publishing: Stonington, Connecticut. 2010.

Holford, Patrick. *New Optimum Nutrition for the Mind-Expanded and Updated. Basic Healthy Publications*, Inc.: Laguna Beach, California. 2009.

Hyman, M.D., Mark. *The UltraMind Solution: Fix Your Broken Brain by Healing Your Body First.* Scribner: New York. 2009.

Laubach, Frank C. *Letters by a Modern Mystic: Excerpts from Letters Written to his Father.* Purposeful Design Publications a Division of ACS: Colorado Springs.2007

MacNutt, Francis. *The Prayer that Heals: Praying for Healing in the Family.* Ave Maria Press, Notre Dame, Indiana. 1981

McMillen M.D., S.J. *None of These Diseases.* Fleming H. Revell, Grand Rapids, Michigan.1963.

Mate' M.D., Gabor. *When the Body Says NO: Exploring the Stress-Disease Connection.* John Wiley and Sons: Hoboken, New Jersey. 2003.

Payne, Leanne. *Restoring the Christian Soul: Overcoming Barriers to Completion in Christ Through Healing Prayer.* Baker Books, Grand Rapids, Michigan, 1991.

Peck, M. Scott. *People of the Lie: The Hope for Healing Human Evil.* Touchstone-Simon and Schuster, Inc., New York: 1983.

Prince, Derek. *Blessing or Curse, You Can Choose. Freedom from the Pressures You thought You had to Live With.* Chosen Books, Grand Rapids, Michigan. 2009.

Sandford, John and Sandford, Mark. *A Comprehensive Guide to Deliverance and Inner Healing.* Chosen Books: Grand Rapids, Michigan, 1992.

Sandford, John Loren and Sandford, Paula. *God's Power to Change: Healing the Wounded Spirit.* Charisma House A Strang Company: Lake Mary, Florida. 2007.

Sandford, John Loren and Sandford, Paula. *Growing Pains: How to Overcome Life's Earliest Experiences to Become All God Wants you to Be.* Charisma House A Strang Company: Lake Mary, Florida. 2008

Sandford, John Loren and Sandford, Paul. *Letting Go of Your Past: Take Control of Your Future by Addressing the Habits, Hurts and Attitudes that Remain from Previous Relationships.* Charisma House A Strang Company: Lake Mary, Florida. 2008

Sandford, John Loren and Sandford, Paula. *Transforming the Inner Man: God's Powerful Principles for Inner Healing and Lasting Life Change.* Charisma House A Strang Company: Lake Mary, Florida. 2007

Scazzero, Peter. *Emotionally Healthy Spirituality.* Thomas Nelson. Nashville Tennessee: 2006.

Schmidt, LAc. Dipl. O.M., *How Rockefeller created the Business of Modern Medicine.* Meridian Health Clinic.com. 2019.

Sheets, Tim. *Angel Armies on Assignment.* Destiny Image Publishers: Shippensburg, Pennsylvania. 2021

Virkler, Mark and Patti. *How to Hear God's Voice.* Destiny Image Publishers: Shippensburg, Pennsylvania. 2006

Virkler, Mark and Patti: *Prayers that heal the Heart (Revised and Updated): Prayer Counseling that Breaks Every Yoke.* Destiny Image Publishers: Shippensburg, Pennsylvania. 2021.

Walsh M.D., William J. *Nutrient Power: Heal Your Biochemistry, Heal Your Brain.* Skyhorse Publishing, New York: 2012.

* Watch for a new book specifically based on Dr. Walsh's research on bipolar disorder. I spoke to someone at Walsh's office who told me the book is nearly ready for publication.

Whitaker, Robert. *Anatomy of an Epidemic: Magic Bullets, Psychiatric Drugs and the Astonishing Rise of Mental Illness in America*. Broadway Books, New York: 2010, 2015.

Whitaker, Robert. *Mad in America: Bad Science, Bad medicine, and the Enduring Mistreatment of the Mentally Ill*. Perseus Publishing: Cambridge, MA. 2002

Whitaker, Robert and Cosgrove, Lisa. *Psychiatry Under the Influence: Institutional Corruption, Social Injury and Prescriptions for Reform*. Palgrave MacMillan, a division of St. Martin's Press, New York: 2015.

Willimon, William H. *Sinning Like a Christian: A New Look at the Seven Deadly Sins*. Abingdon Press: Nashville, Tennessee. 2005

Bibles

Holy Scriptures, NKJ. With "Messianic Study aids by Dr. Michael Brown, "Doctrines of Judaism" by Louis Goldberg, and "The Meaning and Importance of Jewish Holidays" by John Fischer. Sid Roth of Messianic Vision. Bethesda, Maryland: 1986.

Harkavy, Alexander. *The Holy Scriptures*. Hebrew Publishing Company: New York:1951

Life Application Study Bible NIV, Tyndale House Publishers: Carol Stream, Illinois 2011.

Ryrie, Th.D. Ph.D., Charles Caldwell. *The Ryrie Study Bible- New American Standard Version.* Moody Press: Chicago 1978.

Simmons, Brian. *The Passion Translation New Testament.* BroadStreet Publishing Group: Savage, Minnesota. 2020.

Printed in the United States
by Baker & Taylor Publisher Services